Space for wonder

A guide to trekking the mountain frontier of the Pyrenees

Gordon Wilson

This book is dedicated to everyone whom we have met in the Pyrenees who have given us friendship and looked after us. You are far too numerous to mention by name.

Acknowledgements

I am indebted to many people, without whom this book would never have seen the light of day. To:

Angharad, my partner, who has been a constant companion on all the Pyrenees treks, and much more; **Stan** of Gravity Consulting (stan@gravity-consulting.com), whose editing services corrected and much improved successive drafts; **Jenny** who meticulously created the hand-drawn maps. **Judy** and **Trish** who with great care proof-read and commented on the penultimate draft, also much improving it.

Stan, Jenny, Judy and Trish are also long-standing personal friends with whom I have spent many happy hiking days. To these, I add further hiking mates **Steve, Clare, Sharon, Geof, Mick, Jeff, Ellen, Nick, Chris** and **Hazel**. Without you I might never have hiked much anywhere. Finally in this vein, I am deeply grateful to my father **Ernie**, once a marathon runner, who introduced me to mountains when I was 13.

Visit my website at: www.trekthepyrenees.com

This book is also available as an e-book

All profits arising from the combined sales of this book and its e-version will be donated to mountain charities, especially those associated with the Pyrenees.

Chatonnay et moutarde @ sfr. fr] unsolicited email
Marc Chatonnay VIMLA recd 10-1-2017.
info @ pyrenees - exploration .com
www.

Published by Gordon Wilson
www.trekthepyrenees.com

Copyright 2015 © Gordon Wilson

ISBN 978-0-9934422-0-9

British Library Cataloguing in Publication Data. A catalogue record for this book is available from the British Library.

Editorial work by Stan Abbott
Maps by Jenny Ackroyd

Safety in the mountains

Walking in mountainous country may be dangerous and you should always consider the risks that are involved, which will vary from hike to hike and during hikes. While every care has been taken in the compilation of this guide, walkers undertake the Pyrenean traverse at their own risk and the author/publisher cannot be held responsible for any injury, damage, loss or other inconvenience arising from their use of this guide. Note the international distress signal – six short whistle blasts or torch flashes, repeated after a minute's pause; also the international emergency telephone number, 112.

Contents

1
A frame of mind

It was a beautiful Sunday in late July 2008, deep in the Spanish Pyrenees. My partner Angharad and I were in the middle of a lonely, tough, four-day stage of the Haute Randonnée Pyrénéenne – the HRP or High Level Traverse. We had struggled up the sketchiest of paths, traversing two boulder fields, to a narrow pass at an altitude of almost 2,500m. So far we hadn't seen a soul. We had wild-camped the night before and so were carrying a small tent and cooking gear. The pass was the first of three that we had to cross before reaching our destination for the day – an unstaffed mountain refuge. We were behind schedule as we sat eating a late lunch and surveying nervously our descent to the tarn below. It looked to be about 300 metres, almost vertically down a gulley of loose scree and bits of grass. Our English and French guidebooks both warned us to take care. Suddenly, a young Frenchman in his 20s appeared from behind us. We exchanged the usual greetings and off he went, nimbly down. He was more than half way to the tarn by the time we set off on the longest, most agonising descent that we had ever made.

Two days later, as we prepared to leave the Refugi de Certascan, where the Frenchman – Jean-Paul –was also staying, we spoke with him in French and the conversation went something like this:

Angharad: 'You are so fast and nimble compared to us. We wish we had done this [the HRP] when we were your age.'

Jean-Paul: 'I hope that I can still do it when I'm your age.' At the time, Angharad and I were respectively 58 and 62.

The three of us then laughed about the philosophical turn to our conversation, and he was gone. The point had, however, been well made. We never again dwelled on the suspicion that perhaps we should have walked the Pyrenees when younger, and that what we were attempting was really for the super-fit. We were doing it now, in the present and in our own way. That was all that mattered.

In retrospect it was during moments like these that the idea for this book was born. If Angharad and I could traverse this barrier that divides Spain from

France, so could any other reasonably fit person who loves to walk in high hills and who is grabbed by the idea of traversing a mountainous border from the Atlantic to the Mediterranean – whatever their age. Unfortunately, the existing guidebooks to the traverse, while providing generally excellent instructions, give off an aura that this is an extremely tough physical and mental challenge for the super-fit. Following these books to the letter means that you constantly have to put one foot in front of the other for long days (sometimes very long) over at least six weeks. Even this, however, is not sufficient challenge for some individuals who elevate the traverse to an even higher status – that of a combat sport. They try to reduce the overall time to four or five weeks, or even ten days, which is the current 'record', I believe.

If this is how you get your kicks, I am sure that the sense of achievement at the end is immense and you feel great for a while, as would any person who has just stopped banging their head against a brick wall. Without constant reinforcement, however, such a feeling is ephemeral. As noted in several guides to long distance hiking trails, your friends and relations will never quite understand what you have done. They will listen politely to your story and may even say 'well done' or 'that's a tremendous achievement', but these are easy words. Their purveyors certainly won't stretch to erecting a plaque for you, or even putting up bunting to welcome you home. An early edition of one of the guidebooks to the traverse says that you will find out what kind of person you are. I guess that, being a person of mature years, I already knew the answer to that question in relation to my physical fitness and mental stamina before I ever embarked on the great Pyrenean traverse.

What is this life if full of care
We have no time to stop and stare
(William Henry Davies 1871-1940)

This book, in contrast, is for people who, like me, hike because we enjoy it. There is no denying that high mountain days can be physically tough, mentally demanding and require care, because a clumsy trip can do you serious damage. Nor do I wish to belittle the importance of the personal satisfaction felt at ultimately achieving the goal. The first sight from on high of Banyuls-sur-Mer, our finishing point on the Mediterranean, and still three to four hours away, gives a tremendous thrill, not to mention a spring in the step.

Satisfaction, however, is multi-faceted: completion is just one contributing element. A second, obviously, is the stupendous scenery that is habitually encountered – alongside the changing light and other sights that linger in the memory. The panoramas on a grand scale are part of that element of wonder that mountains inspire, as articulated in the final chapter of Robert MacFarlane's 'Mountains of the mind'. There are many other parts to that element: the cascading streams; the woodlands becoming thinner and eventually disappearing as you climb higher; the alpine flowers covering high meadows but sometimes solitary in their own micro-climate, provided by a single rock; the call of those cute, furry, brown mountain mammals, the marmots, perched on rocks above, or scurrying away as you approach; the herd of isards running away at first sight of you; the two eagles swooping round the ridge just as you have stopped a few moments for a snack. Yes, you will gaze in wonder.

[These trans-border footpaths] have become the silent testimony of the passages of hundreds of persons who, during the years of the Second World War (1939-1944), fled from the Nazi barbarianism that devastated Europe. The Government of Catalonia wishes to render a tribute to all those persons who escaped and to all those who helped them and made it possible for the Pyrenean mountain ports to be converted into mountains of hope and freedom.

(Information board at the start of a trans-frontier trail to France from a valley in Spanish Catalonia)

Our experiences over time, however, have taught us that wonder and deep satisfaction do not only concern 'nature'. Further elements shape our constructions of mountains in our minds, and these concern the visible hand of people.

Firstly there are the people you will never meet because they are now dead. Yet, the above quotation illustrates in a few moving words the Pyrenees as a political frontier with a tragic, relatively recent, human history. The board refers to the crossing by refugees from France to Spain during the Second World War. Other boards at the foot of trans-frontier trails indicate a two-way refugee flow, because a few years earlier republican refugees fled in the opposite direction to escape the victorious General Franco in the Spanish Civil War. One particular Second World War route from the French Département known as the Ariège – which borders much of the north side of the Haute Pyrénées – to the Vall d'Aneau in Spain has been inaugurated as a *chemin de la liberté*[1], or road to freedom. It is commemorated by a four-day trek each year that is open to the public.

---

[1] http://tinyurl.com/cheminliberte

A sobering moment at around 1,600m on the *Muntanyes de Llibertat* trail, and also Day 35 of the Brown Route (Chapter 8): Little is known of the details, but a fleeing family during World War II were passing by this spot when they heard a rumble above. The Croix de la Portière (Cross of the Gateway) commemorates their deaths beneath the snow, ice and rocks of an avalanche

You wonder first of all, how the refugees actually did it, inadequately clothed and usually in April or May when deep snow added to the hazards – carrying whatever belongings they could muster, and often with babies. Of course, many didn't make it, but then you wonder about the risks and dangers faced by those who helped them. For everybody involved, this was a matter of life and death. While several books have been written about the Pyrenees and these two wars, reading them will only increase your wonder, not to mention confusion about what really happened beyond what you are told in romanticised accounts. Until recently, these episodes seemed un-mentionable to locals – they were too raw in the memory. Now, however, at least the younger generation is more interested. Complementing the *Chemin de la Liberté*, another four-day trek, this time circular, linking France and Spain has recently been devised, complete with official map and guide – the *Muntanyes de Llibertat*[2].

---

[2] http://tinyurl.com/muntanyeslibertat

Secondly there are the people you meet in the present. Sometimes, as in the opening lines of this book, the meeting is all too brief, but for those moments you are locked into a kind of intense friendship. Occasionally you meet those who eke out a living from this land. Once, at dinner in a mountain refuge, with heavy rain outside, the door opened and in walked a shepherd, dripping from head to toe. He was beckoned silently to a seat next to us and fed. He told us snippets about his life, of the transhumance agricultural method that transforms him from a town labourer in winter to a shepherd in summer. Then he left, going out again into the dark and mountain rain, into a life so different from ours – and we wondered.

Scene: July 2012, and we are with a group of French friends, a friendship that has been forged after a five-day stretch on the same route. We are having dinner together in a small village restaurant. A television is on in the corner, showing coverage of the London Olympics. It takes us to the French studio, seemingly set above the River Thames, with Tower Bridge in the background and a beautiful mellow, evening light. I comment that this must be a very expensive location for the French studio, at which one of our new friends, a Parisian, comments:

'C'est le Photoshop.'

Our most memorable experiences have been the lasting friendships we have forged with co-trekkers. The potential for this is not so great on the HRP because of its long, tough days, and because most trekkers are focussed men and (less frequently) women walking alone. On the two official traverses, however, the French Grand Randonnée 10 (GR10), and the Spanish GR11 (more about these later), the potential is much greater. This is because you start to meet the same people each evening, and soon a group of ten or more may come together to eat, drink and generally make merry. It doesn't always happen, we are told, but when it does, it is enriching and you wonder about other people, about their lives away from the mountains that have institutionalised us all, and how in many basic ways we are pretty much the same.

So yes, again you wonder about more and more things, until at times you feel as if your mind is exploding: the modern livelihoods associated with tourism, especially the intrusion of ski resorts and the roads that have been driven to them; the hydro-electric schemes; the devastation in the valleys caused by floods; the inns, *gîtes* and the first sight of the refuge; the graffiti denouncing the reintroduction of bears; and the mountain dog (*patou*) that guards sheep against bears and wolves. Then there are specific experiences that leave a lasting impression and often questions: the reason for the nine crosses that one suddenly comes across on a high ridge; the *vin doux naturel* that was served to us as an aperitif in a mountain refuge. I could go on indefinitely, but your specific experiences and wonderment will surely be different. Paradoxically, however, wonder at all these things induces a certain modesty, as Robert Macfarlane's Mountains of the Mind also suggests. From landscapes on a grand scale to animal and plant life in its myriad forms, to human trials and tribulations, the total panorama is so vast – and you are so insignificant. Modesty is the other side of the coin to 'feeling great' on completion.

Alas, the existing guidebooks to the Pyrenean traverse allow no time for wonder, whether it be at the marvels of panorama, animal and plant life, fellow human beings creating a history of 'hope and freedom', or the simple enrichment of conversation with those who are sharing the experience. The books provide the walking time only, with no stops, not even to enjoy a snack or dabble in the water. Of course they are right in a sense, because you can't put a number on stop-time, when so many variables contribute, from blisters to the roughness of the terrain, to weather, to contemplating the marvels of nature. Our own recorded actual timings for each day suggest that, to the guidebook walking time, you might add anything between 30 and 70 per cent to arrive at the total duration. Given that a rough average walking time in the guidebooks is eight hours per day, you soon realise that there isn't much opportunity to do anything apart from keeping utterly focused on your feet and falling asleep at night. Full of care to keep to the ambitious schedule, perhaps break a record even, you have no time to stop and stare, or read about refugee crossings, or talk to other people. Perhaps I exaggerate to make the point!

So, this is a book for those whose enjoyment of the traverse also comprises embracing a fuller experience of the Pyrenees beyond the physical endurance. Ultimately, this fuller experience means suspension of everyday reality and immersing yourself in the present with its beguiling simplicity of each day when you walk for several hours, taking in the breath-taking views, the animals and plants; and at the end you relax, perhaps hand-wash a few clothes and dry them on a rock before resuming acquaintance with recently-made chums over dinner. Then you go to bed. There's a bit more to it than that, as I will explain, but that is the essence, when a new rhythm of daily life takes hold.

In other words the aims of this book are firstly to get you interested in the Pyrenean traverse; secondly to get you to want to do it; thirdly to help enable you to do it; and fourthly to ensure you enjoy doing it – in spite of the aches and pains. And that you enjoy the lows as well as the highs, through gaining a full social as well as physical experience.

I started writing, indeed the words that you have hopefully just digested, today, Monday. Yesterday, Angharad and I went for a walk with friends in the South Pennines of England – that tract of high ground that lies between the National Parks of the Peak District to the south and the Yorkshire Dales to the north. The South Pennines do not themselves enjoy National Park status, but they are still fine walking country and a playground that serves the great industrial conurbations to the east and west. Angharad and I live to the east, in the town of Huddersfield, which made its name in the 19th century for the production of fine 'worsted' woollen yarns. The South Pennines, which provided the original water power for the British Industrial Revolution, are thus on our doorstep.

Yesterday we were walking above the town of Hebden Bridge, in Calderdale, towards Stoodley Pike, whose modest height of 400m still imposes itself above the valley. Six months previously I had passed this way in the opposite direction with a friend. We were walking the Pennine Way – the 429 km long-distance path that runs south to north the length of the 'backbone of England'. That was the colloquial name given to the Pennines in geography lessons at school. I mentioned this three-week trek to our friends, pointing out the spot where we had deviated from the official route. We had done so to enable us to descend into the fleshpots of Hebden Bridge where we rested, wined and dined with two of the friends we were walking with yesterday. We had then rejoined the official route about three kilometres further on from where we had deviated. The joking response to my remark was that perhaps we had 'cheated' by not walking the official Pennine Way every step that we took. I responded in turn that a) we had perhaps walked further through our deviation and b) it had never been our intention to be slaves to the tyranny of the painted or engraved acorn symbols that mark the official route. Instead, we had treated the Pennine Way as a 'concept', in which the aim was to walk from one end to the other and certainly not concern ourselves over minor deviations.

I too have digressed from my narrative by describing an incident in my native Pennines of England, rather than focusing solely on the Pyrenees. The reason is – and this is my first tip to those who are buying into the idea of traversing the Pyrenees – that, likewise, you should treat it as a 'concept'. As a concept, or 'general idea' if you don't like that word, you continually adapt your route and expectations. You certainly don't feel obliged to follow at all times the red and white paint flashes of the GR10 and GR11, indispensable as they are when you are on sections of these official trails, or follow the guidebook instruction of the HRP.

Treating the Pyrenean traverse as a concept, you connect with the explorers of more than a century ago, such as the Anglo-French writer and historian Hilaire Belloc (1870-1953) whose goal was simply to be among these mountains and their people, not to mention the inns, which inspired his famous poem Tarantella[3] written in 1929:

> *Do you remember an Inn,*
> *Miranda?*
> *Do you remember an Inn?*
> *And the tedding and the spreading*
> *Of the straw for a bedding,*
> *And the fleas that tease in the high Pyrenees,*
> *And the wine that tasted of tar?*
> *And the cheers and the jeers of the young muleteers*
> *(Under the vine of the dark veranda)?*

Hilaire Belloc also wrote a 1909 Guide, The Pyrenees, in which his aim was to inform others of the things he wished he had known before setting off. I have taken this as the practical objective of this book, in which subsequent chapters will cover:

- Travelling to and within the Pyrenees – aided by Google – and when to go;

- Gear for comfort and weight, together with the pros and cons of different forms of accommodation, from hotels to bivouacs;

- Customising and calibrating to personal circumstance the existing guidebooks, maps, footpaths and waymarks;

- Being aware of and responsible towards the local environment, and those who live and work in it;

- In addition to the stunning scenery, being aware of the cultural, political, social and economic history that has left its mark on contemporary Pyrenean life;

- Being prepared for the full, social experience, while maintaining privacy and independence;

---

[3] http://tinyurl.com/youtubeTarantella

- The routes that Angharad and I have used over the years, during which time we have traversed the entire range twice and walked many variants, and how you might like to create your own route.

While this book provides (Chapters 6-9) daily descriptions of the route and variants, they are not as detailed as those provided in the step-by-step guidebooks. These guidebooks are strong on detail, but generally short on context. They are a bit like walking in blinkers without reference to the overall surroundings through which you travel, and will see every time that you lift your eyes from the ground at your feet. You should also beware because they can never provide enough detail to remove all doubt.

On the other hand, my descriptions are designed to complement the large-scale walkers' maps of the Pyrenees (Chapter 4). These maps demonstrate amply the surrounding physical context, in that they show where you are walking in relation to features such as peaks, ridges, lakes and valleys. Key navigation features along the trail are also apparent.

Thus, this book gives both more and less than the guidebooks and the maps. It gives less detail of the route than the guidebooks and less of the overall physical context than the maps. It does, however, tell you of the nature of the terrain, the places where you might go wrong and an idea of the overall time you will take. To this it adds the human contexts and the spaces for wonder. Finally, it provides links to other sources, should you be seeking more. I, of course, think that the balance is right in that the book provides what I would like to have known before immersing myself in the Pyrenees. On that point, however, you, the reader, are the ultimate judge.

To end this introductory chapter, I tell a little more about regarding the Pyrenean traverse as a concept. First and foremost, it is an attitude in which, sure, the basic-aim is to walk from one coast to the other across the mountain passes – but you are not a failure if you adopt easier routes than those prescribed occasionally, because of bad weather, for example. You are not a failure if you even resort to four wheels on occasion, when a stage in the journey involves a stretch of road. Remember, Hilaire Belloc and others of his generation, never beat themselves up because they hired a mule after a good night in an inn. *'Ce n'est pas un concours!'* I once remarked to some French friends who were marvelling over dinner one night that Angharad and I had

Part of your living mountain: the Pyrenees in Andorra

passed them en route that day – 'It is not a competition!' Nor is it a conquest in the usual sense. Even the HRP as described in the guidebooks only scales the summits of three major peaks in the entire range, all on the relatively easier terrain of the Pyrénées Orientales (eastern Pyrenees). The route of everyone undertaking the traverse – the odd complete head-banger excepted, perhaps – is overwhelmingly over the passes, albeit many of them being high altitude passes.

To put yourself into a frame of mind to do something more enriching than mere conquest, I recommend taking a cue from Nan Shepherd's beautifully written account of immersion over a lifetime in the Scottish mountain range, the Cairngorms. The Living Mountain was originally written in 1944 but lay unpublished after an initial rejection – until a small publisher printed a limited edition in 1977. More recently it has been resurrected, with an introduction by the aforementioned Robert Macfarlane. For the record, the Cairngorms contain the second, third, fourth, fifth and sixth highest mountains in Britain, and five of the nine that are over 4,000 feet (1,219m) in height. For Nan, however, it is not the individual peaks, but the range that becomes your summit and you do not reach this summit by only putting one foot in front of the other with no time or inclination to immerse, reflect and wonder.

As you wonder about a multitude of things while traversing the Pyrenees, you create a story, perhaps the best story of your life. It is a story of considerable subtlety that connects the unique personal experience of the eye of the beholder with quests for beauty and truths about humanity. It is your lived experience of the range. It is a story in the best tradition, which creates a universal out of the local.

You won't create this story-experience if you are on a stage of the traverse that the guidebook says will take you ten hours, not allowing for stops. You won't create it if your focus is to complete the traverse ever faster. You are likely to have an accident if you try to stare without stopping. You will create it if you stop, stare and engage with those you meet during your journey.

Top tips from Chapter 1

1. If you are reasonably fit, used to hill walking, and are interested, possibly fascinated, in walking the Pyrenees from the Atlantic to the Mediterranean, you can do it, whatever your age.

2. Do not be put off by conventional guidebooks that might leave the impression that the traverse is for super-fit, young adults only. It is neither a combat sport nor a competition.

3. Put yourself in the frame of mind that the whole range is your mountain, not the individual summits, which the traverse rarely visits.

4. Put yourself in the frame of mind to treat the traverse as a concept rather than a set route that you must follow slavishly.

5. Put yourself in the frame of mind to have a full experience; that is an experience that is both broader and deeper than the physical endurance of putting one foot in front of the other for hours on end, day after day.

6. Put yourself in the frame of mind to allow the mountains to inspire wonder – wonder at the scenery, wonder at the wild and lonely places, wonder at the wild animals and flowers, wonder at the human history, wonder at contemporary human lives that are created in these mountains.

7. Put yourself in the frame of mind to enjoy the traverse.

2

The Pyrenean traverse: an overview

What are my credentials for writing this book, and especially this chapter, which covers such diverse topics as the geography, the wildlife, the weather, and (for your convenience and safety, as they say) the dangers? I ask this question of myself because, given what I have already touched upon, it is obvious that producing a complete authoritative account would require a large tome of many, many pages and a collaborative effort between many authors, each an expert in his or her chosen field. Please note with relief that I omit the geology of the Pyrenees!

I can't pretend, therefore, that my credentials cover every subject on which I touch. What I can do is write about them from a hiker's perspective, from which vantage I can at least be honest. Existing guidebooks cover many of the topics mentioned above in a few paragraphs in their introductory chapter, as if to get them out of the way before doing the serious bit, which is writing the meticulous route-finding instructions. Having a hiker's perspective, however, is no reason to be unaware of everything else and, like all human beings, we should be prepared to have our imaginations stoked. If at times I give no more than what seems like a taster of the full experience, then that at least hopefully has the advantage of triggering your own wonderment, while leaving some things to your journey of discovery.

Having a hiker's perspective obviously means that I claim to possess an essential qualification for writing a book such as this. My Pyrenean hiking CV runs like this: Angharad and I have long been keen hikers in the UK. Prior to our first two visits to the Pyrenees in the 1990s, we had spent a week of one summer in the Austrian Alps, and a week of another summer in the White Mountains that form the northern end of the Appalachian range in the United States. Both trips involved staying in mountain huts each night.

Those first two visits to the Pyrénées-Orientales, during which we stayed at a friend's house and climbed Pic du Canigou (2,784m) and Pic Carlit (2,921m), set us off. Descending from the former to have a drink and a bite to eat in the Chalet-refuge des Cortalets, and reading on the walls about its role in the French Resistance during World War Two fired our imagination further. Then, back in Britain, we discovered an English translation (the only English translation as far as we are aware) of an early edition of Georges Véron's guide to the Haute Randonnée Pyrénéenne (HRP), the High Level Route that I introduced in Chapter 1, which traverses the range from the Atlantic to the Mediterranean, keeping as close to the frontier as possible. We vowed to attempt the traverse, but our jobs meant that we could not take the 42 days that Véron's guidebook indicated. We were also then in our mid-50s and a little cautious that we should not bite off more than we could chew.

We decided, therefore, to do the traverse in short bursts over a number of years, which turned out to be between six and 11 days each. Rather than start at Hendaye, on the Atlantic, we went to the high mountains first, to do them while we were still 'young', and then worked our way outwards, both east and west, in subsequent years. Thus, on 21 August 2001 we set off from the head of the road at the foot of the shapely, naked-rock Pic du Midi D'Ossue (2,884m) for the six-day trek, via mountain refuges, that would take us to just above the village of Gavarnie, with its famous cirque behind.

We completed the entire range, dipping our feet into the Mediterranean, at Banyuls-sur-Mer, on 15 September 2006, but we did not follow the HRP the whole way. We soon discovered that, away from the national parks, mountain refuges were thinner on the ground and that it would be necessary to wild-camp on occasion. We did not want the extra weight, and anyway we had grown to enjoy the conviviality of evenings spent with other hikers. So we varied our route to take in stretches of the lower GR10 and GR11 trails, where there was accommodation. In other words, we mixed and matched according to circumstance.

We missed out in 2007, because I had broken a kneecap in January that year as we set off for a hike in the dark from a village close to where we live. I tripped over a stone step in the village, which nestles into the Pennines, and so 2007 became the only year since 2001, during which we had not spent at least a week walking in the Pyrenees. In 2008 we returned to fill in some gaps in the traverse that we had not walked between 2001 and 2006 because of bad weather or other circumstances, and also to try wild-camping in a few remote stretches; and 2009 saw us doing other variations.

In 2010 we put down a base camp at a mountain site that had caught our eye in the Spanish Pyrenees – Bordes de Graus, above the village of Tavascan – and explored the area, to which we returned in 2011 with two of our by then six grandchildren and their parents. We were able to persuade the grandchildren to walk an epic day up to a favourite refuge – the Refugi de Certascan – and down again the next day. In 2012 both of us retired and as a joint present we decided to traverse the range a second time, but this time in the 'correct' sequence, from Hendaye to Banyuls-sur-Mer. We were still not prepared to do it all in one go, however, and we finally completed it in

September 2013. In 2014, we returned again to try yet more variations on stages of the traverse, with this book now very much in mind. See Chapters 6-9 for details of our routes, including their numerous variations over the years. See these chapters also for what I consider to be my 'preferred' route, which I would choose if I were to do the complete traverse a third time – weather permitting of course.

That concludes my Pyrenean Hiking CV. As for finding out more, there are many books about the Pyrenees, which fall into the following broad categories:

The detailed guidebooks to the traverse, to which I have already referred in Chapter 1

> Besides Georges Véron's guides to the HRP (all later editions have been in French only), Cicerone publishes separate guides to the GR10 (Paul Lucia), the GR11 (Brian Johnson), and the HRP (Ton Joosten).

Guidebooks to walks and climbs, either over the whole range or within specific regions

> These vary in their level of detail. The Pyrenees: the High Mountains from the Cirque de Lescun to the Carlit Massif, by Kev Reynolds, is a good example and covers a wide area of mountainous country, providing basic instructions for many treks and peaks.

Books that are devoted to social and/or political history, especially that of the last century during the periods of the Spanish Civil War and its aftermath, and World War Two

> Relatively recent examples are Rosemary Bailey's Love and War in the Pyrenees: a Story of Courage, Fear and Hope 1939-1944, and Edward Stourton's Cruel Crossing: Escaping Hitler Across the Pyrenees.

Personal documentary accounts, early examples of which typically wove stories around descriptions of climbs to particular summits

> Robin Fedden's 1950s account, The Enchanted Mountains: a Quest in the Pyrenees, starts with the Cirque de Gavarnie, before moving in later chapters to the highest mountain, Aneto, and the Encantados, in Spain. The book provides an entertaining narrative alongside evocative descriptions but, given that it delights in providing occasional passages in French, requires a certain literacy in that respect. More recently, the emphasis has moved towards people who have bought property in the area, for example Tony Hawks's A Piano in the Pyrenees.

Of course, the list of subjects to cover in an overview of an area as diverse as the Pyrenees is potentially endless, and so I confine the list to:

- Physical geography

- Weather

- The traverse and trans-frontier trails

- Dangers, risks and potential accidents

- Flora and fauna

- The Pyrenees of people, politics and livelihoods.

I think that, among all trekkers, there would be a consensus that the first four are essential topics. Guidebooks often assume that flora and fauna are important, but only a few devote any space to the last of these topics. I include the last two on the list because of the importance I place on gaining a more complete understanding of the area and its special qualities.

Physical geography

People think of the Pyrenees as a high mountain barrier, running eastwards from the Atlantic to the Mediterranean and separating France and Spain both physically and politically. It is a mental map that is reinforced by a physical geography atlas of Europe when you glance at the neck of land, 650 km long as the crow flies, bounded by Spain to the south and France to the north. Unless you live in that area of Europe, the mental map will serve your purposes fine, should you ever be moved to think about the Pyrenees. If you are interested in walking in them, or even traversing them, however, you are likely to want more than this simplification, and so you may choose to read the rest of this description, while checking with the overview map on the inside front cover.

Descriptions and classifications of the whole range tend to be arbitrary. From a trekker's perspective it is usual to divide it into the following sections from west (starting at the Atlantic) to east (ending at the Mediterranean).

- The **Pays Basque (**Basque Country), which comprises rolling foothills, mainly grassy, but gradually building to an elevation of 2,000m, where you also cross an impressive limestone area over two to three days. Their closest parallel in Britain is to be found in mid-Wales and there is no notion of a single mountain range, let alone three or four.

- The **Pyrénées-Occidentales**, which form the western section of the high mountains (Hautes-Pyrénées) from the Cirque de Lescun (with the first 2,500m mountain, the Pic d'Anie) to the Cirque de Gavarnie, whose highest points are more than 3,000m above sea level.

- They then continue with the **Pyrénées-Centrales**, which contain the highest mountain, the Pic d'Aneto at 3,404m.

- We are still in the *hautes montagnes* in the **near-eastern Pyrenees**, a title that is my invention. The guidebooks don't give this section a name, referring to it by its start and end points only. They do, however, make clear that it is a demanding section, owing to a combination of wild and rough terrain, poorly defined footpaths, and few people. Wikipedia lumps it with the next section as a very long tail of the Pyrénées-Orientales (eastern Pyrenees), stretching to the Mediterranean. They are, however, noticeably different from each other (see below) and I prefer to separate them. Thus, the near-eastern Pyrenees end at the eastern extremity of the tiny landlocked Principality of Andorra, sandwiched between Spain and France, still many kilometres from the sea. They contain the last of the 3,000m summits.

- The **Pyrénées-Orientales**, as classified by the Véron guidebook, are very different in character from their near-eastern neighbours. They are smoother and more populous, and the walking is generally easier, although it should not be under-estimated. Their high point is Pic Carlit (2,921m) at the western end, but perhaps the most famous mountain of the section is Canigou (2,784m), which is the Symbol of Catalonia and the last of the *hautes montagnes*. Thereafter, the summits gradually lose height before the range plunges abruptly to the Mediterranean. The Pyrénées-Orientales are also very different from the rolling hills of the Basque country, at the Atlantic end of the range. In the latter, the traverse takes four to five days to reach a height of 1,000m. In the Pyrénées-Orientales, you are still walking at over 1,000m for much of the final day of the traverse.

Taking the Pyrenees as a whole, an agreed inventory, drawn up by climbers on both sides of the frontier in 1990, states that there are 278 'tops' that are 3,000m and above. This total is made up of 129 major and 67 secondary summits, and 82 ridge projections.

From a walker's perspective, especially one who is doing the traverse from west to east, the above classification into 'zones' is neat. Each ends at a village with accommodation and public transport, if not on-site, at least not too far away. They also each involve eight to ten days of walking, ending in, or not far from, valley bottoms, often with public transport. If you plan to do the traverse over several years, they provide a good pointer for dividing trips.

From a physical geography perspective, however, the division is too neat. A glance at the overview map on the inside front cover indicates that the Hautes-Pyrénées (that is without the foothills on either side) comprise three major, overlapping mountain ranges running roughly west to east. While they may be connected by necks of comparatively high land, these ranges are separated by major river valleys. Moving from west to east, the first major division is created by the Vals d'Aran and Aneu. The heads of these two Spanish valleys are a few kilometres apart, but their rivers flow in opposite directions. Thus, the Val d'Aran contains the Garonne which soon enters France where it stays until it enters the Atlantic Ocean at Bordeaux. The Aneu contains the Noguera Pallaresa, which eventually joins the River Segre and flows towards the Mediterranean Sea. The second major valley division is the Vallée de la Têt and the Valle del Rio Segre. Although the Têt and Segre rivers start their flows in opposite directions, they both end up in the Mediterranean.

These river valleys are most obvious to walkers on the HRP, who will descend to the Val d'Aran at Salardu, at the end of the Pyrénées-Centrales section. Twelve or so days later they will spend a whole day crossing the upper reaches of the Têt valley, having 'conquered' Pic Carlit and its massif the previous day.

Walkers on the HRP and GR10 will also note that they descend to a large valley from the Canigou massif a few days later. This is the Tech, which enters the Mediterranean some kilometres south of the Têt. Yes you do have a stiff climb up the other side to what might be classed as a fourth overlapping range. I have omitted it only because it is too low to be counted as part of the Hautes-Pyrénées, its high point being the Roc de Frausa Oriental (1,450m). Don't, however, dismiss this final range. It is full of interest.

Back to the three ranges of the Hautes-Pyrénées: register above all that they comprise real mountains, predominately rock, with soaring ridges and shapely peaks. Some glaciers remain on the highest massifs. They are shrinking, but even after a mild winter, snow will also be seen throughout the year in the high corries. The longest of the three ranges stretches from the Cirque de Lescun, in the west, to the Garonne. It contains the very highest mountains, including all of the 3,000m summits, apart from the Pic d'Estats (3,143m) and its satellites, which form part of next range, east of the Garonne. These two ranges are also the bulkiest, with major incursions of other valleys, and containing massifs either side of the frontier. You may stand and stare from the mountain passes and obtain no sense of the geography that I have just described. All you see is a complex of mountain tops, ridges and valleys – it is easy to forget that you are actually on a traverse from an ocean to a sea. The third, most easterly, range of the Hautes-Pyrénées, which contains the Pic du

Canigou, is slimmer and neater on the map, although not necessarily so on the ground.

The final point I make about the physical geography is that the northern French slopes of the frontier are often much steeper and rougher than the Spanish slopes, which roll away to the south in *sierras*. This northern side also contains the famous cirques of the Pyrenees, such as the hugely impressive rock wall of the Cirque de Gavarnie.

This is all that I have to say about the physical geography and I accept it is somewhat dry. You bring physical geography alive by interpreting it through your own eyes.

Weather

It is July 2013. We are in a taxi travelling from Lourdes railway station to Gavarnie to resume our traverse of the Pyrenees from where we left off in 2012. It is mid-afternoon and a thunderstorm has started. As we climb the valley we notice horrendous flood damage, with barns and side roads washed away. The taxi driver tells us that the flooding occurred about four weeks earlier after several days of non-stop rain. Eventually the present storm and clouds start to clear to reveal rather more snow than we were expecting on the Cirque de Gavarnie, some tongues extending to quite low levels.

We saw more storm damage over the next few days in other valleys, with roads only just (partially) re-opened, driven mainly by people who had come to photograph the devastation. The streams were still in spate, frightening in both sound and sight. Walking down from a mountain refuge to the Val d'Aran on a dirt road, we suddenly came across a bridge that had been washed away. There was no option but to wade across the fast-flowing stream, although with some debate between us as to precisely the exact course we should take. A car driver on the opposite bank watched our progress with interest. You may admire the grace and music of mountain streams but also fear and wonder about their brute power and strength.

The excessive rainfall four weeks earlier was not, we learned, the only reason for the floods. In late March 2013, much of Europe had experienced extremely heavy and unseasonal snow. I can vouch for this from Britain, where many minor roads in hilly country were blocked by huge snowdrifts. The Pyrenees were no exception, with up to seven metres of snow falling – 'the highest snowfall anywhere in the world at that time' an ex-patriate British man whom we met one day told us. Much of this snow was still present in June, although it was melting fast in the hot weather in the run-up to the storms, causing the streams and rivers to be in spate even before the rain started. In other words, a combination of unseasonal weather three months earlier, and hot weather in early summer, followed by three days of storms and perpetual rain, had caused the floods. Two people died in them.

This harrowing story illustrates as well as any that weather everywhere, in mountains especially, can be very unpredictable. Guidebooks often describe a general weather pattern for the Pyrenees. Thus, while undertaking the traverse, you might like to know that it is expected to be hotter and drier towards the east because of the Mediterranean influence and also on the southern sun-basked Spanish side. Further west, the maritime Atlantic influence is more dominant, bringing rain and mist, especially on the French side. Differences in pattern between Spain and France may be abrupt – it may be fine and sunny in Spain, but immediately beyond the frontier 'port' it may become misty. In July 2014 we stood on a Spanish mountain in sunshine and watched the mist engulfing the frontier port just a few kilometres away, threatening to spill over but never quite managing to do so.

The guidebooks also often note the weather by season, sometimes by month: late July is expected to be fine, August hot but stormy later in the day, early September unsettled, but the rest of September fine again. Although it cannot be guaranteed, most snow should have gone from the high ground that trekkers tread by mid-July. Therefore, your window for doing the traverse is from early July (starting with the lower snow-free sections) to late-September when snow might return.

However, as meteorologists are fond of saying, 'climate' is just 'average weather'. In other words, climate is what you expect, but weather is what you get. Climate scientists are also predicting more unpredictability in weather patterns and greater extremes of weather, but that's another book.

Unpredictable, extreme weather has consequences underfoot long after the event has passed. July 2013 was a case in point, the lingering snowfields and streams in spate requiring extra care and occasionally posing a significant problem. Moreover, all of this was challenging us while the weather was actually being 'typical' for the time of year, that is, delivering several days of warm sunshine, which would build up to and eventually be broken by a storm – often a night storm. It would then be followed by more days of warm, often hot, sunshine.

Our overall weather experience in numbers

Overall we have walked 156 days in total on the Pyrenean traverse, of which 139 – or 89 per cent – were generally fine (most of them entirely so), and 17 – or nine per cent – could be regarded as characterised by poor weather because of rain, substantial mist, or both. These stats indicate an excellent reason to go

A storm clears on the descent from Canigou in the Pyrénées-Orientales

trekking or walking in the Pyrenees – the weather between mid-July and mid-September is usually excellent. Our route plans over the years were only disrupted in a major way on three occasions because of the weather that greeted us, and on two additional occasions in 2013 because of the conditions caused by weather earlier that year.

The traverse and trans-frontier trails

The first recorded complete traverse of the Pyrenees was made more than two centuries ago by one Augustin de Candolle, whose primary purpose was to record the local flora. Then, according to the HRP 'inventor', Georges Véron, Friedrich Parrot completed the traverse in 53 days in 1817.

From 1817 to the present era, which started in earnest in the 1960s, information about the traverse is sketchy, so let us fast-forward. As already mentioned, there are currently two officially designated footpaths that traverse the Pyrenees between the Atlantic and Mediterranean, the GR10 on the French side and the GR11 on the Spanish side, plus the semi-official high-level route, the HRP. The usual way to walk any of the traverses is west to east from the Atlantic to the Mediterranean. This is for good reasons: you are likely to stay in the shade longer on hot mornings, the sun is on your back from the middle of the day and the weather improves as you travel east (but see my notes on weather unpredictability above).

The Grande Randonnée 10 (GR10)

This trek starts at the French border town of Hendaye, on the Atlantic, and ends at Banyuls-sur-Mer, on the Mediterranean. It takes 50-plus days to complete, according to the guidebooks and other available information. It stays entirely in France but does visit the frontier with Spain occasionally, so you may step into that country and back if you desire.

Work actually started on the path in 1964, but the GR10 story is never-ending as variations are added and even the official main route changes from time to time. Given that it aims to make the Pyrenees more accessible to hikers, it tends to wend its way below the highest ground, and tries always to land the weary trekker at some form of accommodation (*gîte d'étape*, mountain refuge, *auberge*, hotel) at the end of each day. However, it does not always live up to this aim and you should be aware of the following:

- The main route does climb at one point to a pass at 2,509m, and one of its several official variants climbs to 2,734m. It also crosses several other passes in the Hautes-Pyrénées that are above 2,000m. While avoiding the high peaks, a variant does pass over the summit of Pic du Canigou at 2,784m in the Pyrénées-Orientales. The 2,509m high point on the main route is the Col de Madamète, near the western edge of the Pyrénées-Centrales, while the 2,734m high point is the Hourquette d'Ossue, near the eastern edge of the Pyrénées-Occidentales. The two are not far apart as the crow flies.

- It is intended to be accessible to most hikers and not technically difficult. That said, I note from some autobiographical accounts of the GR10 traverse that the pass, which forms the trekkers' boundary between the Basque country and the first section of the Hautes-Pyrénées (the Pyrénées-Occidentales), might be a bit tricky for those who define the word 'walk' literally. This is the Pas de l'Osque (1,922m), which one description of the last the few metres of ascent on the west side states 'is the closest that the GR10 comes to a rock climb' and another that it is 'quite a scramble that almost feels like rock-climbing'. The only mention that the Cicerone GR10 guidebook makes to the Pas de l'Osque, however, is that it is 'enchanting'. We have been over it twice. It certainly requires the use of hands, but there are plenty of holds and we really had no difficulty. The second time we did it, in 2012, a steel cable had been attached to the rocks, intended to help, but we actually found it easier to ignore, at the start at least. The eastern side of the Pas de l'Osque is easy, on a slanting path heading approximately south.

On leaving the Refuge des Cortalets in the Pyrénées-Orientales

- The GR10 passes through the French Département of the Ariège, a wild and underpopulated stretch of about 15 hard days (essentially the length of the near-eastern Pyrenees section), where staffed accommodation and food can be at a premium. The *gîte* listed in the guidebook might or might not still exist at the end of the day. *Gîtes*, however, can come as well as go, so it's always worth an Internet search for the latest information. Nevertheless, the odds are that you will have to camp or stay in an unstaffed *cabane* on three or more nights while passing through the Ariège, or go 'off-piste'. In addition, not every *gîte* that does exist will provide meals, although it should offer cooking facilities. Be prepared to carry your own food, as shops are also rare.

The consensus on the length of the GR10 seems to be that it is 866 km, with a cumulative total of 48,000m of ascent and descent. This is a lot of up and down, partly explained by the GR10 descending to the valley at the end of most days to seek out accommodation. Moreover, most of these valleys tend to run north-south so you rarely walk along them. Throughout its length it is well waymarked with red and white paint flashes, and you will soon work out markings that tell you when you should turn and those that indicate the way not to go at junctions.

We have not walked all of the GR10, but in our experience there is no need for a detailed guidebook to tell you the way, as the waymarks – plus a good map to provide the overall context and resolve those rare occasions when the waymarks let you down – do a good job. A guidebook is useful, however, for indicating the nature of the terrain – its steepness and roughness – and the accommodation at the time it was being researched. The current Cicerone guidebook to the GR10 also provides some tips for negotiating the 15 days across the Ariège. If you plan to walk the GR10, however, do, as indicated above, seek out the latest information on the Internet. Note that many guidebooks are updated online or on social media sites: you can, for example, subscribe to a free e-newsletter for all Cicerone guidebooks. Much of the accommodation listed has its own website of course, but you also need to check when that was last updated.

Gran Recorrido de los Pirineos (GR11)

The GR11 starts at the frontier Spanish town of Irun (facing Hendaye and the GR10 across the bay) on the Atlantic, and ends at Cap de Creus on the Mediterranean. The latest Cicerone guidebook completes it over 45 days. It stays mostly in Spain but does spend about three days in Andorra. It also visits the border with France occasionally.

The GR11 was developed in the 1980s. At about 840 km or 522 miles, it is shorter than the GR10. It also requires less total ascent and descent: 39,000m[1]. This is because many valleys on the Spanish side run east-west, and, while long enough, it requires six or so days fewer than GR10 to complete. Its highest point, the Collada de Tirapits (2,780m), towards the east of the Hautes-Pyrenées, is higher than anything the GR10 offers on its main route. The GR11 is by repute also rougher underfoot, and although it tries to land you at accommodation with food at the end of each day, on a few stages you only have an unstaffed refuge, *cabane* or camping area unless you take an alternative route[2]. Some lodgings may also be found in *Casas Rurales*, which are local houses offering overnight accommodation, but not necessarily food. Enquire on the Internet or locally. Red and white waymarking follows the same conventions as for the GR10 and is usually adequate, but don't take this for granted.

---

1 This is the quoted figure on several websites, but note that the latest Cicerone GR11 guidebook states 46,000m (although the previous edition stated more vaguely, 'excess of 39,000m').
2 Rerouting of some stretches in recent years has minimised accommodation problems – see also the latest Cicerone GR11 guidebook.

Again, we have by no means walked all of the GR11, but as a proxy for roughness we perhaps have had to put a hand against a rock from time to time to maintain balance, and more often than on the GR10. We possibly also have had to slide down a few more rocks on our backsides than on the GR10, but overall the GR11 that we have experienced is a fine walk. The only time that we have had to use hands significantly, as well as feet, to make progress is on a tough stage on the south side of the highest peak, Aneto, and that was for a few short minutes above a small tarn (*ibón*). Note that this particular stage forms part of an 'easy' variant of the HRP – easy, that is, according to the HRP guidebooks (see Chapters 4 and 7).

The Haute Randonnée Pyrénéenne – HRP (Pyrenean Haute Route in the English Cicerone guidebook, the High Level Route in the only English translation of Georges Véron's HRP guidebook)

Georges Véron and two others made their first high-level trek from Hendaye to Banyuls-sur-Mer in 1968. It took them 41 days, the same overall time as advised in the most recent edition of his guidebook (2007, published posthumously as Georges sadly died in 2005). The current English language Cicerone guidebook (2009) allows 45 days, an increase from the original 2004 edition (42) days after the author, Ton Joosten, agreed with reader comments that some stages were too long. Véron's first guidebook appeared in 1974 and there have been numerous editions since. The only English translation of the Véron guidebooks was published in 1981, with a reprint in 1991.

What one picks up from the Véron guidebooks in particular, but also to some extent from Joosten's two editions (thus far), is that the HRP has always been a developing concept. More so than the GR10 and GR11, the suggested route has changed and evolved over the years and each edition contains many variations. In fact Georges Véron himself suggested that it be treated as a 'concept' and Ton Joosten in his 2009 edition suggests that it should be considered more as an 'idea'. Often decisions as to the exact route have to be made on the ground, according to weather conditions, conditions underfoot and, I would add, your own state of mind.

The total distance for the HRP is stated by the Cicerone guidebook to be 800 km. This is obviously an approximate figure, given the number of possible variations that are described in the numerous editions of the guidebooks. It can safely be said, however, that the HRP is significantly shorter than either the GR10 (866 km) or GR11 (840 km). This is because it takes a more direct line although, to anyone walking it, that might seem to be an odd claim as it lurches from one side of the frontier to the other.

At around 40,000m, it also involves less total ascent and descent than the GR10 (48,000m) because it does not always descend to valleys at the end of each day, but about the same as the GR11 (but less if you take the ascent total from the latest GR11 guidebook). As might be expected, however, its highest points – the Col Inférieur de Litérole (2,983m) and the Coll de Mulleres (2,928m) – are higher than anything on either of the other routes and require great care to descend their eastern sides initially.

Of course, the HRP is generally rougher underfoot. You have to place your hands on rocks to steady yourself or maintain balance more often than on the GR10 and GR11, and some descents are tortuously steep and through rocks. Only towards the eastern end of the Hautes-Pyrénées does it actually go along the frontier ridge for a significant distance, otherwise it switches from side to side. Near the Atlantic end, however, it often follows the same route as the GR10 or GR11 and, towards the Mediterranean, it stays in France and follows the GR10 much of the time, apart from occasional brief excursion into Spain.

We have walked about 85 per cent of the HRP over the years, if you allow for the variations described in the guidebooks. As it is not a formally designated path, expect waymarking – where it exists – to vary. Sometimes it is red and white, other times plain red, or orange, or yellow or green… and probably other colours too. Sometimes the only waymarking is by means of small cairns along an indistinct path. On several stretches, newer red and white paint flashes co-exist with older colours. Despite all this, a wriggly line that the cartographer has deemed the 'standard' HRP is drawn on most French and Spanish maps.

The Cirque d'Estaube, Pyrénées-Centrales, from the HRP

Trans-frontier trails

These paths linking France and Spain have a long history, but, as mentioned in Chapter 1, they are best remembered as two-way refugee crossings – in the late 1930s for republicans fleeing into France from the victorious General Franco in the Spanish Civil War; and, in the early 1940s, for many of the thousands on the Nazi hit list fleeing into Spain, which was actually neutral during World War Two. Recently, many of these paths have been opened up to walkers by providing signposts and red and white waymarks. Information boards at the bottom, and sometimes on the pass itself, tell you about who fled and when.

Some trans-frontier trails provide designated links between the GR10 and GR11, as well as the HRP, because – by definition – they have to cross it at some point. They are useful, therefore, for anyone doing the traverse who has planned their own route as a mixture of GR10, GR11 and HRP. We have walked a few of them for this purpose and we have been led into some truly wild places, although the paths themselves somehow manage to avoid difficulties. Yet, I have always carried a humbling sense of human history and visions of those trying to make their escape in such surroundings. Even the popular name for many of the trans-frontier passes – the ports (gateways) – conjures up images of the desperate human traffic going back and forth.

On the trans-frontier trail below the Port de Tavascan in the near-eastern Pyrenees

Dangers, risks and potential accidents

The first thing to remember when you tackle any of these routes is that you are going for a walk, albeit a long and rough one in the mountains. Sometimes you may feel the need to place your hand against a rock for reassurance, or to steady yourself. Rarely, you have to use hands as well as feet for a short distance to make any kind of progress, but above all, I repeat, you are doing a rough mountain walk. Remember this in order to gain a sense of perspective vis-à-vis the dangers you face in a car, on a bike or walking across a road in everyday life.

Please do keep the above in mind as I give below a potted history of our experiences of risks, dangers and accidents.

Watch where you are putting your feet

You are most likely to have a fall when you are on easier terrain, having relaxed a little. Over 13 years of walking in the Pyrenees – 156 days on the traverse plus several other hikes – Angharad and I have had, between us, three falls that are noteworthy, and none did lasting damage, delivering to me a black eye;

27

nosebleed and broken walking pole; and to Angharad, a badly bruised leg and similar walking pole break. These were all sustained when our guard had relaxed somewhat. My falls were on relatively easy ground and a reward for complacency, Angharad's on the more tricky terrain of a boulder field.

Thunder, mist and snow

You have to accept that in the mountains there are weather-associated dangers that you cannot do anything about. You don't abandon your route because there might or might not be a thunderstorm later in the day. You would hardly ever set off if you did. We have only once been caught out in a storm in a place where we would have preferred not to be. This was in 2003 on a ridge in the Pyrénées-Occidentales. We just had to carry on regardless, but of course you need the appropriate storm clothing that you carry with you, even though you might hardly ever have to resort to it.

Rain is a problem mainly if it is also associated with the cloud descending and shrouding you in mist (again assuming that you have appropriate clothing to put on). Then the temperature drops by several degrees, but on the GR10 and GR11, route-finding should not be a problem because of the waymarks – even when the path on the ground is not obvious, as when, again in 2003, we crossed limestone 'Karst' terrain at the eastern end of the Basque country. Even on the HRP, some form of waymark is more usual than there being none at all. In 2010 in the near-eastern Pyrenees, on a section of the HRP where we saw nobody all day until we were safely down in the valley, the French side of the pass was filled with mist. Moreover, we had a lengthy boulder field to cross slowly, where no path could exist on the ground. The waymarking, however, was good and we just went over the boulders from one red and white flash to another. Only once have we been caught in mist, where route finding has been a problem. We were crossing a rare plateau area when the mist descended, and spent about 20 anxious minutes trying to decide the correct route at a junction – an experience that I describe more fully in Chapter 4.

The other weather-associated hazard is unexpected lying snow that you have to cross. This usually results from a previous heavy fall in spring, as was the case again in 2013 as we traversed the high mountains. We were walking in the Pyrénées-Centrales to the east of Gavarnie, towards the Horquette de Héas, a steep, rocky gap in the ridge. It was a beautiful day with the sun shining, the birds singing and the cowbells ringing when we successfully skirted our first snowfield at about 2,100m. Fifteen minutes later we came across a second snowfield and this one we had to cross. It steepened at its far side, but we coped. That's the problem with snowfields: they might start on an easy gradient but it's difficult to anticipate changes further into them.

The third snowfield a little further on, however, did for us. It was quite long

Sometimes there's no option but to cross the snow: below the Coll de Coma Anyell in the Pyrénées-Orientales

and the slope soon steepened. First Angharad went sliding down, followed by me seconds later, both of us coming to an abrupt halt on grass at the bottom with the only damage being to self-confidence. We had actually checked before crossing that it was not above a ravine and that if we slipped it would be onto grass, but even so it was a sobering moment. With the prospect of worse to come, of which we had been advised the night before by a trekker who was traversing in the opposite direction, we turned back. Plus, we had seen nobody coming the other way and no-one at all for an hour or so.

Back at Héas late afternoon, with the birds still singing and the cowbells still ringing, we hitched a lift to the nearest town – Luz-Saint-Sauveur – checked into a hotel that we knew from previous sojourns and each bought a pair of instep crampons (more on these in Chapter 4).

Rapidly melting snow from the previous spring may also cause innocuous streams to become torrents, as already noted. Take care when crossing. The worst experience that has happened to us was after a storm one night in2012. The next day we were helped across one stream in spate by the leader of another party of walkers. We then had to wade a second with our boots off.

The third was higher up and seemed relatively simple to cross, until Angharad's foot slipped on a wet rock midstream and she shipped a boot's worth of water.

Snakes, wild boars, bears and cattle

You are more or less guaranteed not to come across any bears. The few left are very shy of coming anywhere near humans, and may possibly have all been shot dead by the local guardians of the countryside by the time you read this (see next section).

Cattle with their bells ringing are usually docile. Sometimes you come across them on sections of path, especially the GR10, where they might have eroded it. They will, however, escape to the side at the earliest opportunity. Once, in the Catalan mountains, we reached a hanging valley, where a notice told us to beware of cattle ahead and of the danger of walking between cows and their calves (similar notices are posted in Britain), and generally to give them wide berth. When we eventually came across the herd we saw a way not quite through the middle, but out of kicking range. They studiously ignored us.

We have only seen a wild boar cross our path once, in the Pyrénées-Orientales on the GR10. It didn't charge us. In fact it took immediate fright and went crashing down through the woods that lined the path.

Large horns but usually docile

Finally snakes: the Pyrenees are supposed to be awash with them, including venomous vipers, and this has always been a source of some alarm for Angharad who can't even look at photographs of them in a Sunday newspaper magazine. In all our years of tramping the Pyrenees, however, we have only seen two, and on both occasions they were spotted before we trod on them, thereby allowing them to slither away. Maybe we make too much noise or the vibrations in the ground caused by our walking poles usually give advance warning to clear off.

Drinking polluted water from streams
Generally, pollution of water in the mountains is caused by cattle, sheep and horses, some of which may be found higher up than you would expect. We do take water purifiers with us, but we tend not to use them if we are fairly confident that we are above any cattle, sheep or horses. Also, we did not use them at all in 2013 after it was pointed out that the streams were flowing so fast that they were self-cleansing. Obviously you have to make your own decisions on whether to purify or not, but common sense should get you through without stomach bugs.

Wildlife, flowers and trees

Mammals

Non aux ours! No to the bears! So ran this huge slogan in 2002 on a wall in Luz-Saint-Sauveur, a small town north of Gavarnie at the eastern extremity of the Pyrénées-Occidentales. Lying on the main route of the GR10, Luz-Saint-Sauveur is a friendly place that hosts many tourists and a wide variety of shops, hotels and restaurants. It even boasts an excellent outdoor shop, which is great for things that you have either forgotten or lost or didn't think you would need. We have used it on several of our visits, including the very first one in late August 2001, when we were warned that much snow still lay on the high mountain passes (as usual because of a heavy fall in Spring) and that we should hire ice axes.

Friendly to tourists Luz-Saint-Sauveur might be, but it seems that a vocal part of the resident population is hostile to bears and attempts at their reintroduction to the mountains. The general story is that the indigenous Pyrenean brown bear had been hunted to extinction and this reintroduction involved its cousins from Slovenia. The hostility aroused did cause the local authorities to issue a leaflet defending their action, claiming, among other things, that the bears kill far fewer sheep than the weather and stray dogs, and are very timid towards humans. For more information on the bears and the conflict over their reintroduction try the following articles from an official site promoting the Ariège[3] and the UK's Daily Telegraph[4] newspaper.

The Ariège site notes the (stalled) reintroduction policy, which farmers see as an 'imposition by Parisian bureaucrats' who know nothing about life in the mountains. The author then concludes: 'One might also ask whether, with the situation remaining as it is, the Pyrenees have not just become a bear zoo, artificially managed from Paris.' The Daily Telegraph also quotes someone saying, 'Paris imposes bears on the Pyrenees'. The consensus of websites that mentions bears in the Pyrenees is that about 20 survive across the whole range.

Not accepting the claims of the conservationists, many Pyrenean sheep farmers have reintroduced the *patou*[5], otherwise known as Pyrenean mountain dogs. They are large and white, and are placed among a flock of sheep at an early age. They grow up with the sheep and become very protective of them. We first came across one in 2003 below the Pic d'Anie (2,504m), the first of the high mountains when travelling west to east. It was misty and the dog appeared from nowhere, sniffed us and went away. We have since come across them a few times in the midst of flocks, usually on slightly higher ground, and on the alert. They are unlikely to move from their resting spot or turn aggressive unless you attack the sheep.

Nevertheless, despite this measure to protect sheep, the hunting of bears continues. Two friends once came across a hunting party returning to

A patou guarding sheep from bear and other attacks

3 http://tinyurl.com/pyreneesbears1
4 http://tinyurl.com/pyreneesbears2
5 http://tinyurl.com/pyreneespatou

Landrovers and sporting their kill, which they tied to the bonnet of one. You are extremely unlikely, therefore, even to come across the traces of a bear while traversing the Pyrenees, although tourists in the Couserans area of the French Hautes-Pyrénées were able to view newly born cubs[6] in 2011.

I have mentioned above – under Dangers, Risks and Accidents – our minimal experience of encountering wild boars (*sangliers*). Organised hunts shoot them, but these are managed according to season and even day of the week, so that the population is maintained. In the forests of the Pyrénées-Orientales (wherewe had our sole sighting) we once heard the guns firing away on the other side of the valley.

In fact, the only terrestrial mammals that we have regularly seen on our travels, apart from cattle, horses and sheep, are marmots and herds of isards. Both seem to thrive in the high mountains. The latter (also known as Pyrenean Chamois) bound away at the first sighting, so you're only likely to see them at a distance. Marmots scurry onto safe spots above the path and whistle to each other. We are particularly fond of these furry, brown animals and their distinctive whistles although they too were extinct for many years (due to climatic changes) until their reintroduction from the Alps last century.

To complete the mammalian picture we have seen the very timid *mouflon* (wild sheep) just once. Once also, on a high pass, we came across what the *guardienne* at a refuge two days later described as being like a 'flat squirrel'. We eventually identified it as an ermine.

A sanglier hunt group attempts corporate social responsibility, having restored this picnic site to which the sign refers. It translates as: 'Respect this spot restored by the wild boar hunters of Maureillas'

6 http://tinyurl.com/pyreneesbears3

Reptiles and amphibians

Despite our personal sighting of only two over 13 years (see above), snakes are common in the Pyrenees, and there are several species, some poisonous, some not. There's a good website[7], which provides photos of the different snakes, recording the only poisonous one as being the Asp Viper.

Contrary to our very rare sightings of snakes, we have come across other reptiles and amphibians, such as lizards and frogs, in profusion. High mountain tarns are sometimes teeming with the latter to the extent that it is difficult to avoid treading on them on shoreside paths. We have also sighted toads occasionally. The website in the paragraph above also provides details about lizards, frogs and toads – there is more to these creatures than meets the eye of the careful, watchful trekker.

Birds

In September 2006, we were about to start the long trek (two hours or more) from the frontier ridge to the Refugi d'Ull de Ter in the Pyrénées-Orientales. This ridge is described in guidebooks as a 'classic' through the Catalan mountains, and the HRP trekker follows it for 5-6 km, the height varying between 2,861m (Pic Noufonts) and 2,652m at the point where the GR11 meets it. Although long, the hike, including the ridge, is wonderfully straightforward, except today there had been thunder in the air for the previous two hours and we had been a little apprehensive and keen to descend, away from the exposed heights. So we were happy that the ridge was over for us as we sat down to eat the last of our picnic, when, from around the rocks that marked the end of the ridge, flew two large birds with enormous wingspan, soaring and gliding and coming as close as 20 metres. We had just seen, close-up, a pair of golden eagles – a magical moment.

While never so close as that September afternoon in 2006, we have spotted pairs of eagles several times since, although I wouldn't exactly describe them as common on that basis. Much more often we have seen flocks of that other great Pyrenean bird of prey, the vulture. One way of distinguishing vultures from eagles at a distance is that the latter tend to fly in pairs, the former grouped in larger numbers. In 2012 while we were toiling up a slope we saw almost an orderly queue of vultures waiting to take their pickings from a poor dead animal away to our left. This carried on for a good 30 minutes. More

---

7 http://tinyurl.com/pyreneesreptiles

ominous, however, is when they start to circle over in late afternoon as if waiting for you to collapse of heat or fatigue.

Bird-watchers love the Pyrenees as there are so many to see. We are not bird-watchers ourselves in any dedicated sense, so we can only report what we happen to have come across – especially eagles, vultures and alpine choughs. The first time we noticed the last was in 2008, just after breakfast at the gîte-refuge Jeandel – in the ski resort of La Pierre Saint Martin (summer version, see below) of all places. Like a very large blackbird, but with bright orange beak and legs, it was on the patch of grass in front of the building on which campers had pitched tents the previous night. It was, at most, three metres away. Our next conscious sighting was four years later, only a few kilometres away from the first sighting as the chough flies. Then, we were eating lunch beneath the Pic d'Anie while it swooped bravely around us, landing about ten metres away. There it waited patiently until we cleared off and it could pick our crumbs.

Of course we have seen many more, different birds, but those are the ones that have thrilled us – plus the owls that we never see but hear often at night. It's just as well that birds are *part* of our Pyrenean experience, rather than being *the* Pyrenean experience. From our admittedly only one encounter with serious bird-watchers, expectations may be raised that are not realised, as in the following very short story. It was September 2013 and we were about to repeat the 'classic' Catalan ridge walk of 2006. We had just finished breakfast at the *Gîte d'étape* in Eyne, a small village in the Têt valley on the French side of the ridge, and were talking to two British bird-watchers who were also about to leave the *gîte* after spending a few days there. They had come to see the great migration, for which this part of the Pyrenees is famous. They had, they told us, been sadly disappointed as the fine settled weather covering Europe had obviously delayed the migration and now they had to go home. I don't think that we made them any happier when we told them of our 2006 experience with the eagles on the ridge about 1,600m above them, and that we hoped for similar today (nor were we disappointed).

Butterflies

We know even less about butterflies than we do about birds. All I can say is that, lower down and under the right weather conditions, we have seen colourful masses to the side of paths and dirt roads. Their wings have been of innumerable colours, both bright and subdued, and of patterns complicated and simple. Our most amazing experience was in 2008, near the hamlet of Alós d'Isil, at the Head of the Vall d'Aneu, in the near-eastern Pyrenees. To the side of the dirt road entering the hamlet from the north they were absolutely everywhere – a complete kaleidoscope. For a little more information and photographs, see Hike Pyrenees-butterflies[8].

Flowers

August 2013 saw us in Andorra, climbing on the HRP towards the Col de la Mine, when, as often happens, a steep section ended in a hanging valley before resuming its ascent. This hanging valley was carpeted in what appeared to be hundreds of species of wild flowers. The overall effect, as with the butterflies described above, was of a kaleidoscope of colour, simultaneously bright and subdued in bewildering but beautiful array.

We had not been expecting this sight. Quite the contrary, a hot August day is not the usual time to witness the buoyant freshness of wild mountain flowers in full bloom. June yes, early July maybe, as spring still lingers, but not now. And we had similar sights throughout our three days trekking across Andorra, which the helpful people in the Tourist Information Office at Pas de la Casa (see below) were thrilled to hear about.

The reason for the August profusion was that the much maligned heavy spring snow –which had caused significant problems for us and even greater ones for many of the local population – had only recently melted. Better late than never, a less long-lived version of the mountain spring then appeared, revealing its wares all at once. This is the list we compiled over dinner that night in Andorra, but they represent only those we recognised: daisies, Ox-eye daisies, Yellow daisies, Pink Campion, Bladder Campion, Yellow Vetch, Creeping Buttercup, Irises (various colours), Sea Pink, Squill, Forget-me-nots, Orchids, Gentians (blue and yellow), Thistles, Dandelions, Clover, Cow Parsley (pink and white), Harebells (various shades of blue), Wild Mountain Thyme.

---

8 http://tinyurl.com/pyreneesbutterflies2

Wild flowers in profusion in Andorra

We also came across a multitude of wild grasses and unknown 'fluffy' flowers. Higher up, where snow had only recently melted and where the grass was still flattened, white flowers appeared, clutching the ground and appearing shy in the bright sun. They were obviously the first to do so after the snow had gone, for there were no others. For more information on what you should see (which overlaps with the list above but is by no means equivalent to it) and photographs, see Hike Pyrenees[9].

Trees

The Pyrenees can be densely wooded on their lower slopes, but they are usually bare above about 2,000m. While you will soon note a general pattern of mixed deciduous woodland lower down, and evergreens, such as conifers, higher up, nothing is fixed and the aspect of the land may account for a lot.

We have walked, for example, through a delightful beech forest in the Pyrénées-Orientales at a height of about 1,400m, where seemingly every tree had a tall elegant stem. The same is true in the Forêt d'Iraty, in the Basque

---

9 http://tinyurl.com/pyreneesflora

country, at a similar altitude. Beech and chestnut might also be found higher up, mixed with silver fir, although the last may form forests all of their own.

The transition from evergreen to unwooded mountainside has always appeared to be quite abrupt to me, as fully grown pine and fir turn into stunted variants and then, suddenly, there is nothing.

Although rarely mentioned as being among the most common Pyrenean trees, we have also come across both birch and hazel, the latter appearing as if the trees have been coppiced in the past. However, when we once asked a lady in her 80s who had lived among these trees all of her life about the coppicing, she had no knowledge of it.

The Pyrenees of people, politics and livelihoods

Il n'y a plus de Pyrénées – The Pyrenees no longer exist. So declared Louis XIV of France on the accession of his grandson to the Spanish throne in 1700. He meant, of course, the Pyrenees as a political border between France and Spain. But he was wrong. Over two centuries later, France and Spain might both be members of the European Union, but in every other respect they are separate, with their own traditions, ways of doing things, and, most of all, language.

The Pyrenees also divide smaller trans-frontier cultures into French and Spanish territories, which nevertheless are united by language. Both the Basque Country, in the west, and Catalonia, extending from the Pyrénées-Centrales to the Mediterranean, straddle the frontier, and each has its own language. (At least) two further wholly Pyrenean languages must be added to complete the linguistic count, although to my knowledge I have never heard either being spoken. These are Aragonese, spoken by 10,000-30,000 people and Aranese (in the Val d'Aran of course), which is spoken by about 3,000 people.

Linguists seem intent on arguing forever over the origins of Basque for it appears to be like no other European language, although written down it is immediately recognisable by its prolific use of the letter X. If you understand French (in particular) or Spanish you should be able to get the sense of written Catalan, which belongs to the same branch of the romance language family.

The Basques have a long-held separatist ambition to form their own nation state. Many Catalans too are now seeking independence, especially in Spain where, if you are an English speaker, some will prefer to speak to you in English rather than Spanish. While largely ignored and dismissed as a Spanish problem – at least on the surface - the aspirations, passions and tensions caused by Catalan calls for independence do occasionally emerge in France too, as we witnessed in September 2013 at a *gîte d'étape* below Canigou.

Angharad and I were the only foreigners among about 15 French in separate groups. Half way through dinner a French Catalan at the head of the table rapped it for attention. All heads turned towards him. He explained (in French) that two days later would be Catalonia day, and that in Spain, stretching from the border town of Le Perthus to Barcelona, a human chain was to be formed for independence. He finished his little speech, paused for engagement, but there was none and his co-Frenchmen (apart from his two friends), Angharad and I returned to our food that we had been carefully studying as he spoke..

The following morning, Angharad and I did speak to him, asking more about calls for a referendum in Spain He answered our questions and then enlightened us with a bit more history. The present situation was, he said, in large part caused by the British and Britain's Treaty with Spain, which was signed in 1713. Catalonia was then an independent state, he said, and had an alliance with Britain, which presumably had suited the latter in relation to its ongoing wars with Spain.

The British Treaty with Spain of 1713, however, changed everything because, as a result, Britain abandoned Catalonia, which lost its independent statehood after another year of fighting Spain alone, the final surrender being on 11 September 1714. I apologised profusely for the alleged crimes of my forebears and he did note the irony in my voice and laugh.

Border stone 565 on the penultimate day of the traverse. The graffiti on the signpost translates as 'Neither France nor Spain…. We are Catalans'

Since 1980, 11 September has been marked as Catalonia Day[10]. If you want to read a more complex story of events see Catalan History in 15 Episodes[11] (Episode 7) by the Public Diplomacy Council of Catalonia. Also, the deal that included the abandonment of Catalonia was part of the Utrecht Treaties that signalled the end of the War of the Spanish Succession[12], which you might wish to look up. Interestingly, six years previously, I had engaged in a robust discussion with a Frenchman at the same *gîte*, who had a very different perspective on this and related subjects, a story I recount in Chapter 5.

There's obviously too much human history associated with the Pyrenees to take at face value Louis XIV's comment in 1700 that they no longer exist. Although you will be able to find tomes to read about it, this history is somehow much more interesting and 'alive' when you discover bits for yourself among these mountains, and how they have influenced present day passions and customs. I can give you the statistic that about half a million refugees fled from Spain to France over the Pyrenees in the late 1930s, while the early 1940s saw an exodus of 40,000-50,000 people in the opposite direction. Useful as they are, however, such bare numbers only provide the context for when you yourself embark on these passages, aided by local information boards and plaques. In relation to World War II refugees, one thing among many that you wonder about is why Spain was neutral anyway. After all, both Franco and Hitler were Fascist dictators. Apparently the immediate setting for Spain's neutrality was the very start of the Pyrenean trail in France. Hitler met Franco at Hendaye railway station in 1940, with an agenda for Spain to join the war in alliance with Germany. Franco, so the increasingly apocryphal story goes, insisted on going for a siesta that lasted a few hours, whereupon Hitler took the hump and left, refusing to have anything more to do with him.

This is not to claim that Franco was necessarily sympathetic to many of the World War II refugees who reached neutral Spain. In fact his government was downright unsympathetic towards one Walter Benjamin, a German Marxist philosopher and Jew who was high on the Nazi hit list. A plaque next to the official end of the GR10 in Banyuls-sur-Mer illustrates the route of his escape from France to Port Bou just over the border in Spain, where he arrived in September 1940. He travelled no further. Apparently, although he had papers that guaranteed safe departure from Spain on a boat travelling to the United

10 http://tinyurl.com/catalonia-day
11 http://tinyurl.com/catalanhistory
12 http://tinyurl.com/SpanisSuccession

States, he had none allowing him entry into and travel across Spain to its Atlantic seaboard. Because he was in ill health, the Spanish authorities allowed him to stay an additional night in Port Bou before deporting him back to Nazi-occupied France, where he would surely have been arrested immediately. He was found dead in his hotel room the next day, the Spanish authorities claiming suicide, while others were convinced that he was murdered by the Gestapo. If you have a bit of time on your hands in Banyuls-sur-Mer and wish to discover more, take the short train ride to Port Bou and follow the Walter Benjamin trail[13] around the town.

If you are even hungrier for knowledge about these refugee crossings, a few books are available. As noted earlier in this chapter, we have Cruel Crossing: Escaping Hitler Across the Pyrenees, by Edward Stourton (Transworld Publishers) and Rosemary Bailey's Love and War in the Pyrenees: a Story of Courage, Fear and Hope 1939-1944 (published by Phoenix, 2009). We, however, bought them *after* having our own curiosity roused by what we discovered during the traverse, when they made so much more sense and touched us so much more deeply. My advice, therefore, is to discover this history for yourself in the first instance through keeping your eyes open, listening and talking to people and experiencing at least one of the trans-frontier trails in the Hautes-Pyrénées. What you discover will be rich bits and pieces of individual and partial histories, but a lens as valid as anybody's, through which you may read and interpret more learned tomes later.

You will also undoubtedly discover that, once you scratch the surface, tensions exist at very local levels within communities. Some of these might even have their origins in the Spanish Civil War and Second World War, for not everyone in a community had the same values. And refugee crossings were messy affairs, hard to organise and costly – indeed, some made money out of them, while others informed. Do not, therefore, take the information boards at the foot of the trans-frontier trails – which describe epic journeys over the high passes covered in snow, heroism and the kindness of those who helped the refugees and provided them with shelter – at face value. They tell only part – albeit a hugely important part – of the story.

Other tensions, however, are less dramatic but are manifest in everyday life. Early in 2011, in the midst of the British winter, we received numerous emails about the possibility of a favourite Catalan-Spanish mountain *refugi* in the near-eastern Pyrenees being forced to close because the 'owner of the mountain'

---

13 http://tinyurl.com/wbenjamin

did not like its existence. There was a general outcry, with petitions, the involvement of the Catalan branch of FEDME (the Spanish Federation for Mountain and Climbing Sports), which was accused of not supporting the *refugi* enough, and a television appearance by the *refugi* guardian. We never got to the bottom of it, but the refuge did open again that summer as usual and has continued to do so since. However, there seems to have lingered a related dispute in the valley below the mountain, with the local taxi in the village not being allowed to take us up a dirt road with our grandchildren to where the mountain track to the refuge starts. On the other hand, another taxi several kilometres down the valley, which takes tours up the dirt road, was not allowed to stop in the village. As ever, you wonder what's really going on.

On another occasion, we were stopping at a small hotel in the Ariège in 2013. The *maître d'* was particularly clueless. A pleasant enough elderly lady, she obviously had a memory problem as she forgot on at least two occasions between courses that we were there, apologising each time after we had called her. The *patronne*, a northern European woman who had been running the hotel for over 15 years with her husband (who kept to himself in the kitchen), also apologised profusely at the end, adding sadly: 'It's not easy being here, you know.' The following morning, after the *patronne* had ordered a taxi from the nearest small town to take us to the starting point of our hike, she wearily warned us not to expect it on time. More wonder and speculation; more questions in the mind: is this a community where no outsider will ever be accepted, even after 15 years of living there? Is it a community of mutual obligations, where giving the *maître d'* her job at the hotel was the price paid for a big favour received from someone in her family? We were not there long enough to satisfy our curiosity and maybe we could never be there long enough.

There is also a rich history of Pyrenean mountaineering to discover, dominated by many men and one woman, the English Anne Lister, who climbed the third highest summit, Mount Perdido (3,355m), in 1830, while eight years later she was guided to the top of the highest summit, Aneto (3,404m). Another famous 19th century English explorer was Charles Packe, whose A Guide to the Pyrenees, Especially Intended For The Mountaineers[14] (2nd edition 1867) may be obtained from the Internet Archive.

---

14 http://tinyurl.com/pyreneespacke

Recorded exploration started in the early 1700s by mapmakers, often to serve the military. They were followed by explorers, whose rationale was scientific discovery, following the ethos created by the Enlightenment. Then, from around the middle of the 19th century, when an ethos of Romanticism held sway among European poets, artists and intelligentsia, Pyrenean explorers followed suit with their expressed love of sublime and wild places. Kev Reynolds, in his book The Pyrenees: the Hautes-Pyrénées from the Cirque de Lescun to the Carlit Massif (Cicerone), provides what he calls a 'potted history' of mountaineering in the range, which is as good a summary as any that I have come across. He puts it in the context of *Pyrénéisme*, a distinct ethos that sets the Pyrenees aside from the Alps and other mountain ranges, an ethos that retains Romanticism, where it has been replaced elsewhere by hard-nosed conquest and competition. He quotes Charles Packe (above) and his disdain for the 'doctrine that transforms the mountains into enemies to be conquered, instead of friends worthy of affection'. Kev Reynolds dedicates his book to Jean and Pierre Ravier, the French twins who kept *Pyrénéisme* thriving in the second half of the 20th century, through their knowledge of and dedication to the range. '*Pyrénéisme* celebrates the union of human endeavour with the world of nature without any attempt to conquer it,' he writes.

This book that I am writing endorses the spirit of *Pyrénéisme*. It also adds to it by inviting the trekker of the traverse to try to live in harmony, not just with nature (whatever that might represent in our minds) but with how human beings, societies and cultures have shaped and been shaped by these mountains. And how others, who are not normally mountaineers or trekkers, have represented them. Such representations include seeing the mountains as desperate escape routes to freedom, as a range of human identities with ultimate visions of separate nation-states, or simply as a means of livelihood, whatever that may be.

Livelihoods, even today, have their story too – a story which, if we conduct the traverse with our eyes open, is there for all to discover.

It was mid to late July 2008, the first day of walking in our 'gap-filling' year. We had 'done' the traverse 'in bits and pieces' from 2001, completing it (apart from these gaps) in 2006. On this day, we set off from our hotel in the village of Larrau, in the heart of the Basque Country. The hotel has a reputation for fine dining, and we were aiming for the opposite end of the spectrum, the unstaffed Cabane (Abri) d'Ardané. Standing at 1,332m above sea level, reaching it involved a climb of about 700m from the village. It was a misty day, similar to one that had turned us back in 2003, but the way was clear and we were told that we would almost certainly climb through the layer of mist and leave it below and behind us.

We arrived at our destination – still in mist, but only at one point had the path been indistinct – late afternoon to the sight and sound of hundreds of sheep crowded into a pen. They were being admired by four man-and-wife couples and their children, and two French trekkers. The four families had shared driving their sheep up to this spot, where they were now being counted before being released onto the summer pasture. Judging by the volume of the chatter we were witnessing an exciting moment for both adults and children in the transhumance cycle. Our *cabane*, also owned by the shepherds, was about 300 metres away from their lodging. It was apparently cleaner than usual. The shepherds had recently cleaned it out, having found that cattle had gained unauthorised access!

So, transhumance lives on in the Pyrenees – and not only in the part that lies in the Basque country. In 2005 we came across a shepherd as we walked from Spain into Andorra. She passed us with her dog and we caught up with her again on the first pass, just sitting there contentedly admiring the view. More recently, in July 2013, on the Port de Salau (2,087m) between Spain and France in the near-eastern Hautes-Pyrénées, we came across thousands of sheep that had just been driven up by a shepherd and his dog. The shepherd was standing on a rock, talking on his mobile phone, while we had to flee the sheep, which threatened to mug us for our snack. Transhumance is also practised with cattle, which can be found on surprisingly high pastures. A few days before our Port de Salau experience, we had to walk through a large number of cows, corralled above a valley in the Spanish Pyrenees. They were obviously waiting to be released onto the slopes of the Posets massif, which contains the second highest peak of the range.

The evidence that rough mountain farming and transhumance have declined in importance, however, is everywhere. For example, in the number of *cabanes* that appear as though they are rarely if ever occupied, many of them in ruins. Signs of general depopulation extend to villages, where shops have closed and houses are obviously empty, although in the Ariège of France we have seen a van acting as a travelling *boulangerie* serving various communities. In Spain, on the GR11 in 2005, we passed by two villages on consecutive days, where the first appeared to have one inhabitant and the second none. Sandwiched between was the village of Estaon, above the Vall de Cardós where we stayed the night, and where the *refugi* guardian was one of the few permanent inhabitants, the rest being families from Barcelona who had bought almost the entire place as second homes. Another village in the same region – Alós d'Isil – which could boast no accommodation, no bar and no restaurant when we visited briefly in 2008[15] – seemed similarly to have been acquired entirely as second homes, to the extent that two or three new apartment blocks had been built in quasi-alpine style. They stood in stark contrast to the olde-worlde dwellings and water pump of the original village. The small village of Noarre, which is almost at the head of the Vall de Cardós, is another case in point. We have visited it several times since 2008 and found it entirely occupied by second-homers, even though it cannot be reached by car. In short, where villages are not completely deserted, they have been taken over by rich city dwellers for their holidays.

Sometimes holiday dwellings are away from villages, on the lower slopes of the mountain where, especially in Spain, new *pistas* (dirt roads) have been bulldozed to provide access. The debates around the extent to which the owners are deemed either to contribute to the local economy or wreck the social fabric are complicated and endless because there is no way of knowing what would have happened without their entry into the rural housing market. An apparently buoyant holiday home market, however, does not seem to stop local shops closing. From my own selfish perspective, the closure of a shop that once sold food is not good news for a Pyrenean backpacker.

At least cattle-and-sheep farming still exists in the Pyrenees, even if its contribution to the economy has declined significantly. The same cannot be said about mining for rare metals, which flourished briefly around the start of the 20th century and is now defunct. The only obvious signs of mining that we have come across are on the descent from the aforementioned Port de Salau, in the near-eastern Pyrenees of the Ariège, to the village of the same name at its foot. Here, the relics of old mine workings abound all around the path, with supplementary paths forking off to them (so be careful in mist to keep to the red and white waymarks). Salau, where the Mine d'Anglade opened in 1971, was more recently a centre for tungsten mining. It lasted only 15 years, however, closing in 1986. In Salau village there is a museum about the mines.

It does not require rocket science to recognise as one treks that the mountains and activities associated with them make tourism a large contributor to local economies. Trekking is one such activity, which must make a significant contribution if you take advantage of the accommodation on offer, together with its food. We have also come across coordination among mountain refuges, where they are conveniently placed to create a three to five-day circuit in the mountains. We have seen this in the Pyrénées-Occidentales in France, in the Encantat mountains of the Spanish Pyrénées-Centrales, and in the aptly

---

15 Our latest information (2014) is that a refuge offering accommodation and possibly meals is now available in the village – see Chapter 8 Orange Route Day 33.

named Porta del Cel[16] (heaven's gate) and Muntanyes de Libertat[17] (see Chapters 1 and 10) of the Spanish near-eastern Pyrenees.

Besides trekking, you will also see advertisements for white-water rafting, bungee jumping, canoeing, rock climbing and guided climbs up the high mountains, including the highest, Aneto, and the peak with the largest glacier, Vignemale. Some villages, for example Benasque, in Spain, and Gavarnie, in France, have particular attractions for tourists. The former is the closest settlement of note to Aneto, while Gavarnie is at the foot of its famous Cirque.

Ski resorts are the most ostentatious symbol of tourism, supporting many seasonal jobs in the winter months. We have come across people who are ski instructors in winter and rock climbing or mountain guides in summer. One wonders how reliable the ski economy is, however, for the Pyrenees are further south than, and not as high as, the Alps, and climate change is already reducing the length of the ski season[18].

For the visitor in the trekking season (late June to mid-September) ski resorts provide a weird experience. The year was 2003, the only time we trekked from east to west. We were crossing that day from the Pyrénées-Occidentales to the Basque country, in thick mist. We had successfully negotiated the Pas de l'Osque (see the footpaths section earlier in this chapter) and carefully followed the red and white GR10 marks through the ensuing limestone to reach a dirt road, which we guessed was a ski road from some of the paraphernalia overhead. We walked along it for a kilometre or so, still guided by the GR10 paint flashes, until we reached a suitable spot to stop for our picnic. It was mid-afternoon but we had not wanted to stop earlier, high in the mountains, because of the mist. It was still misty now, but something must have stimulated me – a slight change in the light perhaps – to look behind. The mist was lifting across what looked like a moonscape to a modern town rearing its ugly head, probably another kilometre away but even from this distance appearing deserted. And 'rearing' is the right word, as the tower blocks gradually came into view with the mist rising above them. We finished our salami sandwiches and hastened towards it, drawn by a morbid fascination as much as the fact that we needed to call in anyway, for this was the infamous ski resort of La Pierre St Martin that is referred to in derogatory terms in every book about the GR10. HRP trekkers following the Georges Véron French guidebook will also make their way to it, although he does provide a variant that misses it. The

16 http://tinyurl.com/portadelcel
17 http://tinyurl.com/muntanyeslibertat
18 http://tinyurl.com/pyrenees-ski-season

most recent Joosten English guidebook to the HRP avoids it, but a bad weather variant goes there.

Our sense that La Pierre St Martin was deserted was not far off the mark, the only sign of any life being a *gîte d'étape* on the edge of town. We had not reserved accommodation there (although we have stayed in this *gîte* twice since, see Chapter 6), but at a Spanish refuge about 7km away along a minor road, to which we had already booked a taxi the day before. As we had arrived two hours in advance of schedule (yes it does happen from time to time) we wanted to bring the taxi forward, hence our now unerring steps into the town, following the signs to the Tourist Information Office. We found it, an oasis of humanity comprising two smartly dressed young women, in a mall that was otherwise deserted. I think that we were the only people they had spoken to all day, but they seemed well equipped, with books, music and *petite toilette* (basically a make-up bag) to cope with the enforced boredom. They rang the taxi, which was coming from a real town some distance away, but were unable to re-arrange, so we had two hours to kill in a place where the morbid fascination had already pretty much worn off.

La Pierre St Martin is the most extreme example we have come across of a place that apparently has thousands of visitors in winter but is more or less deserted in summer. As well as the *gîte* and the Tourist Information Office, some books to the Pyrenees mention a bar that is open, but we failed to notice it. It's as if a neutron bomb had hit this monument to the built environment. It is the lack of human life, as much as the fact that ski resorts devoid of snow always look ugly, that gives a depressing feel, albeit a feel that is tinged with ironic wonder with respect to our creative abilities.

La Pierre St Martin is in France. There are five other ski resorts of note that the trekker of the traverse is likely to encounter, three in Spain and two in Andorra. On average over the whole trek, therefore, they appear about every 150km, so it's not as if they overwhelm the place, and the high mountains of the Pyrenees, on the whole, shrug them off quite easily. La Pierre St Martin is the most westerly. Travelling east from there, the first Spanish ski resort encountered is above the village of Candanchu in the Pyrénées-Occidentales, which is just over the road pass and tunnel from France, known as the Col du Somport, and lies at the head of the Valle d'Aragon. The ski station itself is called Astun, and a minor road with a local bus service[19] runs the few kilometres to there from Candanchu. In 2012 the bus left Candanchu at a very convenient time in the morning (about 0900) to save a good hour of road

---

19 http://tinyurl.com/Astunbus

walking, and when we arrived we found a café open for our caffeine hit, before setting off on the day's hike. We were accompanied by a handful of other hikers who had used the bus, but in total we were vastly outnumbered by the bright red plastic chairs with Coca Cola emblazoned across them.

For being open in summer we forgave the café and its chairs everything, which is more than can be said for the next ski station we encountered, which offers no refreshment facilities in summer. It lies above the village of V(B)aquèira, in the Val d'Aran. It also is on the HRP, now in the near-eastern Pyrenees, but your way misses the village, while the ski station itself is nought but a passing blot. The final Spanish ski station that you have to walk through is at Ull de Ter in the Pyrénées-Orientales, where there is also a refuge that is used by HRP and GR11 trekkers. Certainly early in the morning there is nothing open here, but again you are through it quickly.

Although variants abound, one still-popular route into western Andorra on the HRP passes over the Port de Rat (2,540m). Climbing to the Port on the French side is a delight, on a nicely routed and red and white waymarked path, amid the wild scenery of the frontiers peaks. Then, at the Port, you look down into Andorra, and 'enjoy' a bird's eye view of the ski slopes and station of Ordino d'Arcalís – the contrast could not be more marked. It does possess a bar-restaurant that claims to be open, but apparently no later than 4pm (see also Chapter 9). Note that the Véron guidebook claims that it is open until 7pm and that there is a local bus service down the valley, neither of which appear to be true.

You spend three very fine ski resort-free days crossing the mountains, until meeting the second Andorran resort which lies on your route. This is the town of Pas de la Casa, on the eastern border with France, and is probably more infamous than La Pierre St Martin. Unlike other resorts in summer, it may be described quaintly as 'bustling', or rather the crowds are packed together in an orgy of conspicuous consumption. Here you may buy endless quantities of cheap booze and every kind of tat imaginable. Its Tourist Information Centre is, by contrast, a haven of sanity, and when we called in 2013 to enquire about buses into France, its custodians seemed genuinely pleased to be talking to trekkers who had noticed the abundance of fascinating flowers in the remote mountains. They even told us of a pleasant place up a side street to go for a drink while we waited a couple of hours for the bus.

Andorra certainly tickles the imagination. A glance at the map will show that this tiny country is landlocked and surrounded by France and Spain. Topographically it is dominated by the Pyrenees. From the tourist brochures it is the self-styled 'mountain kingdom'. This description also informs us that Andorra is a monarchy or, rather, a principality, and an interesting one at that.

Two co-Princes head it – the Spanish Bishop of Urgell (a Roman Catholic Diocese that covers the whole of Andorra and a significant part of Spanish Catalonia) and the President of France, meaning that the President of the Republic is also a monarch! It also has a multi-party parliament.

The country's population numbers about 85,000 and the development forms a ribbon along the main valley, which runs west-east. The side valleys penetrate into the mountains and sometimes contain ski resorts, but many don't and to enter these is to enter a different world of tranquillity. In the most easterly of these side valleys, the Valle d'Inclés, cars are banned from about 0830 till late afternoon, and a shuttle ferries hikers up and down. Meanwhile, back in the main valley, stands the capital, Andorra la Viella (or La Vella), which I have dubbed the Pharmacy Capital of the World. Pharmacy shops are certainly everywhere and of every size. We have been told that Andorra has the highest standard of living in the world. The extent to which this is a result of the tiny 'island' principality having no responsibilities to the outside world, except to provide a tax haven for the rich and to milk the less well-endowed who flood there for cheap shopping, is a cause for wonder on my part. It is not a member state of the European Union, but essentially the currency is the euro. If you want more, I suggest that Wikipedia[20] is as good a place to start as any.

Pas de la Casa on the Andorran-French frontier

---

20 http://en.wikipedia.org/wiki/Andorra

Pas de la Casa is not the only place where the trekker of the traverse comes across a bizarre, but apparently flourishing, trading economy that is based on the price differential between France and neighbouring countries. At the western end, in the Basque country, GR10 and HRP trekkers will soon discover the delights of the Col d'Ibardin. If you start from Hendaye and trek for four-and-a-half to five hours, you will walk off the hillside path straight into its main drag, as there are no warning suburbs. If you have stopped overnight at Biriatou, as we do, you will reach it in about two-and-a-half hours. The main drag forms the frontier, lined with French shops and cafés on the north side, and Spanish shops and cafés on the south, the latter being significantly more populated. Many trekkers become sniffy at the mention of the Col d'Ibardin and its tat, but we find it a useful spot to have a cup of coffee while opening the map to check our bearings. The GR10 and HRP part company at the eastern end of the main drag, which is about 500m long and has certainly been bustling on our two visits. It is served by minor roads from France and Spain, and we do wonder why it exists and why people put themselves out to drive up here to buy their souvenirs.

So, these mountains have an economy and consequently livelihoods, based primarily on sheep and cattle farming, shopping and trading in cheap booze and tat, second homes and tourism. The mountains also contribute significantly to energy infrastructure in both France and Spain, through the damming of lakes to provide hydro-electric power, although I suspect that the number of jobs this provides is relatively small. We have frequently come across hydro reservoirs, usually accessed by a dirt road. Energy infrastructure, however, requires significant investment and, as with all infrastructure, things occasionally go wrong, as when we approached one half-built dam in the Spanish Hautes-Pyrénées (the Barrage de Campo-Plano), a project which appears to have been abandoned, years ago.

It is easy to condemn uncompleted infrastructure projects, and even completed ones such as the *pistas* that are driven up mountainsides to provide access to holiday homes. It is also easy to condemn the preponderance of holiday homes in villages, the ugliness of practically deserted ski resorts in summer, the crowds who flock into places such as Pas de la Casa and the Col d'Ibardin, and the decline of traditional farming livelihoods. Yet, to condemn out of hand is the privilege of the uninformed. If our romantic illusions of the wild, savage mountain scenery are interrupted from time to time (and the times are actually few) we should pause and question ourselves, and our right to condemn how others make their living. We might do this while drinking coffee on the Col d'Ibardin or at the only café open in summer at a ski resort. For good measure, we might note that the early explorers and trekkers –

people like me and potentially you – played their part in opening these mountains to the outside world.

It isn't of course all about eking out a living and there is plenty of play and laughter among the inhabitants of the Pyrenees. It is probable that, if you stay in villages from time to time, you will come across a *fête* or *fiesta* at some point during the traverse, and if you do, you should add it to your experience. In 2008, our arrival coincided with a fiesta in Tavascan, in the near-eastern Pyrenees. It was a mixture of ballroom dancing early in the evening and disco dancing later, accompanied by a live band. But really, nobody cared how you danced at any time. We enjoyed ourselves so much that we have ensured most years since that we are in Tavascan the night of the summer fiesta (August 5). Also in 2008, we found a similar mixture of dancing at a square on the sea front of Banyuls-sur-Mer, where it seems that there is a dance at weekends during the summer season. In 2009 we found ourselves at the summer fête at Tarascon, in the Ariège, and in 2012 we had a real treat at a fête in Luz-Saint-Sauveur, the town to the north of Gavarnie that I have mentioned earlier in this chapter. We had previously made friends with Sandrine, a French woman who was doing part of the GR10 with a friend, ending at Luz-Saint-Sauveur, where she lives. She and her husband invited us to this special event that was organised by the local municipality and where we enjoyed roast tuna from a spit, yet more dancing, and plenty of bonhomie with the mayor and local politicians. To repeat, if you miss the chance of attending a fête or fiesta, you are also missing a fun experience.

Fellow travellers: I end this chapter with a few sweeping statements based on the people we have met on the footpath, in whatever accommodation we have been thrown together for a night, sometimes several nights, or even touring by other means, such as by car or in a camper van. No overview of the Pyrenees would be complete without a picture of one's fellow sojourners.

The overwhelming experience of other walkers is one of openness and friendliness, undoubtedly born out of our shared experience in the mountains. In 2013, in Andorra, on a footpath descending steeply from the Col de la Mine (in Spanish, the Collada del Meners) (2,713m) we met a Catalan family toiling up. I think that they used speaking to us as a chance to pause for breath. Then they discovered that we were British and middle-aged and became very excited that we were trekking around these mountains. We chatted spontaneously on the spot for about 20 minutes. Our conversation was so open that we could have been long-lost friends who had just met one another again. Friends we certainly were for these minutes in each other's company. That evening at our hotel, we shared more experiences with a group of middle-aged Austrian men.

The communal dinners in refuges and *gîtes*, however, are the best places to meet fellow trekkers and share not only one's experiences of the Pyrenees, but also of life in general. The mountains are a great leveller in terms of age and, without wishing to sound patronising, we have always enjoyed the company of those many years younger than our middle-aged selves. They always seemed to have so much to teach us, about the things we either never knew or had forgotten, in terms of the joy of living and basic human emotions. And in return, if you know something about the Pyrenees from your own experience, you win respect for that and not because of your age.

Twice on our travels – in 2012 and 2013 – we have coalesced as a group with people who are walking the same route over a few days or more (see Chapter 5). These two occasions were while we were on the GR10. The routine of that particular footpath seems to lend itself to this kind of thing. We walked separately, in couples or groups of whatever size, but each evening we greeted each other warmly, shared aperitifs and ate together.

In this way we have made friends with French, Spanish, Catalans, Belgians, Dutch, Germans, Austrians, Americans, Canadians, Australians and other British people. The friendships forged, whether for a few minutes or over several nights spent together, have felt very intense – the shared experience of the Pyrenees does that to you. Frequently email addresses are shared. These friendships, however, are mostly for the moment – in a reality that is bounded by time and place. Back home, another reality kicks in, that is associated with one's work, family and friends – a reality that soon becomes dominant; a reality with people with whom you share lovely experiences but not *that* experience in the Pyrenees. In short, for the most part, Pyrenean friendships easily wither and contact is lost. This isn't to criticise them as having been ultimately shallow, but simply to recognise that the reality in which they were forged can not easily be sustained once one is no longer in it. But is it always the case that Pyrenean friendships soon evaporate? We are still in contact two years later with friends we made on the final days to Banyuls-sur-Mer in 2013.

Openness and friendliness are not restricted to human engagements among fellow trekkers. On occasion we have resorted to hitching lifts on minor roads high in the mountains. The traffic might be sparse, but what there is normally stops, whether it contains local people out for the day on a weekend, local workers or holidaymakers touring by car or camper van. They also make an effort to stop for us. Once, early evening when we were almost on our knees after an epic day, a Japanese-Israeli family (we couldn't work it out properly) made two teenage girls go in the boot so we could be picked up and taken our last 4km. It's not at all unusual for people to move things around so that there is room. We have been overwhelmed by the kindnesses shown, and on at least two occasions people have stopped in pouring rain without us even sticking out our thumbs. Again, those who have picked us up have appeared genuinely interested in what we are doing and why we are doing it.

We could relate a thousand anecdotes concerning our engagements with other sojourners. You will come across some of them in later chapters, especially Chapter 5. It is for you, however, to engage in turn and generate your own stories that will live for as long as you do, and which, in the final call, make you feel good about being human.

Top tips from Chapter 2

1. Be prepared to have your imagination stoked and engage with others who share the experience of the mountains in whatever capacity.

2. The 'season' for doing the traverse is to start no earlier than the beginning of July and finish no later than late-September.

3. The weather is likely to be overwhelmingly good, possibly hot. A period of settled weather sometimes ends in a thunderstorm, but is normally followed by a resumption of 'normal service'. Plan accordingly, even for the few days of bad weather.

4. Previous weather, for example spring snow, may hamper progress months later through enduring snowfields and streams in spate.

5. The trans-frontier trails, as well as having a fascinating history as refugee crossings, create the possibility of doing a traverse that combines the GR10, HRP and GR11.

6. Watch where you are putting your feet at all times. You are most at risk of having a fall when on easier terrain, having relaxed a little.

7. If you would rather not see a snake, the vibrations of walking poles tend to make them scurry away before you get to them. Encounters with wild boar are extremely rare and they are the more frightened. The few bears that survive will avoid you too, and soon there will be almost zero chance of encountering one because it is possible that they have all been shot.

8. Take the trouble to know some very basic stuff about the history, politics and livelihoods of people who live in the Pyrenees, but be prepared to discover for yourselves by keeping your eyes open and engaging with local people and fellow trekkers.

9. If you are staying the night in a village, do not sneak off to bed early if a fête or fiesta is being held. Go to it and enjoy yourself.

3

Planning your trip

Cost, getting there, travelling light and where to spend the night

The first thing most people do when considering an adventure of this sort is to obtain a mental overview. You search and read websites, you look at books – even this one – and any other literature you may come across. You might also talk to others who have direct experience of long distance trekking. Apart from helping you decide whether you are physically and mentally up for the challenge, you also gain an idea of the overall cost, the gear that you will need and the accommodation you should seek en route.

The first substantive action you take, however, is to decide the start and end dates and book your journeys to the Pyrenees and back. These two actions make the intention to do the traverse real, they indicate that you have taken the plunge, and they carry an imperative – you have to fit everything in between the dates on your outward and return tickets. They also trigger the further actions of obtaining the gear that you need and the exact accommodation you will seek each night of the traverse. Hence this chapter.

I covered the season for trekking along the Pyrenees in Chapter 2, but to remind you, it's from July, when most of the snow should have vanished from the mountains, to September. With that in mind, I move straight to the planning details.

Overall cost

This is not necessarily a cheap holiday, or adventure if you prefer to think of it that way. Before you even set off, gear, especially lightweight gear (see below) is expensive, although you might think of this as an investment. Then there is the cost of getting to the Pyrenees and back. During the trek, having a roof over one's head, and a meal and alcohol at the end of each day, rack up the cost significantly. Taking a taxi might be a forced additional expense on occasion.

The following is a simple budget for the traverse based on the costs that we incurred in 2013 and assuming that it will take 51 days overall. It is given in British pounds, euros and US dollars at current exchange rates.

Thus, to scale up per person doing the whole traverse over about 50 days:

Travel to and from the Pyrenees =   £250   €338 $378

Accommodation, meals and drink (assuming a staffed refuge, *gîte*, *auberge* or hotel each night) and internal travel = £2,300 €3,109 $3,482

Total per person =   £2,550 €3,447 $3,860

Relatively speaking this isn't too bad for 51 days away. As an absolute sum, however, it's significant, and if you are doing the traverse over several years, you will be paying extra in travel to and from the Pyrenees for each additional trip.

If you don't want to spend that much, you may trim at the edges, for example by cutting down on alcohol or, indeed, cutting it out completely. If you really want to save money, however, you will have to camp most or all of the way. This will be demanding mentally as well as physically– and think of the extra weight you will have to carry (see below). More importantly, you will miss out on what for us has been an incredible social experience.

Getting there (and back)

It is no longer *de rigeur* that guidebooks provide detailed information on travel options to and from the Pyrenees, given that the large majority of people will simply search on the internet on how to get from A to B for both short and long distances. If planning to do the conventional thing and fly, check out the flights to and from the most appropriate airports in both France and Spain. Currently in France these are Biarritz (Atlantic end), Pau (Pyrénées-Occidentales), Lourdes (Pyrénées-Occidentales and Pyrénées-Centrales), and Perpignan (Pyrénées-Orientales and Mediterranean end). All of these airports are relatively close to the traverse, although you will almost certainly have to take a bus, train or taxi into the mountains in order to complete the journey. You might also fly to Toulouse, but this city is further away and requires a longer subsequent train ride or a combination of train and bus. That said, as befits the capital of southwest France, the city acts as a useful springboard for reaching all parts of the range. Carcassonne also currently has cheap flights from the UK, but again is a little further away.

In Spain you are probably limited to San Sebastian (Donastia to the Basques) on the Atlantic coast, Girona, inland from the Mediterranean and Barcelona a little further south. San Sebastian has a train line running to Irun and Hendaye to start the traverse but isn't much use for other parts of the route. From Girona, you can travel by train or bus to towns along or near the Mediterranean coast that are of similar latitude to the range, but again finding public transport inland might be complicated. Do though search for options. From Barcelona you may use a combination of train and bus to get to the Val d'Aran in the near-eastern Pyrenees. You may, of course, hire a car from the airports, but is it simply going to be parked somewhere during the traverse, to where you will eventually have to return when you've finished walking? It doesn't seem very practical as an option.

You will undoubtedly need to check for cheap flights. These days you are not forced to buy a return ticket to and from the same airport, so you may go out to one and return from another, even using different airlines. In our early years on the traverse we flew to Toulouse and from there took the train to Lourdes followed by bus, taxi or pre-arranged pick-up from a tour company to Luz-Saint-Sauveur north of Gavarnie, which we used as a base. Occasionally we took the train from Toulouse on a branch line to Bagnères-de-Luchon (twinned with Harrogate in the UK) in the Pyrénées-Centrales or up the Ariège valley to L'Hospitalet-près-l'Andorre, as a starting point for the Pyrénées-Orientales. On both of these branch lines, we learned not always to expect a train, but a replacement bus and longer journey time.

Gradually we came to think that this way of getting to and from the Pyrenees was a hassle. Firstly there are the usual airport security issues: walking poles (or perhaps even an ice axe if you're expecting snow) cause extra check-in complications, you have to check in everything that is potentially an offensive weapon and you might have to remove walking boots. Then you have to get from Toulouse airport to the main train station on a shuttle, which is simple enough but is a journey through congested traffic. Next you have to buy a ticket at the large, crowded station, where the machines won't accept your card, and so it goes on. Of course, the claimed advantage of flying that is supposed to make all of this hassle worthwhile is speed of transit. This advantage becomes whittled away, however, by getting to and from airports that aren't exactly placed near where you want to be, and having to arrive well in advance, quite often during anti-social hours. I'm not exactly selling this to you!

An alternative to flying is to go by train the whole way and this has certain advantages in my opinion. After a friend, who ran a small Pyrenean tour company (Chapter 7), told us that those who arrived to be picked up at Lourdes station seemed more relaxed if their whole journey had been by train, we decided to try it that way, and we have stuck with it for many of our journeys from 2006.

Our basic itinerary is Eurostar between London St Pancras and Paris Gare du Nord, followed by a couchette on a night train between Paris Gare d'Austerlitz and our destination. It's not cheap, but it saves a night at a hotel and one arrives having slept and feeling refreshed, ready to grab breakfast in a café and walk. Below are Pyrenean (more or less) destinations for the night trains that depart Paris Gare d'Austerlitz:

Toulouse, a useful 'hub' but you will then have to take another train closer into the Pyrenees, which is simple enough and all bookable through Rail Europe.

Lourdes, which is the closest rail point for Luz-Saint-Sauveur, Couserans and Gavarnie for the start of the Pyrénées-Centrales section. From Lourdes station there are occasional buses to these destinations, or you can take a taxi at a price (€65 to Gavarnie in 2013, the furthest of these destinations).

Bayonne, where there is a rail connection (at least there was in 2013, but check as it may have been replaced by a French Railways (SNCF) bus connection) to Saint-Jean-Pied-de-Port, in the Basque Country. From Saint-Jean-Pied-de-Port, it's 42 km (45 minutes by car or taxi) to Chalets d'Iraty, and 44 km (one hour by car or taxi) to Larrau, both possible stop and start points on GR10 or HRP sections.

Hendaye, which is the start of the GR10 and HRP, and also only just the other side of the frontier from Irun for the GR11. Note that Hendaye is the final destination of the night train that calls at Bayonne, with Biarritz and other places along the coast in between.

L'Hospitalet-Près-l'Andorre (not the final destination, which is a further 20 minutes away at Latour-de-Carol), good for starting the Pyrénées-Orientales, and an occasional bus also runs to Pas de la Casa, in Andorra. Note that sometimes it's difficult to book this through train, which means you have to change at Toulouse (and have breakfast at the Hotel de Bristol opposite the station) while you wait for the connection. Also note that L'Hospitalet-Près-l'Andorre translates loosely as 'the hospitality near Andorra', which is exactly what it is, the 'hospitality' comprising a hotel (where you may enjoy breakfast or coffee if setting off from here), a *gîte d'étape* and a *rapide* refreshment bar next to the station. There is a village of sorts, a hydro-electric installation and the main road from France to Andorra running through. On Saturdays, the arrival of the morning train from Toulouse may cause some interest as French people on a shopping binge to Pas de la Casa rush off it to get their seats on the connecting bus. At the end of the day they return to Toulouse, where they sell on their spoils.

Banyuls-sur-Mer, which is perfect for coming back at the end of the trek. Note that you can not always book the through train and may have to change at Perpignan or Narbonne for the night train to Paris.

Here are some tips for long train journeys from and to the UK.

• Book tickets at least two months in advance for the best deals.

• Use the Rail Europe website[1] for basic information, but it's often better to speak to somebody than book online. Sometimes the website provides more limited options than are actually available. Rail Europe staff are usually knowledgeable and helpful.

• Google, and other search engines, will help with local buses from the above stations. Key in 'Bus Lourdes to Gavarnie', for example, or try this website[2] for Cauterets, Gavarnie and Luz-Saint-Sauveur (Lourdes to Bareges and Lourdes to Gavarnie buses for the last-named).

• Hendaye, L'Hospitalet-Près-l'Andorre and Banyuls-sur-Mer are all stop-points on the traverse so you hopefully should need no extra transport. You are in any event unlikely to be able to hire a car at L'Hospitalet.

• You may hire a car instead of taking a bus or taxi from Toulouse, Lourdes and Bayonne.

• Your outward destination does not have to be the same as the start point of the return journey.

• You don't have to book a couchette on the night train – the reclining seats option is much less expensive. I strongly recommend, however, the couchettes. A major advantage of the train is being able to sleep horizontally. We have never been tempted to try the reclining seats.

• You can go for six-birth couchettes, which are cramped or 'first class' four-berth couchettes for not much more. In recent years, by paying a supplement, you could also have, as a couple, sole use of a four-birth couchette (which is worth asking about as it does not appear as a website option). The bed is usually made up, including pillow, and you receive a little pack containing water, ear-plugs, tissues, and hand or face wipes.

• Treat travelling by train as part of the holiday experience. Don't cut things too fine for the 20-minute journey on the Métro between Paris Gare du Nord

---

[1] Note that Rail Europe is now run by the French Rail Network (still available in English): http://uk.voyages-sncf.com/en/
[2] http://summer.gavarnie.com/organise/how-to-get-here

(Eurostar terminal) and Gare d'Austerlitz (for the night trains), and give yourself time for dinner in Paris if possible.

- The night trains don't usually offer any refreshment.

- Remember the time difference. France and Spain are one hour ahead of the UK.

Our personal preference for travelling by train has evolved over the years, probably a function of growing older. These days we opt for more comfort. Here's how we did it in September 2013, when we did the final leg of our traverse, the 11 days over the Pyrénées-Orientales to Banyuls-sur-Mer.

Monday September 2, 1130. Set off from home in Huddersfield, Yorkshire, and arrived London King's Cross at 1430. Strolled over to St Pancras International.

1531. Caught the Eurostar to Paris, on which we had paid about £15 each extra for 'standard premier', where we were fed with food and wine, and given real plates and cutlery. Arrived Paris Gare du Nord 1847, having 'lost' an hour due to time difference (so actual journey time 2 hours 16 minutes).

Took the Métro Line M5 (colour, orange) Direction Place d'Italie, to Gare d'Austerlitz, arriving 1915.

Called in at the main-line station to check the night train (there was a good reason for this, see below).

Went across the road in front of the station, where there's a string of restaurants. We chose one that we had been in before, knowing that it served fresh salads. We had a large, leisurely salad each and a demi (half) carafe of wine.

2145. Returned to the station and waited to board our train. We had booked a four-berth couchette, sole occupancy, for the two of us, something we did not know existed until the man at Rail Europe told us.

2252. Our train set off as scheduled, arriving Toulouse Matabieu at 0700 the following morning after a good night's sleep.

Tuesday September 3, 0849. After breakfast at the Hotel Bristol, opposite the station, we caught the train up the Ariège Valley to L'Hospitalet Près l'Andorre (1,436m), going higher and higher and slower and slower, arriving 1120. We drank café au lait at the Col de Puymorens Hotel.

1200. We set off walking to the Refuge des Bésines, a relatively easy hike of ten kilometres and about 700m of climbing, which took four hours, including lunch.

From home to L'Hospitalet, the above journey took the best part of 24 hours, but we wined, dined and slept for much of it, and the last bit was through increasingly mountainous scenery. We were totally relaxed throughout.

This was the nearest we have experienced to the ideal journey. It was also in stark contrast to our previous expedition in 2013, from July 17 to August 6, when the journey and accompanying experience went like this:

Apart from the minor inconvenience of having to take a replacement bus part-way on the Métro, all went well as far as the Gare d'Austerlitz. Ninety minutes later, after a leisurely dinner opposite, we got to the concourse. Our train to Lourdes was not showing and staring at the information board failed to produce a result. It had been cancelled due to an accident on the line several days earlier but we could sleep in our couchettes as the train was in the station, albeit not going anywhere. It was now past 2200, but SNCF staff sorted us seats on a TGV from the Gare de Lyon early the following morning. We were given an 'emergency bag' containing some food and water. It was a bizarre way to spend the night.

After a fitful sleep we walked the ten minutes to the Gare de Lyon. Our journey required two changes, arriving at Lourdes around 1430, where there was no other option but to take a taxi for the 75-minute journey into the mountains. We started walking east from Gavarnie at 1615, six hours behind schedule, to the Refuge des Espuguettes. The French and English HRP Guides, and the signpost on leaving the village, all indicated two hours from Gavarnie, without stops. We might just make it for dinner at 1900. Surprising ourselves, we took one hour 40 minutes.

As a postscript, we ended our trek three weeks later at L'Hospitalet-Près-l'Andorre. We boarded the night train to Paris and found our couchettes. I awoke in the early hours of the morning. The train had stopped. This is not unusual because the journey time is over ten hours and the night train often takes a break in sidings. I felt aware, however, that something was wrong. Eventually, I looked out of the window. We were in Toulouse station. I looked at my watch and it was 0300. A quick mental calculation indicated that even if the train set off again that minute, it could not arrive in Paris by its scheduled time of 0722. A TGV, which the night trains are not, takes well over five hours.

In fact, the train did not move at all. There had been a storm in the night further north, which had damaged the overhead cables. We were assigned to a TGV departing at 0900 and given another 'emergency bag'. We finally arrived at Paris Gare du Nord mid-afternoon, having missed our scheduled departure to London by several hours. After hearing our story, the Eurostar man checked that we had not missed the connection because we had been sight-seeing in Paris, and allocated us seats on the next train. We arrived home that night – all was well that ended well.

Yes, trains can go horribly wrong, but so of course can aeroplanes, and these have been our only two experiences on which disaster loomed, although things turned out well in the end. Railway staff in France seem to be very helpful when things do go wrong.

Overall, whether you choose aeroplane or train depends on various factors in addition to cost – convenience for walking destination and of departure and arrival times, and whether you wish the journey to be part of the overall experience or not. Flexibility is a good watchword. On this, note that, just as you may now fly one-way to a particular airport with a particular airline and return from another with a different (or by chance the same) airline, you may also do the equivalent with trains. You may also go one way by aeroplane and the other way by train, which we have done on occasion simply because the timings suited us.

Travelling light

Weight counts. Every ounce counts… even upon the first day, after the first few miles. Weight counts all the time. – Hilaire Belloc, 1909, The Pyrenees.

I remember well in 2012 ordering coffee at a *hostellerie* near the outflow of the Lac de Gaube in the Hautes-Pyrénées. Our trek, that began three weeks earlier at Hendaye, was due to end the following day at Gavarnie. Today we had just started the long hike up the Val de Gaube, which has the highest frontier mountain, Le Vignemale (3,298m), at its head. Our route lay over a pass on the east side of Le Vignemale and down a short distance to the highest staffed refuge in the Pyrenees, the Bayssellance (2,651m). Although only ten o'clock, we had already been on the trail for three hours, albeit some of it spent on a chair lift (Chapter 4), with an estimated six still in front of us.

We talked briefly to the only other customers, a British couple in their 30s, who had set off that morning on the first leg of a four-day round trip. Getting up to leave as our coffee arrived, Angharad and I independently marvelled silently at the large size of their packs. We then spent the 45 minutes we had saved through taking the chair lift to the *hostellerie* chatting, looking at the map, and observing the weather. The day had started dull but now showed definite signs of improving. We departed in good spirits.

We caught up with the British couple – Geoff and Marie – after 30 minutes. They planned to camp that night by the Bayssellance refuge rather than stay inside. They were carrying a tent, a cooking stove and sufficient food for four days. We did not ask what else, but Geoff admitted that the rucksacks were very heavy and Marie especially was moving slowly. We hung back and walked with them to the Oulettes de Gaube refuge below the steep climb to the pass, where we ate our picnic, with the glacier-clad north face of Le Vignemale impressive before us. Geoff told us that Marie was also suffering from back pain and they were going to allow a little time for her to recover. We continued without them.

We arrived at the Bayssellance about 1700, and to our slight surprise at seeing them at all, Geoff and Marie at about 1830. They pitched their tent but, too tired to cook, they ordered dinner inside the refuge.

We saw them again briefly the following morning as we prepared to leave for the substantial descent to Gavarnie. We reached the valley floor in good time where, after a fine picnic and bathing our feet, we saw them approach, Marie walking stiffly in obvious discomfort. As we had no further use for it, we gave her our Traumeel cream – a product recommended by an American acquaintance for relieving muscular aches and pains. She was truly grateful. From the body language, we suspected that this was a fairly new relationship, and speculated how well it would survive beyond their four days in the mountains.

The obvious point of this story is to illustrate for 21st century trekkers what Hilaire Belloc wrote well over 100 years ago. I remember the same message being repeated in my first Youth Hostels Association handbook back in 1959, when I was 13, as I set off for a few days with my father in the English Lake District. *Don't be a beast of a burden* ran the section heading, followed by a couple of paragraphs of handy tips, such as sawing off half the handle of your toothbrush and only carrying a fag-end of toothpaste rather than a full tube. For many contemporary trekkers in the Pyrenees, northern Europeans especially (where the British appear to be among the worst offenders), it's not an unseasonal burst of lousy weather that is the straw that breaks the camel's back and forces you to give up; nor is it one very steep ascent too many after a succession of tough days. Rather, it's the load you have decided to carry, in your risk-averse way, to cover all eventualities. Most obviously, did our British couple have to take four days' supply of food (which they might be too tired to prepare) when their trek would pass through Gavarnie, which has several shops?

It does seem a lesson that has to be learned over and over again with successive generations of would-be trekkers. Either that, or it has to be repeated *ad nauseum* as I am now doing. We have seen the same problem on other occasions, the most recent being in September 2013. A young English guy had eaten and stayed in a staffed refuge with us the night before, but he was carrying a rucksack, again with tent, cooking gear and food to last several days, that I could barely lift. He staggered as he tried to launch it onto his back. I shuddered to think what damage he might do to himself if he had a small trip that propelled him forwards.

Those who do realise the error of their ways before it is too late seek opportunities along the way to send excess gear home. The staff at the infrequent post offices in the Pyrenean villages must see them coming, for they are well prepared with padded envelopes of every size. I know, from personal experience, that one can pack two pairs of mini-crampons in a bag and send them home to England for about €20. (To be fair to us, we had used the crampons, but were now out of the snow zone.)

Hilaire Belloc, who provided the wise words with which I started this chapter, wrote in the same book that all the explorer on foot need carry is:

- A map and compass;

- One set of woollen clothing, with the exception of socks, of which two pairs are advisable because your feet are likely to get wet;

- Sandals, which in the early 20th century Pyrenees were 'cloth slippers with a sole of twisted cord', rather than leather boots, because they are much easier on the feet;

- A blanket to wrap around yourself at night on the ground. Belloc believed a tent to be an unnecessary 'luxury' in summer in the Pyrenees, where you will also find shepherds' *cabanes* in the mountains;

- A pannikin, which is a metal drinking mug, into which will also fit a spirit 'lamp' (actually a small stove) and a container of methylated spirit for fuel;

- A 4lb (1.8kg) loaf of bread, to last between 48 and 60 hours;

- A *saucisson*, which Belloc described as a 'salt pig and garlic' sausage, while also indicating that it was optional;

- Maggi (also optional) – oblong capsules of concentrated beef essence that 'weigh next to nothing' and which can be used to make 'in a few moments a hot and comforting soup'; and

- A leather 'gourd' made from goatskin, with a screw top opening, in which you carry your wine. If you don't want the wine to taste of goat you condition the vessel first by taking it for a few hours' walk at home with the contents of a small bottle of brandy inside that are then thrown away. You attach a piece of string to the 'gourd' and carry it over one shoulder. Belloc obviously thought a good supply of wine essential, stating: 'Half a pound of bread and a pint of wine will carry one for miles, and nothing can take their place.'

Finally…

- A satchel, which you carry over the other shoulder, and which contains a map, compass, blanket, spare socks and food. You strap the pannikin with its contents made secure to the outside of the satchel. Belloc saw no need for the heavier 'knapsack' (the forerunner of today's rucksack), which you have to take off whenever you need something. He gave plenty of advice on packing one, however, in case 'you want to carry weight'.

Belloc obviously took his own advice seriously and, from the above, was a minimalist par excellence. Many items today have come on a long way, especially boots. They are no longer uncomfortable to wear, are much lighter, and can keep the feet dry up to certain limits. Most importantly, I wear them to protect my ankles.

There is also a wealth of lightweight gear available. Trekking poles, clothing made from 'technical' fabric, storm jackets and over-trousers, stoves, rucksacks, sleeping bags and tents all come in lightweight variants. Check out with a web search. Outdoor specialists such as Ellis Brigham[3] and Cotswold[4] provide a good selection. The Pyrenean summer does make it easy to take relatively small amounts of clothing because you may hand-wash, or at least hand-rinse, as you go along. The general rule is three of everything – one for wearing, another that is drying, and a third that is waiting to be washed. In the Pyrenees, however, you can even cut down on these. Only two pairs of thin walking shirts and walking socks are needed, for example. If you arrive at a mountain refuge by 1700, you can usually hand-wash what you need for the next day and have it more or less dry on a warm rock by dinner at 1900. Keep an eye on it on the rock, you don't want it blown away by a gust. While keeping watch, there are other washer-trekkers to talk to, the following day's map to be studied, a hot drink or a beer to sup. We have often gone into this simple routine.

See the Appendix for what Angharad and I normally carry. Note that the total weight we each carry without any water and food is only 7kg. With the water bottles full and food for a picnic, it's about 9kg, which is comfortably light. Note also that we don't take gloves (use walking socks as mittens if desperate, but I have never had the need) and no cold-weather hat.

---

[3] http://www.ellis-brigham.com/
[4] http://www.cotswoldoutdoor.com/

Sufficient water is one item that you must carry, unless you are confident of sources along the way. Font Nostre here is next to the path that leads to the Canigou *cheminée*.

To summarise on kit, I am not trying to claim that one can skimp on survival essentials, such as water, food, wet-weather clothing, boots, maps, compass or GPS, survival bag and first aid kit. Weight can, however, be kept down to a minimum by:

• Weeding out non-essentials, especially in relation to toiletries and clothing, while recognising that an element of comfort is also essential even if it might add a few grammes;

• Obtaining the lightest available gear. Tents, rucksacks, wet-weather gear, walking poles, sleeping bags, stoves, and mugs all come in light versions and don't necessarily sacrifice comfort. We always insist on taking one cotton change of clothes for evenings, and cotton underwear, but we literally weigh the choices open to us. It might seem sad to weigh one's underwear, but it pays to do so.

Finally, don't pack at the very last moment before travelling. Several times we have packed, found our rucksacks too heavy and unpacked them again, 'editing' the contents.

Where to spend the night

By definition, the load is significantly heavier if you plan to camp, which leads neatly to consideration of the accommodation choices (a dilemma for many):

• You camp (often wild) or even bivouac.

• You stay in *cabanes* and unstaffed refuges, which usually have a platform or bunk beds, and for which there is no charge.

- You stay in staffed accommodation – mountain refuges, *gîtes d'étape*, *casas rurales*, *auberges*, *chambres d'hôte*, even the occasional hotel – where you pay for a bed of some form. With the exception of *casas rurales* and *chambres d'hôte* (see below) you may also buy meals in these establishments, or at least have facilities for cooking your own.

- You do a mixture. Hilaire Belloc would bivouac with his wool blanket, stay in shepherds' *cabanes* when available, and after a few days (he only carried food for 48-60 hours) lodge at an inn. Many contemporary trekkers will reach a mountain refuge, but set up camp, where this is allowed, while booking dinner in the refuge, or vice versa.

The general trade-offs when considering the above options are between the weight that you have to carry, flexibility, comfort and convenience, sociability, and cost. Here is my assessment.

Camping or bivouacking

The great advantages of camping or bivouacking are freedom, flexibility and low cost – after the initial investment of buying what you need. You are your private walking home. You don't have to make any reservations or worry about not getting a bed if you haven't done so, and you may adapt your schedule according to the weather and other inconveniences, such as having to go off-route to buy food or fuel. In the national parks, there are some limiting rules, for example, in France you may only 'bivouac' (which also means wild-camp in this context) above 2,000m, at least an hour away from the nearest paying accommodation, not before 1900 and not after 0900 the following morning. These 'rules' do not, however, place severe limits on flexibility in practice. In Spain, a bivouac is more accurately described as 'tolerated' than allowed and, in some national park areas, more strictly forbidden.

As indicated above, you may also camp next to most French refuges (certainly those above 2,000m) and avail yourself of their facilities at a price, such as dinner, breakfast, a picnic prepared for you, or even the human company. Apart from some very popular refuges, they are unlikely to be full even in the high season, so you may also discard camping altogether and share a platform bed with the other inmates, again at a price, of course. If the refuge does happen to be full, it's no great hardship to erect your tent. Sometimes it's worth hanging on before doing the latter, in case someone who has reserved doesn't turn up.

There is something very exciting about camping completely in the wild to the constant music of the stream you are using for water and washing, putting clothes on hot rocks to dry, cooking and eating a dried ready meal (delicious in these circumstances) and retiring to your humble abode as night falls. You might get up in the middle of the night and see the Milky Way, while the following morning you feast on cereal (for us muesli mixed with dried milk powder) and tea before breaking camp and leaving without a trace. You feel simultaneously significant that you are actually doing this and insignificant within the vast scheme of landscape and sky.

The companion to insignificance, however, is a feeling of powerlessness, and powerlessness can lead to (usually unwarranted) fear. At least it does for us, as the following three stories suggest.

Our first wild camping experience was in 2008 above the tiny hamlet of Alós d'Isil at the head of the Vall d'Àneu in the near-eastern Pyrenees. Next to us on our tiny meadow was the infant Noguera Pallaresa river, a torrent both noisy and powerful. The far bank was wooded. The spot wasn't actually that wild, as a dirt road passed nearby. We were clearing up after dinner when suddenly came a loud shrieking from the bank opposite. A large bird, possibly a vulture, had swooped out of the sky and landed on the back of another bird (probably a magpie from its black and white markings). A magpie is a pretty big bird itself, and the two engaged in vicious, noisy battle. It was not a pretty sight as this appeared to be a fight to the death and the bird that had swooped had the upper hand (or wing). It lasted at least five minutes, and then the bird just flew off leaving a wounded magpie behind. Perhaps it planned to return as soon as the magpie had finally given up and died. Perhaps it just wasn't concerned whether it had killed its prey or not. We have often witnessed with amusement blackbirds being horrible to one another in the back garden at home, but the vicious intensity of this fight, the fragility of life, left us sombre and, well, a little afraid. What might dive out of the sky onto us while not giving a toss whether it left us alive or dead?

A year later, only a few kilometres in a direct line from where we had camped the previous year, but at the head of a side valley, we struck camp at about 1,850m above sea level. This was a truly wild spot at the confluence of streams below the southwest ridge of the frontier peak, Mont Roig (2,868m), and en route (the following day) to the Col de la Cornella (2,485m), which is engraved on our memory to share with you in Chapters 4 and 8. We cooked and ate our pasta-based ready meal, put everything away securely so that animals could not get at it during the night, stared briefly at a beautiful sunset, then retired as it began to cool rapidly. We had only been inside the tent for a few minutes, however, when we heard grunting noises from afar, then a rasping noise closer, followed by the sound of movement just outside. We froze. I grabbed the trekking pole that I had carefully laid next to my sleeping bag, although I was not exactly ready to fight off all comers. There was, however, no more sound or apparent movement and eventually I fell into a fitful sleep. I awoke in the early hours to Angharad going outside. She re-entered after a few minutes, announcing an amazing night sky that included a very clear Milky Way, and also reported no sign of any visitors. We both soon fell back to sleep again.

Again in the same region two years later, but now on the east side of Mont Roig, we were wild camping by the Estany Xic, a small lake before the final short climb to the Port de Tavascan (2,217m), on the frontier. Also known in France as the Port de Marterat, the trans-frontier trail that crosses it is likewise etched on our memory as an epic trek in both 2013 and 2014 (Chapter 8). We chose our spot (always a subject of some discussion, so be prepared to give time to it), pitched the tent, cooked and ate and went to bed, all as usual. We were both awoken in the early hours, however, by bright light filling the tent for a second, followed by complete darkness, then another bright light, and so it continued. We waited for the sound of thunder, but there was none. Nor was there any rain that could be associated with a storm. We wondered if the lights were torches being carried by people, silently, in some kind of ritual. And, might we be sacrificed as part of this ritual?! There was still nothing, and eventually, after about 30 minutes, the light show stopped and we went back to troubled sleep. We arose at 0700 and climbed to the Port and back before breakfast and a morning sunning ourselves. It was a perfectly lovely Pyrenean day. Down in the valley we were told that there had been an electrical storm during the night, a storm so far away that nobody had heard any thunder.

If you decide to go wild-camping in the Pyrenees, no doubt your experiences will be different, although I can almost guarantee that something will happen to ensure that the night does not pass without incident (real or perceived), tickling the imagination. I guess the more you do it, the more you get used to these happenings.

Given the obvious advantages, what are the drawbacks to camping or bivouacking? To bang my drum once more, the most obvious disadvantages are the extra weight that you must carry and the inevitable loss of comfort. Even if you are camping only occasionally, and using staffed accommodation with meals most of the time, you still have to carry at least a tent, stove and eating and drinking utensils. This extra weight is a big price to pay. Yes, you can buy a small lightweight tent and a lightweight sleeping bag that may be stuffed into a small sack, but having practically no indoor space to move around in isn't exactly comfortable. The tent that we bought for backpacking in the Pyrenees weighs less than a kilo and is easy to erect. The sales information describes it as sleeping one to two persons, but it only manages the latter if you know each other very well. We actually found that head to toe is the best way to lie at night. It's just as well that we are well-organised, because rucksacks, boots, stove and so on have to be packed into the entrance area of the tent which is side-opening, while, above all, no food should be left lying around.

Then, in the morning, you find that, whatever you have done to minimise it (for example leaving a tiny opening to the sleeping compartment), condensation is rife, both on the inside from your breathing, and the outside from dew. If you're lucky, it dries off while you have breakfast and pack away everything else, taking the tent down last. If there is still significant water on it when you are ready to leave, you have to fix it loosely onto the back of the rucksack, along with whatever clothing you still need to dry.

It is almost obligatory to carry food in dried form when camping, which certainly reduces weight. I have mentioned above mixing breakfast muesli (or other cereal) with dried milk and the reasonably edible dried ready-dinners. In July 2013 we met a lovely young Belgian couple doing the HRP and wild-camping from time to time. They were carrying many days' supply of dried food, specially produced from fresh ingredients using the man's own dehydrator back in Belgium. We too have experimented (pathetically in comparison with the Belgians), our most delicious meal in the wild being in 2014 when we mixed leek and chicken cup-a-soup powder with crumbled stock cube and couscous, and poured on boiling water.

You may reduce your backpacking weight further by eating only cold food that doesn't require cooking, and drinking only cold water from the streams. You may also buy ready meals that heat up when you open the packet. In 2012, sitting outside the *gîte* late one afternoon at the Chalets d'Iraty, in the Basque country, we met two French women doing a section of the GR10, who had just bought such a meal from the site shop. It was their first experience of this delight and they were busy amusing themselves and us with the instructions on the packet. We eventually left them, about to open the packet precisely according to the instructions, while we went to the restaurant. The following morning we asked after their meal, to which they replied that it was an interesting experience. Their body language indicated, however, that this was also a bad experience, confirmed that evening when we met up with them again, this time tucking into the meal provided at the next accommodation.

So, cold food and water might be a better option if you don't want to carry a stove, fuel and associated utensils. Would you really want to do it, however, for more than one or two nights in succession? We have met people who do this, but personally, I would find it a cheerless endurance rather than something to be enjoyed. Even if I had the wherewithal to prepare hot food, I would also soon be pining for a good meal that wasn't created entirely from tipping a packet of dried ingredients into hot water.

The final potential camping discomfort is weather-related. If there's a storm in the night, you should be fine, providing the tent is erected properly (and a lightweight tent is always not far above the ground even at its highest point), you have packed everything away with rainproof covers over rucksacks, and turned your boots upside down. If it's still raining in the morning, it multiplies by several times the discomforts of having breakfast and breaking camp. This, however, is where the flexibility of camping might come into its own. You simply stay put until the weather brightens. In 2006, we spoke to an English guy nearing the end of the HRP. His worst experience of the traverse, he said, was in the Basque country towards the end of June, when he had to stay three days at the same spot in his tent because of snow. I should stress, however, that we have never experienced bad weather while wild-camping.

By themselves, the above represent probably minor discomforts for which the freedom, flexibility, adventure, wonder and magic associated with wild camping more than amply compensate. All of them, however, apart from those related to bad weather, are repeated in combination each day and I suspect that they become tedious after a while. In particular, the extra weight that you are carrying has the potential to wear you down. On the other hand, you become more adept at handling and living with the inconveniences the more you do it, so they become accepted as a normal part of daily life. This to some extent is conjecture on my part because I have wild-camped in the Pyrenees on only six occasions, and that spread over four years! I do know that, for myself and Angharad, we would start eventually to yearn for human company beyond each other, a bed, even if only a platform bed in a refuge, a shower, and a decent dinner.

Cabanes and unstaffed mountain refuges

Cabanes are generally old stone huts in the mountains that were originally built for shepherds and are often still used by them. If there is no padlock on the door, you may safely assume it's fine for a trekker to use it for the night too, but of course check if shepherds are present.

Unstaffed mountain refuges tend to be newer and sometimes they are made of shiny metal and can be spotted from some distance. They are of course intended for those who travel by foot in the wild and isolated mountains. At one, however, we came across a couple of guys from Barcelona who were spending a week of summer holiday there, having carried their food and drink from the nearest road-head, about three hours away. If this happens to you, do not let it prevent you from using the refuge. It is not a private holiday let and the two aforementioned guys we stayed with were very accommodating and friendly. They accepted fully that some nights they might be by themselves, others not.

Cabanes and unstaffed refuges are both free of charge and they offer similar facilities (or lack of them), namely:

• A roof over your head;

• A platform bed for several people or bunk beds (refuges may have a few more spaces than cabanes);

• Usually, but not always, a water source very close;

• No electricity and therefore no lighting. Moreover, the only natural light is likely to be through a tiny window, or the door when open.

• No cooking facilities, although refuges may have a stone table on which to place a stove indoors and a few shelves for storing food;

• No washing or toilet facilities.

They are, therefore, a small notch above camping in terms of comfort, the main difference being that you don't have to erect and remove a tent. You stay dry and have no worries about rain during the night or condensation moisture, and you have at least a mattress to lie on. Trekkers who back-pack tend to combine camping with staying in these places where they exist, so the weight issue does not go away as you are always carrying a tent and stove. Also, on the rare occasion that a cabane or unstaffed refuge is full, you will undoubtedly pitch your tent close by as the backstop.

My final word about cabanes and unstaffed refuges concerns their state of cleanliness. We first stayed in a cabane in July 2008, to the east of the Basque Country, where the first 2,000-metre mountains start. Staying there that night in addition to us were a young French couple, and two amazing Swedish guys who had no hearing and communicated by sign language. It was clean, but the shepherds a few hundred metres away told us that a few weeks earlier, at the start of the summer season, it was absolutely filthy because cattle had let themselves in. The shepherds had, in fact, cleaned it (see Chapter 2). We then stayed in the Refugi Enric Pujol in the near-eastern Pyrenees a couple of weeks later. This too was generally clean, with a few items of unwanted food on the shelf, such as salt, pepper and cooking oil. Most recently, in September 2014, we were the only two staying the night at the Cabane de Marterat, on the French side of the 'port' of the same name (see above). The place was incredible, having been renovated by the local *commune* (roughly equivalent to an English parish council) a few years ago and now maintained by it. It was scrupulously clean and even provided an emergency food ration.

Inside the clean, comfortable Cabane de Marterat (altitude about 2,150m), a short distance into the French Ariège, over the frontier from Spain

Our personal experience of cabane and unstaffed refuge cleanliness, therefore, is that mountaineers and shepherds are generally considerate and well house-trained, but don't count on it as being an absolute truth. We have heard that some places have not been clean, and it only takes one group or one person to spoil them for others.

Cabanes and unstaffed mountain refuges are marked on trekking maps, the latter having a different symbol from those that are staffed and provide meals.

Staffed mountain refuges

The end of July 2011 found us climbing up the final stretch of mountain path to the Refugi de Certascan, in the near-eastern Pyrenees. We had two grandchildren (then aged nine and seven) in tow, origin East London. They were bounding along over the rough terrain after liberation from a long stretch on dirt road in the heat of the day.

First grandchild: Mamgu [*Welsh for grandma*], what will be the choice at dinner tonight?

Mamgu (i.e. Angharad): There won't be any choice. Everybody will have the same meal.

Second grandchild: But that's not fair! Why will there be no choice?

Mamgu: Because they have to carry the food loaded on a donkey every day, so they can't allow any choice. You have to eat what you're given.

First grandchild: But what if we don't like it?

Me (intervening): Then you will have to eat it anyway or go hungry. You can give me what you won't eat because I will be very hungry.

We duly arrived at the refuge and after some negotiation over who was sleeping next to whom on the platform bed, we settled in. Dinner started with a clear soup containing bits of chopped *saucisson*. The grandchildren sniffed at it, decided they liked it and the whole dinner was a resounding success, nicely sealed by the guardian's young female helper taking them to feed the donkeys at the end.

It is because of this and other good experiences that we have a soft spot for the Pyrenean staffed refuges. The first night of our first trek in 2001 saw us lodged at the Refuge de Pombie, next to the imposing rock triangle of the Pic du Midi d'Ossue (2,884m) in the Pyrénées-Occidentales. We arrived, having misjudged the time our hike would take, only a few minutes before dinner, where a French lady and her young son, with whom we were sharing a table, helped us gain our bearings and bought us wine.

A few refuges are private, but mostly they are run by the various Pyrenean mountain clubs, associations and federations on both sides of the frontier.

Although a few popular places open in winter for cross-country skiers, snow-shoe walkers and snow and ice climbers, the staffed refuge season usually ranges from mid-June to the end of September. They tend to be about 2,000m above sea level, but there are a few outliers. I have already mentioned the highest one – the Refuge de Bayssellance, at 2,651m. When the guardian arrives in mid-June there is usually plenty of snow still on the ground – it is not uncommon to have to clear six metres of it drifted up against a refuge.

During winter, an unlocked area may be provided for people to huddle into, but there are no facilities. During the summer, the refuge is often open all day, serving coffee, lunches, tea and alcohol. Those that are not too far from road-heads may attract significant day-tripper trade this way. Don't be concerned, therefore, if you arrive at one before 1630 and find many people milling around. Most of them will have departed within the hour.

Refuges come in all shapes and sizes from small (30 bed places or fewer) to large (well over a hundred bed places). Many have platform beds sleeping several people in a row, but others have two or three-tier bunk beds. Dormitories can be large or small, spacious or cramped. You don't need full sleeping bags – just liners, because blankets or duvets are provided. Because of our advancing years and the necessity of getting up at least once during the night, we have tried to negotiate with the *guardien* a bottom bunk or platform and generally it works. In French refuges I tell the *guardien* or assistant straight, with a smile, as when we arrived at the Bayssellance in August 2012: '*Pourriez-vous nous aider s'il vous plaît? Nous avons marché au moins neuf heures. Nous sommes trop agés et en panne. Pourriez-vous nous offrir un lit en dessous?*' This translates as: 'Could you help us please? We have walked at least nine hours. We are too old and

Platform beds don't have to be austere and purely functional. This one at the Refuge de Mariailles, in the Pyrénées-Orientales, has colourful blankets arranged very tastefully – a touch of real style

broken down. Could you give us a bed below?' The Canadian couple of about the same age, with whom we ate dinner that night, loved the playing of the 'age card'.

Facilities vary enormously too. In one refuge you will find hot water, showers and flush toilets with toilet paper provided. The next refuge might only have cold water from an outside tap or hose running into a stone basin and, needless to say, no shower. It will also have only a squat, long-drop toilet with no paper. If showers are available, you sometimes have to pay extra, book a slot, and be prompt because there is pressure on them. In some the washing and toilet facilities are in a separate building.

The communal dinner is usually taken at 1900 in French refuges, 1930 or 2000 in Spain. Occasionally, where the dining room is small, there are two sittings. What we told our grandchildren about there being no choice is not strictly true.

Although they are not provided as a matter of course, you should be able to negotiate a vegetarian meal but do so at check-in, not when the dinner is just about to be served. Speaking solely from personal experience, allergies can also be accommodated. We once trekked up to a French refuge with two friends who were renting an apartment for a week. One of the friends has a gluten allergy (coeliac disease). We explained on arrival at the refuge and the *guardienne* understood immediately that this was a medical condition and negotiated with the chef, her husband, for a gluten-free version of the dinner. She could not, however, provide a bread substitute for breakfast or the following day's picnic, but our friend had anticipated this and brought her own. If you have a special diet, organise it in good time, preferably when making a reservation in advance. Be prepared to bring your own substitutes for anything basic, such as bread.

For dinner, usually, six to ten people sit at a table together. The atmosphere is warm and convivial and the meal overwhelmingly good and sometimes excellent. It is wonderful trekking and mountaineering food: not short of carbohydrates, with plenty of protein and tasty liquid to rehydrate you. Usually it comprises four courses: soup, main course, cheese and a dessert. You clear the table at the end of each course, although the French custom is to keep hold of cutlery and even dishes and plates from the previous course. Overall, a Pyrenean refuge dinner is the perfect place for meeting like-minded people and making friends. Whatever else, you have the shared experience of the mountains on which to build conversation. Often you will find that there is much else in common besides. See Chapter 5 for more on the social gatherings in the Pyrenees.

Wine with, or a coffee at the end of dinner costs extra, although Spanish refuges may continue their tradition of including wine in the overall price. Don't ask for a wine list, it's house wine only, which tastes brilliant at 2,000m after a long day.

Breakfast tends to be more spread out and therefore private. It is also usually very light – bread, biscuits, jam and a choice of hot drinks (tea, coffee or chocolate). You will usually be asked the time at which you require breakfast either on arrival or at the end of dinner.

The exceptions to the eating arrangements described above are in the large Spanish refuges, of which we have experienced three: the Refugio Respomuso (105 places) in the Pyrénées-Occidentales, Refugio de Estós (145 places) in the Pyrénées-Centrales, Refugio de la Renclusa (110 places) also in the Pyrénées-Centrales and the main 'base camp' for climbing Aneto, the highest mountain of the range. At these, meal service tends to be industrialised, and served from a hatch by table number. The first time we visited the Refugio de Estós (2005), we were even allocated a table number in advance of serving, which abruptly broke up conversations with new friends, although this particular practice seemed to have been discontinued by the time of our second visit in 2013. At the Respomuso, during our only visit in 2012, we were given all courses together on a tray from the hatch, which did not make for any conviviality at the table. I should add that we have stayed at one ostensibly large refuge in France, The Wallon, which unfortunately is the next stop on the traverse from the Respomuso. It has 120 places, although much of it appears unused and the whole place is somewhat dilapidated. I don't think that enough people stay for an industrialised system to be in place – certainly not on the two occasions that we have lodged there (2001 and 2012).

I should stress, however, that these large refuges are exceptions. Also, while their size, state of repair and eating regimes might make them less inviting than the smaller refuges, the staff have been overwhelmingly friendly.

Over the years, we have decided that we should plan our stages, where possible, to arrive at the refuges by 1630 and no later than 1800 in France, or 30-45 minutes later in Spain. This allows time to do at least some of the following: check in, claim a bed, get your bearings, wash yourself, wash whatever clothing needs treatment and put it out to dry, write up your diary (or, in Angharad's case, draw attention to yourself by knitting), have a drink and talk to people. If you order tea to drink British-style make sure you ask for *cold* milk. We also carry a small supply of teabags brought from home that we use, to the amusement of onlookers, to supplement the weak tea that we are supplied with.

We have in recent years grown into the habit of ordering an aperitif 20-30 minutes before dinner. Usually this is a kir, and French refuges will sometimes offer a choice of fruit for the accompanying liqueur. We were amazed to discover that a favourite refuge, the Arrémoulit, in 2012, offered raspberry, blackberry or bilberry 'cassis', and a dish of black olives too. This refuge has a romantic position just above a lake bearing the same name, among the high mountains (including the 3,144m Pic de Balaïtous) of the Pyrénées-Occidentales and is often surrounded by snowfields even in late August. It is reached by an exciting trek from the Refuge de Pombie, while the following day there is a choice of two routes, each traversing rough and exciting passes (Chapter 7). The refuge itself is small and basic. The washing facilities are from a hose at the rear, and the squat toilet is several metres away across rough ground. A rope fixed to one rock and hooked to another across the approach indicates when it is occupied. Don't rush or you may trip over the rope and fling the toilet door open with your head! The refuge's 30 places are on two platform beds, one on top of the other, so cramped together that you can barely sit up on the bottom bed without banging your head. The dining room has very little natural light. Yet, the atmosphere is wonderful, as is the range of kirs!

Towards the Mediterranean, however, kirs die out as an aperitif. We discovered this simple fact in September 2013 at the Refuge de Mariailles, on the western side of Canigou. No, the *guardien* had no kir, but he could offer a Maury, which is a *vin doux naturel* (a natural, red sweet wine). In Britain and the rest of northern Europe we would normally have such a wine with dessert, and we might prefer it to be white rather than red. In this corner of France, however, it is traditionally drunk as an aperitif, and very good it is too. Maury is a cousin of the better known Banyuls, also a sweet red wine drunk in these parts as an aperitif. You will walk through the vineyards that supply the grapes for the latter at the end of the trek. Where else could they be but above Banyuls-sur-Mer? We now have several bottles of a vintage (1928) Maury at home, supplied by UK The Wine Society.

Once upon a time at many refuges you weren't allowed into the dormitories until shortly before, or even after, dinner. In 2005, we arrived fairly shattered at the Vallferrera refuge, the last stop on one variant of the HRP before crossing over to Andorra. We were told at check-in that we could not go upstairs to the single dormitory until after dinner, about 2100. We could see why, as access to the dormitory was from the middle of the area acting as both dining space and common room via a rope ladder and trapdoor. In fact, dinner was not served until gone 2130, and we eventually made it up the rope ladder at 2200. A German couple, in particular, were unimpressed! From 2012, however, the renovation of some of the more cramped refuges, including that of the Vallferrera which now has modern dormitories and toilets upstairs, seems to have changed this policy, and nowhere have we been denied access until after dinner.

In general, people start going to bed around 2100, having viewed the sunset over the mountains. They get up from 0600 onwards, apart from guided trips. For us it's generally about 0700.

At all refuges bar one that we have visited, you may order (at check-in) a picnic or, if that seems too much, just a sandwich, for the following day. You certainly are given various extra goodies in a picnic. We have sometimes found that one is sufficient for both of us. Some of it, however, such as plastic spoons and cartons of yoghurt, creates more rubbish. You rarely find bins at refuges and, apart from what you buy and consume at them, you have to 'pack out your trash'. Be prepared for that. Crossing a road with a parking area is often a good spot to find a bin. On the traverse, the one exception to providing a picnic is the Refuge de Pombie. The refuge almost seems to pride itself on its reticence to supply anything other than a few nibbles. This was the

Refuge rules:

1. Remember you're in a refuge, not a hotel.

2. No admission for our doggy friends.

(Pinned to the wall in the Refuge des Cortalets at the start of the tourist track to Pic du Canigou).

case when we stayed there in 2001 and 11 years later in 2012, the latter occasion causing me some irritation as I tried to argue with the guardian over the policy. For those doing the traverse, however, the Pombie allows the exclusive privilege of using the shower.

You should have plenty of euros available to pay by cash when you leave a refuge. French cheques are valid in France, but if you're reading this you're unlikely to have a French bank account! Some Spanish refuges pride themselves on being able to take a debit or credit card, although in practice there may be nerve-wracking moments while waiting to connect. As indicated above, the bill won't necessarily be cheap. If you consume everything that I have noted (afternoon tea or beer, aperitif, dinner with demi-carafe of wine and small black coffee at the end, breakfast, and a picnic or two sandwiches) it will come to about €55 per person per night (2014 prices).

I have painted, with a few noted exceptions, the staffed Pyrenean refuges as wonderful, often quite distinctive places that go far beyond offering a roof over your head. But what are the drawbacks?

First, obviously you don't have the same flexibility and freedom to organise things how you would like. You could add a good deal more flexibility, however, if you, as many do, just turn up without having reserved. From my observations, this course of action is fine 90 per cent of the time, but that still leaves a ten per cent risk that the refuge is full. This may even happen at usually less busy refuges if, for example, a large party has reserved.

You, the reader, might feel differently, but for Angharad and me a risk is a risk, even if it's a small one. Maybe it's a matter of our age, but we just don't want the anxiety of not knowing if we have a bed until we get there, so we have always booked our accommodation well in advance, before leaving home. An in-between option, which we have seen others do, is to book the next accommodation by mobile phone the night before your planned arrival, although that too carries a risk in remote areas that you might not have a signal.

Booking accommodation in advance means that you are prepared to lose a large degree of flexibility and freedom. Although we have cancelled on just two occasions, the pressure is on to get to the next reserved place by whatever means possible and whatever the weather. Booking in advance also has one other advantage – it tells you whether a place is still open or not. Refuges do close for renovation sometimes. They might also close down completely, although this is more likely to happen at a *gîte d'étape* in the valley than a refuge.

In the early years we used a Pyrenean tour company (now defunct) to book accommodation for us, and it also arranged for pick-ups and drop-offs at each end of the trek. If you want to try doing it this way, it's best simply to enquire of an existing Pyrenean tour company because the service is unlikely to be advertised in its brochure.

As my French has improved, and Angharad has learned some Spanish, in recent years we have reserved for ourselves. I usually feel nervous picking up the telephone the first time, but soon get into the swing. Note that most refuges don't answer their telephone between about 0900 and 1700 their time, and sometimes you are switched from ordinary phone to radio phone.

The Internet has also made things easier. Just about every refuge has a website of sorts, containing a summer contact number (which is that of the refuge) for reservations. Many sites have English translations. Use Google (or another search engine) to put in the name of the refuge, for example 'Refuge d'Arremoulit'. Although with French refuges, you always end up telephoning (emails not being received in the refuges themselves), you may often book Spanish ones electronically through the site, just as you might book a hotel.

The second drawback of staffed refuges is that, while they save significant weight compared with camping, and offer luxuries such as a bed, a lovely dinner, alcohol and coffee, they do have some discomforts of their own. A few (and I stress 'few') can be pretty cramped. In 2005 at the Colomers refuge in the Encantats area of the Pyrénées-Centrales, the dormitory mattresses were on the floor at right angles to each other. I found myself that night with my head next to the feet of a stranger. You won't have this experience because a new Colomers refuge has since been built. Some refuges alleviate possible congestion by providing a locker for everything apart from what you need that night, which is placed in a basket that you put at the end of your bed space. Renovated, rebuilt and more recent refuges are, however, better designed.

While enjoying the communal dining arrangements, some people don't like the same when applied to washing, toilets and sleeping. Personally, I am happy to treat these as part of the experience, and I don't mind the loss of privacy that comes with platform beds – at least Angharad has been on one side of me. I don't welcome, however, waking up in the early hours because the dormitory is too hot and stuffy (Spanish refuges especially like to close windows at night) and the noises that my compatriots make (I never use them, but ear-plugs may come in handy). Mostly this is snoring, but other noises are unmentionable in a book as averse to scatology as this one is!

Our most memorable story of the early hours in a dormitory concerns a night at the Refugi de Certascan in August 2009 (two years before our trip there with the grandchildren). Dominique, a larger-than-life French guy, was snoring so loudly that I think the whole dormitory of 20-plus people must have awoken, apart from him. Various attempts were made to divert him, including whistles and other noises. As he carried on oblivious, people started to snigger and giggle until the dormitory was vibrating – Angharad next to me was certainly in convulsions. Then some started to mutter to each other that they needed to '*faire un pipi*', and so head torches were switched on and off as they trooped to the loo. Somewhere along the line I must have become immune to it all, because the next thing I knew was that it was seven o'clock.

Location, location! the Refugi de Certascan in the near-eastern Pyrenees

We must, however, put these drawbacks into perspective. To me they are tiny and it's not often that I have been awoken this way, certainly not enough times to consider ear-plugs. Further, as described above, I am prone to being awoken by 'happenings' in the night while wild camping, which might be more interesting than snoring, but also at times a little too interesting. In the end, I often wonder with amazement and am thankful that such a chain of refuges on both sides of the frontier exists at all. They are a precious resource.

Gîtes d'étape

Gîtes d'étape (*gîtes* for short) are privately owned accommodation in France that meet criteria that you would expect to find in a hostel, such as a bed for the night, toilet, washing facilities and a kitchen for cooking your own food. They are usually accessible by road and near a village or hamlet. Most also provide meals, including a picnic for the following day – we have only come across one in the Pyrenees that doesn't. This was the Gîte de Mounicou, above the Ariège valley, where we stayed in 2008, but we were able to cook our own food using its facilities.

Generally speaking in the Pyrenees, we have found gîtes to be a little better than refuges in terms of space and other comforts. Do check, however, that they provide meals if you want them. Most provide dormitory sleeping accommodation similar to that found in refuges, but some also provide private rooms at extra charge. A few have entirely private rooms and feel, relatively speaking, almost luxurious.

Gîtes are often to be found at valley heads. While some are stand-alone dwellings, others may be attached to an *auberge* or a *bar-restaurant* through, for example, a barn conversion. Having road access introduces another option if you are prepared to pay for it – you have your baggage transported by vehicle from one gîte to the next and you only carry a day sack on the daily trek. Check out through a website search if interested.

Where meals are provided, the communal dinner at a gîte is on a par with that provided by a refuge and you will find similar conviviality. I mentioned above the two French women we met in 2012 at the gîte of the Chalets d'Iraty in the Basque Country, who had decided to try out a self-heating dinner. Well we met them again on each of the next four nights, by which time a 'gang' of eight of us were congregating to have dinner together and knock back a fair bit of wine. Some of us had labels: Angharad and I of course were *Les anglais*, a couple from Paris *Les deux Parisiens*, and two who were having their baggage transported, *Les deux avec les baggages*. Similar happened at the other end of the range a year later, where during the last seven nights to Banyuls-sur-Mer, 12 of us bonded as a strong group that wined and dined together each night, while continuing to walk in our separate groups (see Chapter 5).

You will gather from the above that many permutations are possible in gîtes d'étape. Being privately owned, they may come and go, however, especially in remote areas of France, such as the Ariège. You should check their websites for more details on the accommodation offered, meals service, and indeed whether they even still exist. Usually you have the facility to send an email to state reservation requests. If there is no response, possibly the website has outlived the gîte!

Casas rurales and chambres d'hôte

The casas rurales that you might come across from time to time in the Spanish Pyrenees are not really the equivalent of the French *gîtes*. They are generally rooms in private houses, a bit like British bed and breakfast, except that many provide no meals at all or even cooking facilities. The only time we stayed in a casa rurale, at Parzan in the Pyrénées-Centrales in 2004, we had to pay for a minimum two nights even though we only stayed for one, and buy dinner and breakfast in a bar-restaurant attached to a service station on the edge of the village. The room was smart and clean, as were the toilet and washing (including shower) facilities, but that was all we got. Like French *gîtes*, casas rurales may have their own websites, or the local tourist information website will provide a list, or you may ask at the bar if you arrive in a Spanish village.

The French chambres d'hôte are similar to casas rurales in that they do not provide meals, except the only one we have stayed in (in the village of Lescun, in the Pyrénées-Occidentales) did provide breakfast, not only for us but also for residents of the nearby refuge that has the same owner. That was in 2012, and we had to go to a restaurant in the village for dinner. They are not in private houses, however, but often have been hotels in a previous life. In fact, our *chambre* in Lescun, which had the full en suite facilities and a bar downstairs, was previously the Pic d'Anie hotel, where we had stayed and eaten in 2003. Then it was run by an elderly lady who had possibly seen better days there, telling us as we entered in our trekking gear, *'Vous savez que ce n'est pas un refuge.'* (You know that it's not a refuge.'). She was still in evidence in 2012, although it seemed that now her son and his partner ran the place. After expressing pleasant surprise that we had returned after nine years, she explained that, like many other rural hotels in France, increasingly stringent food regulations had forced the change from hotel to chambre.

You may usually check out chambres d'hôte on a website, send an email with reservation requests, and occasionally even book online.

Inns (*auberges*) and hotels

Whenever we are able (which isn't that often), we stay in an auberge or hotel simply to give ourselves a bit more comfort, some privacy and a break from dormitory accommodation. We are also provided with luxuries, such as towels and guaranteed hot water as a matter of course. Many rooms are en suite, others require a short walk along a corridor. You may, of course, also take your meals in private on a table for two, although if there are other trekkers staying you might share with them. Trekkers walking in the opposite direction to you are mines of information about the route ahead. For example, at an auberge in the Pyrénées-Centrales on the second night of our trek in July and August 2013, we met a British trekker who had come from Banyuls-sur-Mer over the previous 20 or so days, and who told us over dinner about the abnormal snow conditions that we might face (Chapter 7). The year before we stayed at an auberge in the Basque Country, but our new-found French friends were staying in the *gîte* attached to it. We ate dinner with them and had a good laugh, not to mention being the butt of some jokes about our attempt at luxury.

Whether you go for privacy or sociability is of course entirely up to you and your mood of the moment. Being smaller than hotels, auberges tend to push people together more. Do be prepared, however, for a variety in hotel standards. Many are smart and relaxed with a nice atmosphere, others (especially in Andorra where, if you are not camping or staying in an unstaffed *cabane*, a hotel is the main option) corporate and larger, with buffet meals. Some take you into a time warp in a nice way, such as one hotel in the Basque Country with a mainly elderly clientèle, which gives you a place at dinner with your own cloth napkin. At the end of dinner you fold the napkin neatly and leave it at the place to which you return at breakfast. A few, however, take you into a time warp in not such a nice way – they are dirty, the bed sags and food service is poor.

Yet other hotels have a reputation for fine dinners, and they don't disappoint. One such is at Biriatou, our first stop inland from Hendaye. We have stayed there twice. The first time was in early June 2006 and we arrived on a Thursday public holiday in time for late lunch, which we duly took along with extended families, whose members had arrived by car. Then we went for a nap in our room, getting up at about 1800 to shower and repeat the experience. When we returned to the hotel in July 2012, we made sure that we had already eaten a small picnic en route and sensibly took only the evening dinner. We appreciated it all the more because of our afternoon abstinence. It's a wonderful place if you want to splash out a little at the start of the trek, and we are not the only middle-aged trekkers who do this.

It goes without saying that auberges, and hotels in particular, have their own websites, on which you may usually book electronically or at least send an email containing a reservation request. Some you may also book through sites such as Booking.com, but if the site states that no rooms are available, take a

Dinner at Hotel Les Jardins de Bakea, Biriatou:

I know of no better way of celebrating the completion of Day One of the traverse after a gentle stroll out of Hendaye

tip from us: it's always worth checking with the actual hotel or auberge site, or telephoning.

I have one final point to make on booking accommodation in advance in auberges, *gîtes*, refuges and occasionally even hotels in the French Pyrenees. Over the telephone they may ask for a deposit, which isn't much, but is a bit of a hassle to provide if they don't take credit cards and you don't have a French bank account and hence a French cheque book. The only way to do it is through international bank transfer. They seem to be geared up for this, with their IBAN and BIC numbers, and it's easy if you do internet banking yourself, but be prepared for it.

Top tips from Chapter 3

1. To traverse the Pyrenees on foot is to customise your holiday or adventure. Don't, therefore, expect it necessarily to be cheap. You may cut the costs significantly, but only if you are prepared to carry a tent, stove, fuel and food for a large part of the journey.

2. If flying, don't forget to check in even the smallest item that might be deemed a security risk if you carry it on board. Angharad likes to take some knitting to wile away the time, and she always asks at check-in whether it's OK to carry the needles on board the aeroplane (the answer varies).

3. Taking Eurostar to Paris and then a night train south is possibly more expensive than flying. However, it is more relaxing in our experience, especially if you consider it an integral part of the trip, which includes wining, dining and a good night's sleep.

4. If you do opt to go by train, don't relax so much that you let your guard slip. The lessons from our experience of things going wrong occasionally are: always check the night train on arrival at the Gare d'Austerlitz before you go for dinner opposite; have spare euros to throw at a taxi if needed; and give yourself a first day of walking with plenty of leeway in terms of time.

5. Don't be a beast of a burden. Most people who give up on the Pyrenean traverse do so because they are overloaded. Weed out non-essential items and go for lightweight gear. Take few clothes, washing and drying them as you go.

6. Staffed mountain refuges can be great fun with a delightful communal atmosphere. They provide meals as well as a bed and other basic facilities. Sleeping may sometimes be difficult, however, in stuffy dormitories surrounded by noises from co-habitees. If you are a light sleeper, ensure that you have ear-plugs.

7. You need to decide whether you want security of accommodation, in which case you try to reserve in advance, or if you want to maintain flexibility, in which case you arrive at the accommodation hoping for the best. A half-way house is to book for the next night as you go along (make sure you have the telephone numbers that you need). If you book in advance you will almost certainly have to spend time looking at websites. Sometimes you may also be able to book electronically, but don't count on it – you might have to telephone. Checking websites also usually indicates whether your chosen accommodation is still open, or not.

8. While you will usually be able to do so in hotels and *auberges*, and some *gîtes* and Spanish staffed refuges, don't count on being able to pay by credit or debit card. Have your euros ready.

4

The daily trek

From the drawing board to the high trail

This chapter concerns the level of fitness and the numerous trekking aids that you might need. The latter range from things you wear or carry – boots, maps, compass, GPS, directional guidebooks, walking poles, first aid kit and possibly also crampons and/or ice axe – to features of the walking environment, such as footpaths, waymarks, and local transport (orthodox and unorthodox). These aids help you to walk each day and to do so without getting lost. I have no more to say about tents, stoves, sleeping bags, and clothing beyond what I wrote in Chapter 3 about your hopefully light, daily load.

Level of fitness

There is no point in beating about the bush: you have to be fit to trek in the Pyrenees, yet it is a level of fitness that should be attainable by any mobile person. In addition, you develop stamina as you get into the routine after the first few days and the muscles gradually strengthen. Don't be put off, therefore, if the first full day is a shock to the system. What will possibly suffer over time are joints, especially knees, but the simple way of looking after these is to take it slowly downhill. Poles also help preserve the joints (see below). Some people also wear knee support 'bandages', although I gave up on them years ago hiking in Britain when they chafed the area around my knees badly. Maybe they have improved in this regard.

The best preparation is obvious: walk as much as you are able, whether to work, to the shop, with a dog, with friends, or by yourself at weekends. Choose walking as your preferred exercise. If you need to travel faster, or if the walk to work is too far, cycle instead, which will at least build stamina. When I was working full-time in the UK, I used a folding bike for commuting, about 6.5 km each way.

Angharad and I are both keen hikers, and have been for a long while. Many of our friends hike too. When I was working full-time – up until the end of 2011 – I would ensure that I achieved a decent hike almost every weekend. That, coupled with cycling 13 km each day when commuting, kept me fit for the Pyrenees between the ages of 55 and 65. Since I have retired, I take an additional modest hike of five or six miles most weekday afternoons. Angharad, also now retired, does rather less. Having other priorities, she accompanies me occasionally on a weekday, but not often. She manages quite adequately in the Pyrenees after the first day, so you don't have to be as obsessed with walking as I am.

I have calculated that the Pyrenees account for about three per cent of all our walking, whereas the South Pennines on our doorstep, which are more like high hills than mountains, account for 80 per cent. Elsewhere in the UK, the Yorkshire Dales and Pembrokeshire come in at about seven per cent each and the English Lake District at two.

From this, you can see that, although we walk a lot in rough country, it hardly constitutes bounding around among mountains for the most part. In many ways, the start of the Pyrenean traverse in the Basque Country is similar to much of our UK walking – over rolling hills and along grassy ridges. This is one reason for doing the Pyrenean traverse the conventional west to east direction, as the Basque Country hills provide a gradual and familiar introduction, although some of the distances can be long.

Boots

Despite what Hilaire Belloc recommended in his 1909 book (Chapter 3), I believe that good hiking boots are essential. I have little to say, however, about choosing them. Each person is different, and each will choose the most comfortable for her or himself. You obviously need a sturdy pair of reasonable quality that will last the trek, as they will receive a hammering. If you have already used them a significant amount, check that the tread has not worn away anywhere on the soles as they need to grip well, especially when walking downhill. I also like mine to give adequate ankle protection.

I found in July and August 2013 that I had to apply butter from the breakfast table every day to stop my almost new, expensive leather boots from drying out completely, and hence cracking. The reason was that we had been forced to wade through streams in spate due to rapidly melting snow, which had washed out the oils from the leather, and then the boots had dried rapidly in the daily heat. The downside is that several months later they still smelled a little of rancid butter, so you might consider olive oil from the dinner table instead.

Maps

The map is the best route aid and you should remember that, whatever you read below. I assume that you can read a map. If not, there's a problem! You should also learn to trust the map, as the following short story illustrates:

It was a late afternoon in August 2005, and we were at the foot of what the map told us is the frontier pass into western Andorra – the Port de Rat (2,540m). We had to climb 500m over the Port, having already been over one pass followed by a long descent into the Vallée de Soucelm, at the head of which we now stood. Although the map indicated that we were correct, I had a slight niggle caused by a combination of factors. Firstly, I could not see the Port which was allegedly above us. Secondly, we were following red and white waymarks yet the Véron French guidebook to the HRP made no mention of them (yes, waymarks may sometimes sow seeds of doubt). Thirdly, I was concerned that the path, which was heading roughly east, might turn south into the head of a side valley, which was ringed by some very fierce-looking mountains, with no way out. Then we met three French-speaking Belgians descending and I asked, simply for reassurance as I was sure that the map must be right, if this was the path to the Port de Rat. The man of the group answered with a resounding, 'Non' and then spent about 15 minutes suggesting places where the Port de Rat might be, all of which meant retracing our steps down the valley.

He was so forceful that, once the group had left us, I said to Angharad that we had to take him seriously. We then descended for 15 minutes the route we had already ascended in order to gain a broader panorama and hence locate not only our exact position but also that of the Port de Rat. Further intense discussion followed as we stared at the map, before we finally decided that we were on the correct path after all and only buttresses ahead, which the path would surely circumvent, prevented us from seeing the Port. Angharad also ventured that the man was almost certainly a visitor like us, and not necessarily knowledgeable about the area.

We had lost about an hour late in the day. The map and path with its red and white waymarks led us unerringly to the Port de Rat.

A cautionary tale about trusting the map, but let me now move onto the different maps available and their content.

In addition to large scale trekking maps, an overview map to cover the whole range is useful to track progress and to help you exit from the traverse should you ever need to do so. We have a 1:250,000 Rough Guide map which has been worth its weight in gold on the occasions we have resorted to it. (See the Appendix).

Things become complicated when it comes to the daily trekking maps, of which there is a proliferation at different scales. A further complication is that you are dealing with maps produced in two different countries, and the French maps don't stray far over the frontier. On top of that, as mentioned in Chapter 2, the Pyrenees are blessed with a variety of spoken languages – French, Spanish, Aranese, Aragonese, Catalan and Basque. This means that names of passes, mountains and other significant features may vary from one map to another (and from the names given in guidebooks). Often the multiple names for the same spot are similar, whatever the language, but occasionally they are not. For example, the frontier port, which lies between the Spanish village of Tavascan and the French hamlet of Bidous, in the near-eastern Pyrenees, is called the Port de Tavascan on Spanish and Catalonian maps, and less obviously the Port de Marterat on French maps. The latter name derives from the Tuc (Peak) de Marterat, just along the ridge to the southeast.

For British trekkers, you should not expect any of the Pyrenean maps to deliver the standard of detail that you find on Ordnance Survey ones. Being so much higher and complex than anything that you have to negotiate in Britain, there is simply too much detail to put into even a 1:25,000 map. Thus, you will find that contour lines are often spaced at too large an interval to give a proper sense of gradient and its fluctuations. Boulder fields, cliffs, and other features that have to be circumnavigated are not shown. At best, there is general cross-hatching, but on some maps even this doesn't exist. For example, a 1:25,000 map of the Posets massif, boasting the second highest mountain in the Pyrenees (3,371m), makes it look like a Pennine moor in England, which I assure you it is not!

For following waymarked trails, especially the GR10 and GR11, we have found the 1:50,000 maps perfectly adequate for providing the context and orientation that you need to complement the red and white marks on the ground. Where your way is not thus marked, you might feel more secure with a 1:25,000 map, although in my view it doesn't give significantly more detail. On one section we have found a Spanish 1:40,000 map useful.

The Appendix section on maps contains two tables. The first aims to help you through the confusing array of maps at different scales that cover both sides of the frontier. The second, with a little accompanying text, lists in order the maps that we actually used during our 2012/2013 traverse.

It might seem like sacrilege, but to save weight and bulk we have literally cut from some of our maps the areas we don't need, and where there are overlaps with the previous or next map. The most extreme example is the 1:50,000 Mapa Excursionista 24 Gavarnie-Ordesa, of which you only need a small corner for a few hours because of such overlaps. If you do decide, however, to cut away the bits you don't need on any map, be careful to leave enough either side of the intended route to allow for assessing context (passes, peaks, ridges, lakes and valleys) and possible variants. In other words, don't turn it completely into a narrow strip map, otherwise one of the benefits – to provide an overall sense of context and orientation (where you are in relation to everything else) – is lost.

As part of home planning, checking routes across different maps that cover the same ground through their overlaps may be a useful thing to do if you are going away from the beaten track of the standard routes. This is because, although maps are generally accurate, especially in respect of the GR10, GR11, their variants and other waymarked paths, none is infallible and errors might creep in, or they might show different details. However, I don't wish to overstate a problem that I have found to be minor. No discrepancies between the maps have ever thrown us badly off course. The most likely error, to which guidebooks are at least as prone, is that details may change after publication. Especially lower down, dirt roads and even the occasional tarmac road may appear on the ground where previously there was none.

As well as checking between different maps, the routes may also be checked against guidebook instructions. The information flow is not, however, necessarily, one way. For example, if the guidebook tells you to turn left off a hitherto waymarked stretch, the map will give meaning to the instruction and also help to identify the spot on the ground, which might not be obvious otherwise. The map also helps resolve ambiguities in guidebook instructions, and suggests alternatives. It is a good idea, if following them, to trace the route indicated by guidebook instructions on the map in advance of setting out. But now I am straying onto the next topic.

Directional guidebooks

As previously stated, the guidebooks to the GR10, GR11 and HRP provide detailed day-by-day instructions of the route to be followed. Each day's entry includes a short overview of the terrain you will be covering, how much climbing there will be, and the approximate walking time, without stops. The GR10 and GR11 guidebooks also provide the approximate distance that you will cover.

We have the GR10, GR11 and HRP English language directional guidebooks that are published by Cicerone on a light Kindle, which certainly saves weight. Kindle is not so good if you are continually checking the instructions en route. For that purpose you need something handy in front of your eyes that can be fished out of a convenient pocket, such as a sheet of paper that comprises a photocopy of the guidebook instructions for the particular stretch that you are walking.

That is not, however, how we have come to use these guidebooks, as a rule. Rather, we go through the following steps on the Kindle versions, cross-checking with photocopied pages from the Georges Véron French guidebook, which is not available electronically.

1. When planning our route at home, if we are following a particular stage in the guidebook, we check the walking time that it gives for the trek. If it is nine hours or more, we know that our total time spent trekking is likely to be at least 12 hours (see step 4 below). Do we want to spend that long on a trek, especially if the previous and following days are likely to be just as long? If not, is it possible to divide it in two? Is it possible to do part of it differently so as to make it shorter?

2. On the traverse, at our lodging either the evening before or over breakfast, we scan the appropriate guidebook for its overview of the terrain and the basic stats of ascent, descent and walking time. We then look at its detailed instructions for any part of the day that may cause problems, such as route-finding or having to scramble over rocks. We do the latter in conjunction with the map, where we check for possible alternatives if the weather turns bad or if we simply want to shorten the day.

3. Having traced (not necessarily literally with a highlighter pen, although you may do that) the route indicated by the guidebook instructions onto the map, we estimate the distance that we will travel. I know that the guidebooks to the Pyrenees tend to stress walking time rather than actual distance, but I personally find it useful to have an approximate idea of the latter. Until recently, I calculated very roughly. I simply laid the scale that is provided on my compass along the route without worrying too much about minor angle deviations and turns, and added 50 per cent to allow for meanderings and gradients. I now have a hiking app on my iPad mini that measures walking distance accurately and provides other stats such as ascent, descent and walking time (plus, on completion, a route profile and a trace of it on a satellite image). Checking a few of my previous crude approximations against this app, I have found that they were only deviant by about five per cent.

4. Next, I calibrate the walking time that the guidebook provides with the likely overall time that the hike will take us. In other words, I customise the time given in the guidebook to what I know about myself and Angharad, to the nature of the terrain, and to the likely length of our stops. Thus, we may add anything between 30 and 70 per cent to the guidebook walking time, depending on length of stops, weather, ease of terrain, the nature of the path, whether streams to be crossed are in spate or not, how fast we normally

ascend or descend, and other questions of personal context. In this calculation, we have learned from experience over a number of years that we keep better to guidebook walking times during weather closer to what we are used to at home (for us, cooler, 'British' weather), in lower country on dirt roads, and when ascending well-maintained and waymarked paths in the mountains. We lose time when it is very hot, when paths are barely traceable on the ground or very rough, and when descending. On the last of these, knee and other joint problems affect us more as we become older, and we are more cautious. Thus, to put the above another way: for us, a 21 km walk takes about seven hours in the Basque Country, while in the high mountains such a distance takes up to 12 hours. To illustrate this point, September 2015 saw us doing the 4-day *Muntanyes de Llibertat trek* (Chapter 1). This is how Days 2 and 4 went. Day 2 was 19 km and involved a combined 3,600m of ascent and descent. Day 4 was 18 km with a combined 2,800m of ascent and descent. So, there was only a kilometre difference in distance, yet Day 2 took us 15 hours, while Day 4 took 9.5 hours. Part of this difference may be explained by the greater combined up and down on Day 2, but mostly it was due to the state of the footpaths. On Day 2 there was no path, or only traces of one, for most of the time, through some very rough terrain. On Day 4, there was a good waymarked path virtually all of the way that ingeniously wound its way around every difficulty.

5. We then pack the Kindle away, while keeping it easily accessible in an outside pocket of the rucksack. We usually only take it out when we are having a break during the trek, simply as a reassurance and double-check to the map as to where we are and what lies ahead. Very occasionally, if, despite scrutinising the map, we are not sure where to go at a junction, we will take it out to see whether the guidebook can cast some light on the issue. Otherwise, we use the map in conjunction with our compass for general direction (see below) and the waymarks that exist on the large majority of our routes. To be honest, as I mentioned in Chapter 2, on the waymarked GR10 and GR11, I don't think that a detailed directional guidebook is needed for finding the way, although it remains useful for overviews. You still need a map, of course, on these trails. On the HRP (where it is not the same trail as the GR10/GR11) you might like to use a guidebook more often.

The preparatory steps, 2-4 of the above, might appear to require a lot of you at a time when you would rather relax. In reality, however, they total 15-20 minutes over a drink in your overnight lodging. It is time well spent.

Finally, the directional guidebooks, like maps, are not infallible. For example, landmarks in guidebooks may change over time, especially lower down. Is, for instance, the building on the left the one that the guidebook indicates as the reference point for turning right, even though it is now a complete ruin? Or should we carry on until we come to a building that is still worthy of the label? Sometimes, especially on the GR10, the official route changes after the publication of the guidebook, and even on the HRP, new paths appear. Then there are ambiguities with respect to left and right. For example, 'Pass the *cabane* to the left'. Does this mean that the *cabane* should be situated to your left, or you should you be to the left of the *cabane*? While on left and right, note that the right and left banks of a stream correspond to facing downstream – the guidebooks usually explain this, but the explanation might be tucked away somewhere and not necessarily read. Thus customising guidebooks includes updating them where necessary, and noting potential ambiguities.

Compass, GPS and whistle

As with maps, I assume you can use a compass and there is no point in carrying a GPS unless you know how to use it without having to read the instructions.

We had set off walking one September day in 2013 an hour or so earlier from the Refugi d'Ull de Ter in the Spanish Pyrénées-Orientales. We were on the HRP, en route to the Refuge de Mariailles, in France, at the western foot of Canigou, which we expected to take nine hours in total. We were crossing a large plateau at an altitude of about 2,300m. Plateaux are rare in the Pyrenees and the worst thing possible occurred – the mist that had been threatening since the start of the trek descended, restricting vision to a few metres. Still, it was possible to follow the path until we came to a fork that wasn't marked on the map or mentioned in the guidebook. Two men who had been following, caught up and went straight on, but appearances suggested that we should follow the right fork. This was fine, with waymarks for about five minutes – until the path petered out on what appeared to be a grassy pass. Fleetingly, we saw a large cairn to our right and went to it. We could, however, see no further and the compass now suggested that we were walking in the wrong direction. We therefore retraced our steps to the junction, looking without success for signs of a path that might lead us in the right direction. Back at the junction we were discussing what to do, when a lone hiker appeared through the mist walking towards us on the path we had just walked up and down. He was Catalan, happy to speak English, and confirmed that our original supposition was correct, but we should carry on at the cairn where we had turned back. He too had been confused for a few minutes, but we should soon find ourselves on a good path again, heading in the right general direction. He also pointed out that we were about 30 minutes further back compared with where we thought we were. We, in the meantime, had spent about 20 minutes at this hiatus and endured a great deal of angst.

We managed the next seven or eight hours without trouble as the mist came and went. Without trouble, that is, apart from the rain, hail and thunder that accompanied us, and which is a story to be told later (day 45, Chapter 9). It was not as if we hadn't been forewarned about this plateau section. Georges Véron states in the French HRP guidebook: *'Parcours très délicat en cas de brouillard'* [very tricky route in fog]. Joosten states in the English HRP guidebook: 'Be aware that route-finding can be very difficult today in poor visibility.'

We were lucky that the knowledgeable Catalan appeared when he did. It was the only occasion on the 156 days that we have walked on the traverse that, I reflected afterwards, I should have had a GPS. The compass, map and two guidebooks combined were not enough to resolve the situation at the junction of paths on that plateau. Because of the mist I did not know quite where we were on the map. And because I did not quite know where we were, the compass was only of use for general direction (which could have been either fork), not the local details. If the mist had not been down, I could have gained a more accurate position on the map from the surrounding peaks and valleys. But then, if there had been no mist, I would have seen the true path ahead of me, winding its way onwards in the correct direction. While not being completely foolproof, a GPS could have told me within metres where I was and where to go.

I still don't have a GPS as I write these words over a year later. We had crossed that same plateau without any problem seven years previously when the day was clear. Two days out of 156 on the only plateau that the Pyrenean traverse encounters, and on one of those days the mist was down. I also know that should I return to that plateau in mist, I will know exactly where to go at that junction, and after a few more minutes the route-finding will be straightforward.

If you have been brought up on a GPS, please ignore the previous paragraph. For others who are perhaps like me, you need to make your own informal 'risk assessment'. The chances that you will really need a GPS when you already have a low-tech compass are slim. If, on a single occasion, you do need one, however, the consequences might be severe if you do not have it to hand.

As for my compass, I still find it indispensable, in fair weather as well as foul. I keep one in the breast pocket of my walking shirt. I use it to check that the direction in which we are travelling is correct and in accordance with the map or guidebook instructions. I also use it to check change of direction further along the path. I have even used it on minor roads to check direction when new roads that are not marked on the map have been constructed and cross at an acute angle the one on which I am travelling. And, of course, you do need to use it more intensely and accurately if you are caught in mist – as long as you know where you are!

Finally don't forget the whistle. We have never had to send out a mountain distress signal – six blasts in quick succession, followed by a pause before blasting again. (Note that in the dark, the same sequence of torch flashes does the same job.) Many modern trekking rucksacks come with a whistle permanently attached to an accessible strap. It's not always that obvious, so ensure you know where it is. Otherwise, bring one to put in an outside pocket – a light one of course.

Footpaths

Over the whole range, footpaths vary enormously in terms of quality and ease of recognition on the ground. That said, you will find in the popular Pyrénées-Occidentales and Pyrénées-Centrales, and much of the Pyrénées-Orientales, that they are very obvious. Some paths have eroded sections, although work has been carried out on others to prevent further deterioration. In the near-eastern Pyrenees there are a few wild days around Mont Rouch/Roig when the path is not always obvious, it is rough and progress is slow (see also Chapter 8). Points to note about footpaths are:

Zig-zags on paths ascending or descending steep ground are important for ease of movement, carrying heavy loads and saving your knees when descending, but shortcuts have ruined many popular routes, contributing to footpath erosion. In the worst cases, it's difficult to make out where the carefully graded zig-zags of the original path went. For example, at the eastern end of the Pyrénées-Occidentales, the final climbs to the high passes of the Hourquette d'Ossue (2,734m) and the Col de la Fache (2,664m), are both described by the Joosten English HRP guidebook as being steep and on loose scree. The former, however, has largely kept its zig-zags, while on the latter they are hard to trace. There is no doubt which climb is easier.

High above Gavarnie on the HRP

Paths may be very rough, especially in the high mountains. Traverses of boulder fields in particular are tortuously slow. Use every means to cross the worst parts, even if it means sitting on your backside. Some of the boulder fields that we have had to navigate are etched on my memory (but these are not the only ones and Angharad will swear to and at others!) and recorded here:

o Below the Col de Peyreget (2,300m) and with the Pic du Midi d'Ossue towering above en route to the Refuge de Pombie, in the Pyrénées-Occidentales. This is memorable because it is the first boulder field we crossed on the first day of our first traverse of the Pyrenees, back in August 2001. Having set off late morning, and not acclimatised, it felt at the time like the last straw. See Chapter 7 for the route that avoids this boulder field.

o   From the Refuge de Pombie, the HRP goes east to the Refuge d'Arrémoulit. The next day there is a choice of routes, the easiest being via the Col d'Arrémoulit (2,448m), which is what we did in 2012. We were tortuously slow on the steep, rocky descent from the col into Spain and the Lacs d'Arriel below, but we made it without mishap. Then, as we reached the Lacs and a stretch of ostensibly flat terrain, an awkward boulder field again felt like the final straw.

o   The boulder field towards the end of the day on the GR11 route through the Encantat mountains, which is where Angharad had the accident I describe in Chapter 2.

o   The obscure Col de la Cornella (2,485m) on the HRP in the near-eastern Pyrenees (Purple Route Day 34 Chapter 8). On the trek to it from above Alós d'Isil, at the head of the Vall d'Aneau, you follow a path that is often faint. Below the final climb to the col, you then have two awkward boulder fields to cross in hanging valleys, one above the other. The first time we did this route in 2008, we tried to avoid the worst of the first boulder field by climbing above it on the south side. That proved to be a mistake and we lost an hour.

o   The equivalent of two long days of walking roughly east from the Col de la Cornella will bring you to the frontier at Port de l'Artigue (2,481m), the pass that provides the link between the Refugi de Certascan and the Gîte de Mounicou, in France (if open, see Chapter 3). On the French side of the 'port' you will soon reach an extensive boulder field, where you need to keep your eyes open for the red and white waymarks to guide you for what seems like an age. With the help of the waymarks, we negotiated it successfully in mist in 2009.

Of course, boulder fields are not the only impediments to progress in the high mountains. As hinted in Chapter 2, you might have to cross snowfields, but I deal with these in the section on crampons and ice axes, below. On other occasions, you have to use hands on rock, not just to steady yourself but to make any progress at all. Here are some of my most memorable 'hands-on-rock' experiences (again, Angharad has others).

o   The last few metres onto the Pas de l'Osque (1,922m), marking the start of the high mountains as you travel west from the Atlantic. These have

An occasionally steep, but relatively easy stretch of the HRP in Andorra

been described already in Chapter 2 as being close to a rock climb in some eyes.

o   The Passage d'Orteig, which is the final hurdle before reaching the Refuge d'Arrémoulit, en route from the Refuge de Pombie, in the Pyrénées-Occidentales. It is a traverse along a ledge, on a vertiginous rock face. When we traversed it in 2001 we did not find it difficult. Nevertheless we kept hold of the steel cable bolted to the rock face and did not look down. The Passage d'Orteig may be avoided by a descent from the prior Col d'Arrious (2,259m), followed by an ascent to the Refuge, and we went that way in 2012 (Chapter 7). See a photograph of the Passage d'Orteig at: http://tinyurl.com/Passage-Orteig

o   The Port du Lavédan (2,617m), which is an alternative HRP route from the Refuge d'Arrémoulit, that we took in 2001. As you approach across rough ground and possibly snowfields, the rock ridge ahead looks impenetrable. Then the only weakness appears – a boulder-strewn scramble up to the Port du Lavédan. The name is engraved in the rock to the side of this perfectly formed notch. When we climbed it, Angharad became stuck on a huge boulder on which she was spread like a giant insect. I had to come up behind her and give a shove with my head – my hands being otherwise occupied keeping my own balance – in a part that I would not care to mention. People like me, with longer legs, will find the climb easier, but the whole of this day's trek is rough and tough (see Chapter 7). The Port is simply the crowning glory.

o The short, sharp, rocky descent to the Ibón Superior de Vallibierna, on the GR11/HRP variant, which passes to the south side of Aneto, in the Pyrénées-Centrales. There are also large boulders to cross hereabouts, remembered by Angharad but not by me. (The GR11 and HRP guidebooks mention them so they must be there and substantial!). When we passed this way in 2005, I remember that we had to take a little care but overall it was OK. The rocky descent, and indeed the whole trek for the day, was memorable. We were following a GR11 stage that is also an HRP variant described in the Joosten and Véron guidebooks. In the Joosten guidebook, his overview of the Pyrénées-Centrales is headed 'The hard or easy way…', and the easy way consists primarily of this variant and two preceding days. Well, I have never done the 'hard way' so I can't vouch for it, but in my memory this particular day with its short, rocky scramble and many hours over rough terrain is not 'easy' (see Chapter 7)!

o On the HRP in the near-eastern Pyrenees, having negotiated the Col de la Cornella (see the section about boulders, above) followed by two more cols, the rocky descent to the unstaffed Refugi Enric Pujol (2,287m) at the foot of Mont Roig. Véron describes it as 'admirable, polished glacial terrain'. It is actually a wide area of polished, glaciated, brown boulders, so large that you might as well treat them as a series of rock faces over which there is no obvious, single path. The Joosten guidebook suggests that cairns will lead you down, but I sense more a profusion of cairns that have the potential to lead you round in circles. You should pick your way down slowly, and that tiny spec glinting in the distance, which represents the Refugi Enric Pujol, will gradually loom larger. There is, however, a sting in the tail. The *refugi* is situated on a rocky promontory above the outflow from the most northerly of the Gallina lakes (you will have made brief acquaintance with two other Gallina lakes en route). To reach the crossing point, you have to edge round from the lake for a few metres. Then there is a step across that is made awkward by the fact that you are clinging onto the rock above it. The two occasions that we have crossed we have been helped by another person grabbing our hands. See the Purple Route of Chapter 8 for more on these experiences.

o The rocky scramble the next day between the Refugi Enric Pujol and the Refugi de Certascan (or the next day but one if you choose to break the journey by staying at the refuge and campsite of Bordes de Graus, roughly one third of the way into the trek). This scramble comes shortly after you emerge above the trees when ascending from the valley below. The best and easiest way up is to ensure that you follow the painted arrows. It is possible to avoid it by turning left and following the stream to the Estany de Flamisella, before doubling back to the Pleta Vella and small lake at the top of the scramble, but this is a long way round. After taking the scramble in 2008 and 2009, we tried out the long route in 2010. I don't think it's worth it.

o   En route from the Refugi de Certascan to the Port d'Artigue (see boulders section, above) you pass by two lakes – the Estany de Romedo de Dalt and, lower down, the Estany de Romeda de Baix, at the end of a dirt road ascending from the village of Tavascan. At this second lake, before reaching the dirt road, you have to scramble over a steep rocky section. It's manageable, and there is a rope fixed to the rock some of the way to help. Just take a bit of care.

Paths may be blocked by fallen rocks, especially after spring avalanches, and trees –as well as by overenthusiastic trees that are still upright. Such blockages are, however, usually minor and easily circumvented.

Cattle, found especially on the lower reaches of the GR10, may wreck short sections of paths, but again this is generally a minor inconvenience. Cattle themselves may occasionally block paths, but you can usually get them to shift as you approach.

Paths may be rerouted occasionally. We have noted this especially on the GR10, in France. In Spain, lower down, paths might be disrupted by new *pistas* under construction (see Chapter 2). Such occurrences will probably incur no more than a little head-scratching and gazing at the map.

Finally, on paths, I repeat what I wrote in Chapter 2 on 'Dangers, risks and potential accidents' – always watch where you put your feet. This should go without saying, but stumbles are most likely to occur when you drop your guard, and you tend to drop your guard on easier terrain or when tired at the end of the day. Stop to admire the view and don't be in a hurry.

Waymarks and signposts

I have referred already to the excellent waymarking on the GR10 and GR11. The waymarks consist of red and white painted stripes, usually on rocks, but sometimes on posts and trees. Turnings left and right are clearly marked, and a red and white cross at a junction indicates the way NOT to be taken.

In recent years, several trans-frontier trails have been freshly waymarked, and these paths may be used to link the GR10, GR11 and HRP. Their red and white stripes also follow the GR10/GR11 conventions for left and right turns and 'wrong way'. The waymarks do, however, appear to be more conspicuous in France than in Spain. In both countries, older marks of different colours sometimes still dominate. Again, the red and white stripes are painted directly on rocks and sometimes trees or posts. We did discover one variation on this, however, when descending the French side of the Port de Salau (2,087m) above the Ariège, in 2013. Many of the red and white stripes were on metal and screwed into the rock. They appeared to have been placed recently. Being on metal made them highly visible, but already a few had been removed by persons unknown, while others were loose or appeared to have been vandalised

The HRP often does its own thing, but sometimes it follows the GR10, the GR11 or even part of a trans-frontier trail. In these situations, it too is marked by red and white stripes. As previously noted in Chapter 2, at other times it will follow waymarked paths with older markings. These may come in many colours, including orange, yellow, purple, blue, green, red, and even red and white, to name but some. There are also locations on the HRP where only a few cairns accompany the faint path. Here, Angharad and I perform our civic duty by adding an extra stone to make them a bit more visible. This is something we have always found unnecessary on the well-trodden paths of the English Lake District, but in these isolated parts of the Pyrenees, the cairns take on added importance.

GR and trans-frontier trail signs and conventions for 'turn right' and 'not this way'

Other points to bear in mind about waymarks are:

• Occasionally they may be sparse, especially where you most need them: for example, where the path is across grass and not obvious on the ground, or along a dirt road where multiple dirt roads branch off. Waymarks on trees are, of course, vulnerable.

• Also, occasionally, they may be confusing, seeming to send you off in different directions – for example, on the Col d'Osin, in the Basque Country, on the first full day of walking. Very occasionally, they are actually wrong.

• If the official route has changed, and the waymarking has also changed to match it, the new route may not be shown on the map. We came across this, again in the Basque Country, in 2008 on the Port de Belhay (1,732m). Clear red and white waymarks pointed south, yet both the Véron and Joosten guidebooks indicated that we should go east on a vague track. Nevertheless, we followed the waymarks for about 15 minutes, before deciding they were wrong. We retraced our steps and followed the route indicated in the guidebooks. We realised later that we should have trusted the waymarks when we met two other trekkers who had stayed with us the night before in the Cabane d'Ardané. (Note that Véron often uses the term 'abri' (shelter) in place of *cabane*). They had followed the red and white waymarks leading to a path, which our route eventually joined. Their route may well have been faster.

Signposts usually appear either at significant junctions of paths or to indicate the summit of a pass. While important and useful, unfortunately they may also on occasion sow seeds of doubt and you then spend some minutes staring at one while you try and make sense of it. For example, at one multiple junction in the Basque Country, a signpost indicates the route to the same place in apparently different directions, and also different directions for the GR11. Perhaps they all end up converging! A second example is for the signpost to give the correct general direction, while the immediate direction is in a large zig-zag starting at right angles to the one indicated. This is easy to work out when it is clear, but in mist in the high mountains there is a danger that you will step into an abyss. Our memory of this issue concerns a crossing we made of the Hourquette de Héas, to the east of Gavarnie, in the Pyrénées-Centrales in bad visibility in 2002. The Hourquette itself is rocky and quite narrow. The way off is to slant down to the right across the rock, not go straight on as the signpost seems to indicate. We crossed the Hourquette de Héas a second time in 2004 with two friends, and in sunshine and clear weather we found the pass delightful and it was obvious where to go next.

Signposts usually indicate times to the destinations to which they point. As with the guidebooks these are walking times only (that is, without stops), but, allowing for this, treat them with suspicion or even as fiction. Most quoted timings seem hopelessly optimistic, but a few can catch you out and the times then appear, conversely, to be generous. On the latter, I have already mentioned in Chapter 3 of our 2013 experience, climbing from Gavarnie to the Refuge des Espuguettes in an hour and 40 minutes, when the signpost out of Gavarnie indicated two hours (without stops). Pathetically, we felt really good at having beaten the wooden signpost!

To end this section, always remember that waymarks (for sure), and probably many signposts, are the work of volunteers. Our hero, Georges Véron, gave up much of his time to paint the first waymarks on the western section of the GR10 before he 'invented' the HRP. To paraphrase the author of the original Cicerone GR11 guidebook, Paul Lucia, please be thankful to them every time that you are reassured by seeing one, while forgiving them the occasional glitch.

Walking poles, crampons and ice axes

Apart from those who are attempting to jog the traverse in record time, most trekkers use walking poles. In fact, this is 'normal' for almost everybody who hikes in these mountains.

When we set off on this adventure in 2001, only Angharad used poles because she had a long history of problems with knees and feet. By 2003 I had joined her, but was using one pole only. I persisted with this until our completion of the traverse in September 2006, despite being gently scolded by a couple of French hikers while on the steep descent from the Hourquette de Héas in 2004 (see above) who suggested that one-pole trekking was next to useless. Perhaps they were right, but somehow the pole reassured me.

By 2008 I was equipped with two poles. The reason for the conversion was a bit bizarre. As part of my recovery from a broken knee cap the year before I went on short hikes in the English South Pennines, using my two elbow crutches. In this way, I acquired the habit and the technique and I saw the value of two poles for a fully fit Gordon.

I continue to use them for hikes in mountainous country, that is mainly the Pyrenees plus a few occasions in the English Lake District, and longer hikes in the English Pennines. I would not now be without two walking poles in the Pyrenees. They definitely help when descending, but also give extra power when going up.

Poles of course add weight to the load. For our 2009 trip, we discovered lightweight poles (if you Google 'lightweight trekking poles' or 'lightweight walking poles', you will be spoiled for choice), which we have used ever since. I have an exceptionally light pair that weigh in at just 285gms for both, including their sack. They fold like tent poles when you are not using them, which means they may be carried without them poking out of the top of your rucksack (a definite advantage on the Paris Métro). They are not, however, as strong as heavier poles. Lean on them heavily to save yourself after a stumble and they will deform. In 2010 in the Pyrenees – not actually on the traverse or indeed anywhere dangerous, but on a rough dirt road – I stumbled and one of the poles bent almost double. I am now onto my third pair since 2009, but given the amount of hiking I do, that's not bad.

My very lightweight poles come in various sizes (I have the longer pair) and they don't adjust. I don't find this a problem, and anyway adjusting my previous poles always seemed to pose a challenge – either the adjustment action was stuck and sweaty hands would not turn it, or I pulled a pole out too far and the whole thing came apart. Angharad, however, likes to adjust as she walks up and down and so has a heavier (but still lightweight) pair. These will not bear the weight of a bad stumble either. When Angharad had her accident among the boulders in 2013, one of her poles actually snapped.

A further point about any poles is that they are easily left behind at a refuge, picnic spot, café, etc. Folding poles that you can tuck into a rucksack are in fact a boon for those of us prone to leaving things lying around. Angharad and I do have our own little techniques for ensuring that 'leaving behind' doesn't happen and try to look out for each other.

Overall, poles in the Pyrenees have been good for us, although I am not so sure that we have always been good for them. As well as helping when ascending and descending, they also help a bit with balance and steadying yourself on snowfields. In our experience, however, they are unlikely to arrest you if you fall on snow and ice. Unless the snowfield that you encounter is minor and has at most a slight gradient, I think that you require something more.

This 'something more' brings me on to crampons and ice axes. I have already recounted our hairy experience when we slipped on snow below the Hourquette de Héas in 2013 (Chapter 2). Here I tell of another occasion of a snow encounter when we were inadequately equipped.

After hiring ice axes at the last minute because of significant snow before we started our Pyrenean adventure in 2001, the next six years lulled us into a false sense of security. We came across only occasional small patches on gentle slopes and by the time we finished our first traverse in 2006 we had abandoned this extra load.

Thus in August 2008, while we were filling gaps on the 2001-2006 traverse, we had neither crampons nor ice axes. We expected warm and settled weather. I was slightly perturbed as we worked our way across the Pyrenees west to east, as there seemed to be more snow than usual on the mountains. This, I was informed, was the result, as in 2001, of late spring snowfall followed by a cool early summer.

I have mentioned above the little rock scramble that year en route to the Refugi de Certascan. Well, after this hazard, we toiled to the Col de Certascan (2,605m) in changing weather. Clouds had built up and there were sounds of thunder nearby. Still, it was now mostly downhill with the *refugi* a good hour away. Given that the time was seven pm and dinner was scheduled for eight, we couldn't hang around. In any case, the thunder had grown louder and there was a storm in the next valley.

The start of the descent was steep. After a few minutes we came to a snowfield that had not been visible from the top, which we were able to bypass on the scree to one side. Then, as a few large drops of rain arrived, we came to a second, larger snowfield. We were able to get round some of it, but the last third gave us no option but to dig our heels in and descend gingerly, making it to the bottom with manifest relief as the rain stopped. It had been a sobering experience. We arrived at the *refugi* late, but the guardian produced a meal. As we ate, the ground turned white outside under heavy hail stones and thunder now directly above.

We now always carry mini-crampons for treks in the Pyrénées-Centrales and the near-eastern Pyrenees. They have six spikes instead of the 12 on 'full' crampons and they do not require special stiff boots. They are good for snowfields but are not advised for long glacier treks. By 2013, mini-crampons had advanced in design, having a simple instep and strapping system. A pair weighs 500gms. They have always held fully firm on the snowfields where we have worn them. I should further note, however, that they must not be confused with some brands that call themselves mini-crampons that have no spikes but metal teeth around their perimeter, a chain criss-crossing from one side to the other, and which are attached to the boot by a simple strong

The instep, six-spike mini-crampon that we use: suitable for snowfields but not extensive treks on glaciers

elasticated system. These latter are NOT suitable for crossing mountain snowfields, although they are fine for the high hills of the English Pennines that we cross in winter snow.

Perhaps we suffer more than most because we have never skied and do not have the appropriate balance. Whatever the reason, I do recommend a pair of mini-crampons for the high mountains as far east as the Col de Certascan. You can always post them back home once you are confident that you are not going to meet any more snow – if you can find a post office that is.

In addition, note that we have never carried crampons *and* an ice axe together; it has been one or the other. Mini-crampons plus poles have been sufficient for us, although I concede that an ice axe offers security if you do slip.

The first aid kit

This is something else that adds weight. Hopefully you will barely use it, apart from plasters, Compeed blister relief and something for pain relief if your joints are playing up,. Some people apply plasters and Compeed blister relief before they even set off for the day. Yet, a first aid kit is not something you can sensibly do without. The Appendix lists the items in our first aid, which weighs in at 400 gms.

While not strictly 'first aid', we also carry a water purifier tablets, which we actually rarely use (see Chapter 2), as well as sun tan cream and lip salve, which are both essential.

When all else fails: public transport, taxis, hitch-hiking and chair lifts

It was 0830 as we set off in August 2004 from the Casa Rurale in the Spanish village of Parzan, in the Pyrénées-Centrales (mentioned briefly in Chapter 3). We descended to the main road that bypasses the village. The sky suddenly turned black. I have never seen anything like it before – reasonably bright one moment and now almost dark. The blackest of the black was up a side valley. We looked anxiously at each other and wondered if we should wile away some time over coffee in the café attached to the petrol station about 100m along the road, until the sky brightened again. We did not have to wonder for long. Up the side valley appeared a huge flash of lightning followed by an immediate, frighteningly loud, thunder crack. We sprinted towards the café as the rain tumbled from the sky in bucket loads.

Two hours passed before we ventured outside. The thunder and rain had stopped, but the sky still appeared ominous and everywhere was dripping wet. We had an estimated nine-hour trek ahead of us to the Refugio de Viados, which faces the Posets massif (see the Maps section of this chapter above). We might arrive in time for dinner if we were lucky. On the other hand, that ominous sky did not bode well. It started to rain again, not heavily, but enough to make up our minds. I examined our 1:250,000 map, which covers the whole of the Pyrenees (See Maps, above, in this chapter). I noted that, if we headed south down the valley, we could then go round and up the next main valley to the Refugio de Viados, a trip of an estimated 50 km, most of it on tarmac but the last few kilometres on dirt road. Thus, we decided to hitch from Parzan. As we walked down the road to a hitching spot, we exchanged greetings with a French guy, encased in his wet weather gear and obviously about to set off hiking somewhere.

A car soon stopped and we did the whole journey in two lifts, the second being with a young Spanish couple in an old camper van who drove us to just below the Refugio de Viados, including the section on a very wet dirt road. It was neither the first nor the last time that we were subject to incredible kindness and help from people in the Pyrenees. We arrived at the Refugio at about 1400, just before another deluge that was accompanied by thunder. That evening, as we were eating dinner, the Frenchman whom we had met in Parzan, walked in, wet but relieved, having done the walk that we had intended to do.

To remind myself as much as you, the reader, I return to a basic premise. The traverse of the Pyrenees is not (or should not be) a competition, a trial of strength or an extreme sport. It is a concept that you have to treat flexibly on the ground for all kinds of reason. The point is to complete the route while having a wholesome experience. Be prepared to accept non-walking aids from time to time. Seeing the Frenchman enter, we knew that perhaps we could have walked it after all, although he appeared to be much younger than us. But there's no point in getting upset or feeling guilty about it. Our decision had been finely judged and made only after some discussion.

We returned to do the walk from Parzan to the Refugio de Viados in our gap-filling year in 2008 (described in Chapter 7).

As in the story above, weather is usually the main reason, but you might also use road transport aids when you:

• Have a road walk of a few kilometres at the start of the day and want to gain time and save energy on a tramp that might take an hour or more. Hitch-hiking to the *start* of a hike, however, feels a bit risky to me, and it's worth checking out if there are buses – French or Spanish. Google (or use other search engine) 'X to Y by bus'. Alternatively, you might pre-book a taxi, but this is likely to have to travel some distance before it collects you and the fare will reflect this.

• Find yourself on a stretch of road at any time of day, but especially at the end, and are running late, are too hot, very wet, have sore feet, or are simply done in. In these circumstances, we have put out our thumbs up while walking, without feeling at all guilty or conscious of our age. Traffic is likely to be minimal on minor roads, but often the first vehicle with room will stop for you. Sometimes, in inclement weather, you don't even have to stick out your thumb as the lift is offered. In pouring rain in September 2006, a van stopped and the workman driver offered a lift as we were walking up the minor road between the border town of Le Perthus and our accommodation that night, the Gîte d'Albère, on the penultimate day of our first traverse. We accepted! Conversely, on major roads, where there is more traffic, drivers are less likely to stop.

That covers the road transport options. I have also added, however, 'chair lifts' to this section. In fact, we have only once taken a chair lift, in August 2012. This is mentioned in the section on Travelling Light, in Chapter 3, but not the circumstances that occasioned us to use it.

We had spent the night at the Refuge Wallon in the Marcedau valley of the Pyrénées-Occidentales and set our alarm for 0600, knowing that we had a long trek ahead of us to the Refuge de Bayssellance, high above Gavarnie. We had planned to do the HRP over the Col de Mulet (2,591m) down to the Refuge des Oulettes de Gaube (2,151m) and then over the Hourquette d'Ossue (2,734m) to the Bayssellance refuge (2,651m). That's some up and down over rough terrain in the *Hautes Montagnes*, including our highest pass of the whole traverse. The Joosten guidebook indicated seven hours 20 minutes, the Véron guidebook seven hours exactly, both of course being without stops. Using our usual rule of thumb, we estimated it would take us at least ten hours in total. Leaving after breakfast at 0700 meant an approximate arrival time at the Bayssellance of 1700-1730, which would allow enough time to do our jobs (wash, change and sort our bed space) and recover in time for dinner.

It was horribly gloomy as we ate breakfast. Outside was thick mist. It wasn't actually raining, although the humidity was so high that it made little difference. We decided to do what we did in 2001, which was to go down the Marcedeau Valley to Pont d'Espagne (1,496m), take a GR10 variant up to the Refuge des Oulettes de Gaube, and then follow our planned route over the Hourquette d'Ossue to the Bayssellance Refuge. In 2001, however, we had only gone as far as the Refuge des Oulettes de Gaube. Today we were adding around two hours plus a significant climb to that journey.

The descent down the Marcedeau valley was easy and uneventful. Also, there were signs that the mist was lifting. We remembered there being a chair lift at Pont d'Espagne and wondered – only half-jokingly – whether it would be running; perhaps not on such a cloudy day with the mist quite low.

In fact, there was a God. When we reached the chair lift, the mist had risen significantly and, despite it being not much after 0900, it was indeed running. Our decision to take it was a no-brainer given the climb ahead of us. We were ferried upwards some 250m, watching the other unoccupied chairs trundling up and down, and the ground below us. We were deposited on a level path that, in 15-20 minutes, led us to the Lac de Gaube to meet the GR10 variant. We then lost the 45 minutes that we had gained by having coffee and a chat at the *hôtellerie* on the northern shore of the lake, but we were refreshed and able to pursue the rest of the trek with vigour, unlike the two Brits we met carrying the overloaded rucksacks (Chapter 3). We arrived at the Bayssellance refuge at our originally scheduled time.

This is a useful reminder of the circumstance in which you might decide to take whatever form of transport is on offer. We found the chair lift fun, we found our subsequent leisurely coffee break fun, and as we trekked upwards we were never too tired to stop and admire the imposing north face of Vignemale and its glacier, as the day continued to brighten.

Top tips from Chapter 4

1. Get yourself fit. The best training is walking in rough country but do it sensibly. You don't have to be super-fit to do and enjoy the traverse of the Pyrenees.

2. Wear good quality boots which protect the ankles and have a good tread on the soles. If they dry out, oil or butter administered daily will help keep them supple and stop them cracking.

3. You may reduce the weight of the maps that you carry by cutting away what you don't need, although leave sufficient area either side of the route to enable you to see where you are in relation to mountains, passes, valleys, lakes and other physical features. You may also discard maps as you travel, once there is no longer need for them.

4. Maps are generally accurate. They are most prone to inaccuracy lower down where, for example, new dirt roads have been created since publication. This applies also to the directional guidebooks.

5. Consider carrying the directional guidebooks that you think will be useful on a light Kindle or iPad mini (or other tablet). Another way of reducing their weight is to photocopy the pages that are needed and discard as you travel. If you carry a complete guidebook, you may rip out and discard the pages that are past their use-date.

6. Note that the guidebook times are walking times only, that is without stops. You need to customise them a) to your own trekking speed on different terrains, and b) by adding on the length of time you stop over a stage (which often is longer than you think). We add anything between 30 and 70 per cent to the guidebook times to give our overall time on the trail.

7. We have never travelled with a GPS, only a compass and map (and whistle). Only once, in thick mist on a plateau where the path became indistinct, did we wish we had a GPS. This is really a matter of personal choice for you.

8. The GR10, GR11 and linking trans-frontier trails are waymarked in red and white stripes, but the HRP waymarks, where they exist, may be in a variety of colours. Learn to recognise the waymark conventions for 'turn' and 'don't come this way'.

9. You may encounter, especially in the near-eastern Pyrenees, some routes that barely exist on the ground, have a few cairns to guide you, but no waymarks. Progress is slower on such routes.

10. Look after the zig-zags on the more popular paths.

11. Signposts are usually erected at passes and other significant places. They are reassuring but may sometimes be confusing, with an overload of information.

12. Where signposts give times to destinations, treat them as you would guidebook times (6 above).

13. Walking poles provide extra power going uphill as well as helping knee joints going down. Lightweight poles are available and good, but they are inevitably not as strong as conventional ones.

14. Crampons and/or ice axes are important in the high mountains if there is a lot of snow around. Buy light mini-crampons, but choose those with six spikes each and not those that use a metal teeth and chain system. You may post them home once you have no need for them.

15. Carry a first aid kit with plasters, a good bandage with safety pins, ibuprofen and anti-histamine tablets, Immodium, antiseptic wipes, cream for muscular and joint aches, sachets of rehydration salts, and survival blanket. Also don't forget sun tan cream and water purifying tablets. (See Appendix).

16. Remember at all times to treat the traverse as a concept that enables a wholesome experience that you can enjoy. This means being flexible from time to time about how you proceed. Never beat yourself up afterwards if you have to resort to transport of one kind or another. Hitch-hiking on minor roads is usually easy in the mountains, although the traffic will be sparse.

5

Being socially aware and being sociable

My first attempt to distinguish in an introductory paragraph the difference between being socially aware and being sociable provoked the following comment from my editor: 'This sounded too much like a sociologist's tract!' Fair point, so I'll leave you to work it out as you go along. It won't be difficult.

Being socially aware

For many people who go for long distance treks in remote places, being socially aware means treading lightly, that is, packing out your trash, buying locally (the only option anyway when you are trekking), and not picking flowers or collecting butterflies or disturbing birds' nests. For me, however, being socially aware in the Pyrenees includes all of this but is something more. Basically it's about understanding the complicated human interaction with 'nature' in these mountains. I must admit that I try to avoid using the word 'nature' where possible because, to me, it represents an ideal state that is untouched by human hand. Such a state exists only in our imagination. Even the most unsullied and wildest parts of the wild Pyrenees are not free from human influence – although the causal chain may be long with many links.

Take for example the shrinking glaciers, which are an issue in the Pyrenees as they are in the Alps, the Andes and the other high mountain ranges throughout the world. As the British Meteorological Office says, shrinking glaciers are consistent with 'fundamental laws of physics'. In other words, a warming world will make ice melt faster! I also understand the evidence that our warming world is a result of increasing carbon dioxide concentrations in the atmosphere. This has not always been the case. For example, not long ago in terms of the huge timescales that meteorologists usually work with, 1816 in the northern hemisphere was dubbed 'the year without a summer' because it was so cold. The year was the finale to about 300 years of relatively cold weather in the northern hemisphere, called 'the little ice age', during which glaciers actually increased in size. They have been generally shrinking ever since.

One of the biggest jobs for scientists has not been to determine whether our world is currently warming (it is), but to separate the influence of carbon dioxide and other human-induced emissions from the non-human factors.

After all this has been done, the large majority of scientific opinion is that human emissions are having the major impact, over and above non-human factors.

While I endorse personal environmental responsibility through treading lightly, I try to think of it in terms relative to my 'normal' life. On the traverse itself I am walking primarily and visiting rarely, if ever, a big supermarket or travelling any significant distance in a car. My personal footprint, including my carbon footprint is low. Even the rubbish that I carry will have been acquired locally, especially from picnics that I have bought at refuges, *gîtes* or other accommodation, where I end up with plastic spoons, yoghurt cartons, an empty drinks can and so on. I get rid of it, as you will also do, locally in the first rubbish bin that I find. My rucksack can't simply become a mobile rubbish bin by the time the trek is completed.

I also think, however, that it's important to be aware of the context of the Pyrenees in all of its social, economic, political and cultural aspects. Despite the creation of national parks in the most popular parts of France and Spain, my personal footprint is insignificant compared with that of the ski resorts, deforestation in some areas without apparent sign of re-planting, the new roads being driven into the mountains and the new apartments being built, and the overall tourist economy. It is also insignificant compared with the hydro-electric dam projects, which, while claiming to be relatively carbon-friendly, present other environmental issues.

Yet, as I indicate in Chapter 2, ski resorts, new roads, new apartments and hydro-electric infrastructure are all attempts to breathe fresh economic life into a region that has become depopulated and, of course, to make money by earning a return on that investment. This does not mean that such investment provides decent jobs and other social benefits. The person selling morning coffee in summer at the only café open at the ski resort possibly hates his or her job and the immediate surroundings of plastic Coca Cola chairs as much as anyone. Nevertheless, the modern developments do offer some kind of livelihood, however exploitative they might be of both people and the local environment. Not all jobs are bad: the young man we met who was a ski instructor in winter and a mountain guide in summer seemed to love his work.

In Chapter 2, I make the plea to condemn not if you understand not. Elsewhere in Chapter 2, I note that farmers in the Pyrenees don't want the reintroduction of bears, and one of their most sneering ripostes is that the mountains have become a 'zoo for Parisians'. More generally, they and others claim that the Pyrenees have become little more than a wilderness escape for tourists, including trekkers.

Why, however, did the region become depopulated in the first place? There exists a simple explanatory model, named after the economist William Arthur Lewis, which applies to all countries as they move from an economy based on agriculture to one based on industry and, more recently, services. It postulates that people will tend to migrate from the countryside to urban areas because of greater opportunities in the latter. These opportunities are not necessarily good in an absolute sense and urban areas have many problems, but they only need to be marginally better than those in the countryside to create depopulation of the latter. Of course, as with many models created by economists, the Lewis Model is a simplification of what actually happens on the ground. In China, for a long time, a law prevented rural people migrating to cities. In the present-day Pyrenees there are some signs that people who left when young are returning in their now-wealthy retirement. Yet, as a general rule of thumb, the model holds.

Even if the complexity of it all does your head in – it certainly does mine from time to time – it is important, and I believe ultimately enriching, to be aware of what is going on around you as you walk through these mountains, and certainly before you pass any kind of judgement. And there is more of which to be aware than present-day economics and livelihoods. There is too, as Chapter 2 again introduces, the history, the politics, understanding Basque and Catalan separatist movements (and their separate languages), and imagining the two-way refugee flows that were created by the Spanish Civil and Second World wars.

I agree that the Pyrenees are large enough to shrug off both their contemporary blemishes, and historical ones, such as abandoned mine workings. It is because one comes across them rarely that they stick out like sore thumbs, but for the same reason they are also easily forgotten. If judgement is passed at all, it is perhaps only fleetingly before awe at the scale and grandeur of the mountains, lakes and valleys takes over once more.

Some trekkers seek out only the very wildest places where few people tread and, in our 2008 and 2009 treks of the HRP over the passes on the south side of Mont Roig, we did the same. We sought to 'tame' the Col de la Cornella (Chapters 4 and 8) and its ilk, while at the same time being knocked out by the wild, untamed beauty of our surroundings. This combination of taming the mountains yet leaving them pristine has gripped many a trekker. It possibly finds its ultimate articulation in the United States, where romantic notions of rugged individualism in relation to wilderness form defining features of what it is to be 'American'. And, I should add, this same mix has given rise to great American National Parks whose job is to preserve wilderness. Although I haven't done a systematic survey, it is interesting in this regard that the majority of people we have met who are doing the HRP are solitary trekkers, for whom 'communing with nature' trumps communing with other humans.

I find nothing wrong with any of this. Angarad and I have found the wilderness areas of the Pyrenees both exciting and inspirational. It's just that we need to be aware of these escapes, that they are 'mountains of the mind' as Robert Macfarlane calls them, and be thankful that we can be among them, while understanding what might be happening in the valley a few hundred metres below. We should also remember that the earliest trekkers were scientific and leisure explorers. They were the first visitors and it is they who introduced the potential of the mountains to a wider audience. Nor is there a completely right or wrong solution to the dilemmas that are raised, but a classic trade-off between environmental footprint and the regional economy. Whether we like it or not, we the contemporary trekkers are a part of the contribution to the latter.

Being sociable

The notion of the sole trekker, 'communing with nature' while being cut-off from the messy business of life brings me to the other theme of this chapter – being sociable.

I remember arriving one Saturday in early September 2013 at the Refuge de Mariailles (1,710m), at the foot of Canigou, in the Pyrénées-Orientales, at around five o'clock. This was the day, described in Chapter 4, when we had been lost for about 20 minutes in mist on a high plateau, and it had subsequently rained, hailed and thundered for the rest of our hike. We entered the refuge looking like proverbial drowned rats. Inside appeared to be mayhem and the cacophony of human noise was phenomenal. The common and dining room was full of groups of people talking excitedly and ever more loudly as they tried to make themselves heard. We were bewildered. Since the Catalan man who had helped us find the correct route about seven hours previously, we had not encountered a soul. We had been alone together… communing with the weather.

Luckily the *guardien* spotted us through the steamy crowd and took us to the drying room. That was hardly any better, being full of a group of Spaniards changing into dry clothes, noisily and not standing on any ceremony – I had to avert my eyes from one woman. Angharad sat down on the bench among the dripping clothes, then almost as soon stood up and went outside without saying a word. She had had enough and I could tell from her face that she just wanted to weep. The toilet next door was mercifully free and the quietest spot in town.

By the time she returned, the Spaniards had departed and the *guardien* had shown me the facilities and the dormitory – a nicely done room circled by just one layer of platform beds, with different pillows and blankets of many colours hung decoratively on a single nail above each mattress (see photo in Chapter 3). He was impressed by our trek in the wretched weather. I had also talked to the Spaniards briefly. They were day-trippers who had planned to climb the Pic du Canigou, the famous 'symbol of Catalonia' and, at 2,784m, the last peak of the *Haute Montagne*. This is a common excursion from the Refuge de Mariailles, but they had been forced to turn back because of the weather. Now they were returning to their vehicles at the nearby roadhead, as indeed, or so it seemed, were most of the human contents of the common room. After another 15 minutes, peace and quiet reigned, much to our relief.

I first met Minouche about 30 minutes later. I was alone in the dormitory. Angharad had recovered, washed, changed, and was at that moment in the now spacious common room talking to a Dutch guy and a British man whom we had met on previous nights. They were sharing accommodation at a nearby foresters' cabin and had come to the refuge to buy wine. Minouche and I simply exchanged a few greetings and comments about the weather outside.

At dinner we sat by chance with Minouche and her husband, Gérard. The conversation was completely in French, for they had no English. They were trekking a section of the GR10 to Banyuls-sur-Mer. They looked to be a few years younger than us. Given the relatively small number (18) staying at the refuge, we had dinner on the same table and at the other end I vaguely noticed a group of four – three men and one woman – also middle-aged. None of the conversation was raucous, although there seemed to be a relaxed conviviality. Perhaps we each had endured a similar experience during the day.

The following morning we were probably the last to leave, partly because we had to retrieve gear from various nooks and crannies where we had left it to dry and partly because we chatted to the *guardien* about our anxiety when we arrived, about the Maury aperitif that he had served us before dinner (Chapter 3), and about the nice atmosphere in the refuge.

We set off along the GR10 and later passed and exchanged greetings with the group of four I had noticed the previous night. They were eating a picnic. Then, about three quarters of the way to our destination, we caught up with Minouche and Gérard. We offered them the last of the Welsh cake we had been carrying since we left London, explaining to them what it was. They ate it with interest. Then we made our own way. As we approached our destination for the day, the Cortalets refuge, one of the group of four caught up with us. A few years younger, and sporting a greying pony tail and a roving twinkle in his eye, he seemed fascinated that we were walking so well. Yves, as he was called, was also traversing the GR10 with another of the four, Denis. The remaining couple (Sylvie and Jean-Claud) were friends who were walking with them on this final section.

That evening we had dinner with Minouche, Gérard, Yves, Denis, Sylvie and Jean-Claud. The following day, we met them again at the Gîte de Batère, having more or less now completed a circuit of the Canigou massif. It also marked the end of the *Hautes-Pyrénées*, and completion of the traverse was in sight. Over dinner we were joined by another group of four – Lise and Eric, and Bob and Josy. Lise, a retired history teacher, wasn't short of expressing an opinion or two, including on past French-British conflicts, namely the battles of Waterloo and Trafalgar. I eventually said to her: 'Madame je pense que vous croyez que votre avis est la vérité absolue.' *Madam, I think that you believe that your opinion is absolute truth.* Bob banged the table and gave me the thumbs up, the others laughed in agreement and the ice was broken, with Lise included. We were now 12 in total. The only silence during dinner thereafter was when a French Catalan at the head of the table harangued everybody about Catalan independence (see Chapter 2).

Our route following the HRP and that of the new friends on the GR10 diverged the next day, but we all met again at the Hostal dels Trabucyares at the frontier village of Las Illas two nights later. We took the new local aperitif together – the better-known red *vin doux naturel*, Banyuls – and by the end of dinner we were truly bonded. They seemed fascinated by Angharad and me and, being provincial middle-aged French, had an interesting view of Britain, asking us more than once if there was still always fog in London.

Dinner with the 2013 French friends at the Cabane d'Albère

So to the penultimate day, picnicking by chance together in a square in the border town of Le Perthus, where the main highway from Barcelona enters France on stilts. We were reunited later at our accommodation – the Cabane d'Albère (actually a *gîte*) – for more Banyuls, wine and dinner. On the last night in Banyuls-sur-Mer we duly arranged to meet by the plaque that commemorates the GR10 and sat down to eat at a seafront restaurant, accompanied by a huge carafe of Banyuls. They told us that we weren't at all like what they expected the British to be and we reciprocated about our expectations of the French. We told them bits about our life histories, about our grandchildren and the irritating leniency of their parents, and again they did the same. Towards the end we swapped contact details. Angharad asked: 'Avez-vous une plume?' They roared with laughter. She wanted to ask if they had a pen, but the word 'plume' originates from when pens were ink quills and has not been in use in France for decades (although my editor tells me that it is still in use in French-speaking Canada, rather than stylo, bic or biro). I explained that many years ago, when we started learning French at school, the teacher went round the class, pointing at an object such as a table or a pen, and we would respond, 'C'est la plume' or 'C'est la table' as appropriate. Then they ventured that their English teacher used to walk around the class pointing likewise and asking, 'What eeze it?' and they would respond, 'It eeze the table', and so on.

And so, with the Mediterranean lapping a few metres away, it ended…

Having just written about this tale and the warmth it still engenders, I reflect that friendships spring up spontaneously and shouldn't be forced. We never expected 12 of us to bond over a period of days.

When it does happen, it is incredibly satisfying – the simple engagement of people who are sharing an intense experience, yet probably live very different 'normal' lives. You get to discover other lives in a way you might never do in your own country, and to share similarities as well as differences.

Of course it all works best when you are all following a standard route, such as the GR10, for several days, and your movements are in sync with each others'.

But to a large extent the friendships that are forged are ephemeral, and tend not to outlast the occasion, as I noted in Chapter 2. We have kept in touch with a few of the 2013 crowd, but it is occasional. We have lost touch completely with a similar crowd that we met in 2012 (see later in this chapter), but that doesn't mean it wasn't a good experience at the time.

Fin: the team of 2013 comes together for the last time in front of the GR10 plaque in Banyuls-sur-Mer

Of course, many deep and meaningful conversations and good times can take place on just one evening, or just one footpath, as Chapter 2 has also noted. Let me tell you a bit more about some of the people we have met and the conversations we have enjoyed. All, I hope, will reinforce my point that taking the trouble to be outward-looking and engage with others while on the traverse can be extremely enriching and is a big part of the 'total experience'.

It was August 2001 and we arrived at the Refuge de Larribet mid-afternoon after a seven-hour exciting but bruising trek from the Refuge d'Arrémoulit (see Chapters 4 and 7). It was the third refuge of our first ever trekking experience. We had not given a thought to the possibility that we might on occasion be sharing with other Brits, but at about half past five, eight of them turned up, each with a 'plummy' English accent.

As I had anticipated, we were put together on the same table for dinner. Not only were they Brits, but they were retired soldiers; SAS in fact, officer class of course. In their 70s to a man, they had trekked that day from the Refuge de

Pombie. In other words they had done in one day what had taken us two. More, over the course of 18 days, they had trekked from Hendaye. They were planning to do half the HRP this year and the rest next. They had not been without casualties, however, two of their original party having given up because of bad knees and feet.

Like us, they were using the Véron guidebook (Joosten's English guidebook had not been published in 2001), a later but original French version rather than the English translation we owned. 'What does Véron say about tomorrow?' one asked. They had found today tough. I was not surprised. Still, they were in high spirits and had plenty of style. They polished off a good quantity of wine during dinner, then came the moment common to all refuges when the table has to be cleared and cleaned. Angharad made some motion to start, but they intervened. 'No, just leave it to us, we'll show you how it's done,' said one and within a minute, plates, cutlery, glasses, jugs, bowls had been stacked perfectly and cleared, and the table wiped spotless. I was impressed; Angharad, who knows a thing or two about clearing tables after dinner, even more so. Then they went outside to the tents that they had erected when they arrived – they preferred to sleep in a tent, rather than a bed in a stuffy dormitory, they said. We talked briefly to the man who appeared to be the youngest. He was the exception in not being SAS and the others referred to him as The Brewer. He was probably the ex-managing director of a large brewery, rather than someone who made his own at home!

We spent time with them again the following night at the Refuge Wallon, where my black eye was beginning to form after a trip while descending from the Col de la Fache (Chapter 2). At dinner, one of them talked about the problems associated with mixing with Royalty.

At our next refuge, the Oulettes de Gaube, we learned that they had arrived early in the afternoon and had decided to push on, over the Hourquette d'Ossue, to camp outside the Bayssellance refuge (which was closed at that time for refurbishment).

We never met them again but we had internalised something that we had only known in an abstract way before: it's unwise to base preconceptions about people on stereotypes, including national stereotypes. Indeed, being away from home may even give you the opportunity to enjoy time with people you might not even dream of socialising with at home – and learn from them.

A year later (August 2002) we met two French families, with children aged ten to 12, at the Refuge des Espuguettes, east of Gavarnie. We started talking to the parents over dinner. An hour later we were still talking, now about the European Union and the then relatively new euro, Britain's place in the EU, and French populist right-wing politics epitomised by Le Pen's strong showing in the presidential elections (dismissed by our French counterparts as only being important at presidential election time). The conversation was partly in French and partly in English. Angharad and I were relying on GCE O-level French of 40 years previously. We could get by, but this conversation required a different level. Yet it was also very interesting. In a mountain refuge at about 2,000m you really are back to the basics of human interaction. You are either silent or you engage in conversation. The latter is much more fun, as well as enlightening of perspectives different from your own. Back home I decided to go to evening class to brush up my French. This interaction also impressed on us for the first time that knowing something about French, Spanish or European politics and being able to link to similar issues at home helps oil the wheels of conversation, taking one beyond asking people where they live, how many children they have and what jobs they do.

August 2003 saw us at the Refuge d'Ayous, facing the full grandeur of the Pic du Midi d'Ossue in the Pyrénées-Occidentales. Sharing the dinner table were three French women, mature but younger than us, who were doing a circular trip involving four refuges. The conversation was stilted but Angharad persisted with her usual lack of fear when speaking a foreign language, including Welsh, which she partly learned over the phone from her father. She asked them in French were they came from. 'Nantes,' they replied. 'Ah, Nantes,' ventured Angharad. 'Comme Liverpool.' The women looked perplexed. Why should Nantes have anything in common with Liverpool, other than being on the western, Atlantic coast of the country? Sensing their confusion, Angharad tried to explain that the two cities were involved in the transatlantic triangular trade of the early 19th century. She got as far as sugar and cotton, then stopped, looked at me and yelled across the table in English, 'Gordon, what the hell is the French for slaves?' I didn't know (I do now!), and the conversation stopped dead there and then. Which may go to show that, while some command of a Pyrenean language may be useful, you may still end stuck up a cul-de-sac.

The following year (2004) we were at the Refugios Viados and Estós on the GR11 in the Spanish Pyrénées-Centrales. On consecutive nights we engaged with an unassuming French couple, about the same age as us. The second night we talked about the fascination of the Pyrenees historically and it turned out that they had read a French translation of George Orwell's Homage to Catalonia, his account of joining the International Brigade to fight in support of the Republicans against Franco in the Spanish Civil War. A gentle empathy was created between us. The last time we met them was after lunch the next day, down the valley from the Estós. We were waiting for a local bus when they appeared and the woman burst into tears, showing us the bloody leg she had suffered when she had tripped. As Angharad hugged her and cleaned her up, I watched our bus disappear at the road junction a hundred metres away. But at least we had found areas of common interest!

In August 2005, we were at the Refugi de la Restanca, in the Spanish Encantats mountains, Pyrénées-Centrales, sitting for dinner at an 'international' table, at which the default language was English. London had recently beaten Paris to host the 2012 Olympic Games. A young Frenchman berated me, implying that London had cheated because Prime Minister Tony Blair had gone personally to the deciding meeting to plead the case. 'Whatever happened to British fair play?' he asked, repeating an oft-heard caricature. Then we settled down to an amicable conversation about the relative degree of cosmopolitanism among European and North American cities. Be prepared to take criticism of your home country on the chin.

Fast forward 13 months to the Gîte d'étape Mines de Batère, which I mentioned earlier in this chapter in the context of bonding with our 2013 friends. Our first visit to this roadhead gîte, at the eastern end of the Hautes-Pyrénées, however, was back in 2006, when we sat down for dinner with about a dozen fellow trekkers, some of whom knew each other from previous stages of the HRP. We were Belgian, Dutch, Catalan and British, I think. As we tucked into the first course, a larger than life Frenchman made an impressive entrance, dressed in motorcycle leathers and carrying a helmet. The table went quiet as if he were an intruder. He asked for a bed and food and sat next to me at the end of the table. He was relatively local, from the Ariège, and doing a four-day tour on his motorbike. It was, as in 2013, when we stayed here, close to Catalonia Day, and I mentioned the conversations we had had the previous two days about Catalonia's claim to be a nation with its own traditions, which spans both France and Spain. He responded huffily that I had to understand that 'in France, everyone is French first and Catalan, Basque and so on only second, unlike you Anglo-Saxons where you are English, Scottish, Welsh and Irish first, or in Spain where you are Basque and Catalonian first'.

In a few words he had summarised wonderfully the principles underlying the Napoleonic State after the French Revolution 1789-1799, but then he went too far: 'In my opinion it is Anglo-Saxon multiculturalism that is responsible for world terrorism.' Now I admit that multiculturalism has its problems, but I wasn't having this, so I asked him whether the North Africans in the Paris suburbs and other French conurbations who had rioted across the country for several days 11 months previously considered themselves to be 'French first'. The argument, which has added poignancy as I do my final edits two days after the sickening Paris outrage of 13 November 2015, escalated, with him banging the table, and I managing to stay calm only because I was pleased that my French had improved sufficiently to be able to maintain this lively discussion. The others at the table who had been carrying on their quiet conversation about trekking experiences started to glance at us. Then, the *patronne*, Annie, handed round glasses of after-dinner *eau de vie*, and everything calmed down. It was brilliant timing on her part, as we moved to safer, amicable conversation, shook hands and headed eventually to our rooms.

The Refugi Certascan in the near-eastern Pyrenees features perhaps more than any other in this book. This is not surprising as we have stayed in it more times than any other and our stays there have been framed by some epic treks. Its first mention was at the very start of Chapter 1 in relation to our philosophical conversation back in 2008 with the young Frenchman, who was skipping along the HRP. We even took two grandchildren there in 2011 (Chapter 3).

Now, in August 2009, we were investigating an HRP variant that is described in the Véron guidebook, which would take us the next day from the Certascan over the frontier Port de l'Artigue and down to the Gîte de Mounicou, above the French Ariège. Here we were reminded that the simplest little coincidences can melt the ice. That evening, I thought that I vaguely recognised a French group, but could not say from where. Then, at breakfast, one of them asked me if I had ever worked in France because he thought he recognised me. I hadn't, but at that moment it clicked. The previous year, when we had been 'filling in gaps' many kilometres west, at the infamous La Pierre St Martin, we had stayed at the Refuge Jeandel. There, a Frenchman was doing the HRP by himself, but his daughter, other family and friends had joined him to walk over a weekend. This was the group now staying at the Certascan and, although we had barely exchanged words the previous year, we greeted each other with whoops of laughter. They too were going to the Gîte de Mounicou, although they must have set off probably an hour before us.

We arrived at the *gîte* at about eight o'clock, having hitched a lift the last 3 km from a camper van of young French people, whom we had seen earlier appearing to pick fungi on a pasture. We entered to a large cheer from the group, while I announced that I was too old for this and next time I came it would be for an easy holiday with the grandchildren. They responded, 'Non, non,' I would never be too old, and so it went on. New friends had been made. Back home, I corresponded with the father, helping a little in his quest to find an au pair placement for another daughter.

In August 2012, we finally parted ways with the group of friends we had made along the GR10 who have previously made cameo appearances above in this chapter and in Chapters 1, 2 and 3. We were now starting a week of staying in refuges on the HRP, as we trekked from Candanchu, a ski village on the Spanish side of the Col du Somport to Gavarnie. The only other people staying in Candanchu were two Frenchmen, possibly a little younger than us. They lived in the Ariège and were doing a round trip of a few days. Our conversation with them over dinner was almost poetic. It was certainly philosophical, as they declared, *'Plato est notre seul livre.'* Plato was indeed the only book that they were carrying. We all agreed that the Pyrenees were mountains of *l'espoir et la liberté* (hope and freedom) and reflected that it was good to share together our love of the Pyrenees, and that would be irrespective of whether or not we'd read Plato.

Although I say that we had parted from the friends that we made along the GR10, we did on the path the following day, meet and chat to *les deux Parisiens* (Chapters 3 and 7). Seven days later, we were also reunited with one of the French women who had amused us with their self-heating meal two weeks previously (Chapter 3).

The following July and August, we were back in the Pyrenees and were reminded that the trek levels out barriers of age as well as culture, when we met two young Belgians doing the HRP. They were camping some nights and staying in staffed accommodation on others. I mentioned in Chapter 3 how the man had dehydrated his own food for the trek. We had dinner with them on a couple of evenings at a small hotel in Parzan and at the Refugio de

Viados (both in the Pyrénées-Centrales). They were lovely people; very honest not only about their apprehension concerning the many snowfields they had had to cross and the weight they were carrying, but also in their very positive overall vibes about everything. We bumped into them again several days later, at the village of Salardu, the starting point for the near-eastern Pyrenees. We were returning to our hotel at about nine after dining at a restaurant, and they were just leaving a *gîte* to find something to eat. In a short, intense conversation in the street we exchanged tales of derring-do, and the woman gave us her email address. We must have written it down wrongly, because weeks later when we tried to make contact it bounced back. I do hope they made it to the Mediterranean.

Also at Parzan, we made friends with two British who had emigrated to Australia about ten years previously. This was their annual European holiday – doing a section of the GR11. We met them again on the path the following day and had dinner together – alongside the Belgians – at the Refugio de Viados. We last saw them on the GR11 between the Refugio de Viados and the Refugio d'Estós. They had a stove and offered us tea – elevenses by a mountain stream.

Then, while at the large Refugio d'Estós on the same trip, we were assigned a dining table with a group of young Catalans. Pleasantly surprised, they embraced us. One of them was living and working in England, and we chatted to him about the Catalan independence movement. It was a fun, but also serious conversation. We told him of Orwell's Homage to Catalonia, which, unlike the middle-aged French couple at this same refuge eight years previously, he hadn't heard of. He told us wistfully that we probably knew more about the history of Catalonia than he did.

This reminded us that knowing a little about Catalonia and its independence movement may oil the wheels of engagement with Catalans. You only need know enough to ask sensible questions and to be prepared to learn from the responses.

I have told in Chapter 2, rather later on the same 2013 trip, of our spontaneous meeting in Andorra with two Catalan families who were toiling up the Col de la Mine, or Collada del Meners (2,713m). About 30 minutes after we parted company to continue our descent, the two women in the party caught up with us. They had left the men and sons to scramble along the ridge from the *collada*, while they were going to prepare a barbecue by an idyllic small lake. Full of smiles and laughter, they exchanged life histories with us as they decided the exact spot on which to spread their blanket. I learned so much from just watching them. They had a wonderful sense of unadulterated being, living for the moment. Despite the effort required, the Pyrenees for them were a place for enjoyment – a total experience, and they were giving themselves the time to make it so. We should all remember that message from our Catalan chums that day.

In September 2013, we stayed at the Refuge des Bésines – our first stop travelling east in the Pyrénées-Orientales. This was an unscheduled second night there because Angharad was feeling ill. From mid-afternoon a French extended family spanning three generations and friends turned up in dribs and drabs. The final members to arrive were a very old couple. They, and everyone else in the party, had walked from the valley, a climb of about 700m that had taken us four hours two days previously. Before breakfast the following morning, the old couple approached us. I suspect that they recognised us as the second-oldest in residence, and that earned the privilege of speaking with them. That day they were going to climb to the pass above, the Coll de Coma d'Anyell (2,470m), a rough-at-times ascent of a further 370m, and then return to the refuge – a round trip that had taken me four hours the previous day while Angharad recovered. He was 87 and she 84, so we were giving them almost 20 years. They became our role models there and then and I told them so.

At the Gîte d'étape Cal Païxa (or *du Presbytère*, in French) you may be in for a bit of a shock as, when busy, it provides no human reception – only a blackboard showing names and the location of rooms for those who have reserved. But this *gîte* has a wonderful atmosphere. The dining room table is set as if for a banquet, complete with candles, and all guests sit around it. The food is exquisite, including home-grown salad vegetables and, on the night we dined, leeks and beautifully cooked fish. Red wine is provided in jugs.

At the end of the meal on this occasion (September 2013), several of us, all trekkers, retired to what in a previous era might have been called the parlour (indeed the word comes from the old French, *parloir*, to speak, or 'speakery') for coffee and biscuits. The gathering was international, and I remember that, alongside us Brits, were young Germans, Dutch, French and Catalans. English was the default language. We simply chatted of our experiences, especially with a German man who knew the early Véron guidebook, the English translation of which we possess. We lamented together about the routes it describes on paths that have since been lost through lack of use. Like us, he was a great fan of Véron. Everybody was very interested in our experiences and that this was our second traverse. We were a centre of attraction because we were so obviously older than the rest of the gathering, not being trumped this time by any octogenarians!

Oiling the wheels of social intercourse

Throughout our 2012 and 2013 treks we found it incredibly easy to talk to everyone we met. It might be that our memory of routine encounters in earlier years has lost its sharpness, but I suspect that partly this profusion of chums has been a function of our experience accumulated over the years in the Pyrenees. We have had plenty to tell and plenty of opportunities for engagement, even if we have ended up discussing Plato! It is almost impossible to convey the atmosphere of these conversations. Words on a page are dry and inadequate compared with the spontaneity of spoken words and accompanying body language which transform what may appear mundane or banal. I hope with the above, however, that I have been able to give you a flavour and inspire you to engage with people you meet on this amazing traverse.

I have mentioned above that sociable occasions tend to happen rather than be deliberately created, and in a *gite* or refuge they happen very easily. You cannot force them, but you can make yourself ready for them and help create the environment where they not only happen, but are also enriching.

There is no recipe, but it's worth remembering that:

If you are nice to people, they are generally nice back. You don't have to say much to appear warm and open. Your body language will do most of the work.

It is most easy to give 'do not engage' signals when you are a large group of friends who have planned to do the traverse together, or are part of an organised tour group. Of course, you might be having a ball with friends or the tour group, which is great, but do be aware of possible limitations if your main company is restricted in this way.

And remembering to:

Give yourself the time to enjoy the trek and the people you meet. This inevitably involves not trying to break records for how long it takes to do the traverse. Many days described in the GR10, GR11 and HRP guidebooks are too long for socialising at the end of the day, and that applies even when keeping up with their theoretical timings. After several experiences of arriving late at accommodation, feeling stressed and having to get to dinner without wash or change, I do not recommend it. While not always possible, nowadays we try to arrive at our destination by late afternoon, which gives us time to take in the air with a beer or tea, wash and change, and even wash and dry some clothes on hot rocks (see also Chapter 3). This might mean shorter stages than those given in the guidebooks, although our total number of days on the traverse isn't so many more.

Try to gain some basic knowledge of the region, its history, politics and current issues. Nobody expects you to be an expert. It's more about knowing enough to able to ask sensible questions if topics arise. Many national issues are likely to be similar to those in your own country – for example, the pressures on public services, employment and pensions.

And not forgetting:

Language skills. You can almost certainly get by without speaking any French or Spanish, except for knowing the traditional mountain greetings, appreciations (for when someone has helped you) and farewells. Miming and pointing will eventually be understood, and usually there is someone around who knows sufficient English to interpret, even if that is not the person you are addressing. However, some French and/or Spanish is wonderful, not just for getting by, but for if you seek company and wish to enrich your experience. You can't always expect that other English speakers will be staying at the same place as you, and anyway why should you want to restrict your company to them alone? I also personally find it an embarrassment to expect French or Spanish people to speak English to me when in their own country. Note, however, that the first language of the locals you meet along the route is likely to be either Basque or Catalan. It might even be Aranese or Aragonese. Whatever their first language, however, they can usually speak Spanish or French fluently. Some may even prefer to converse in English for political reasons. As already noted, at multi-national gatherings, the default language tends to be English.

The social ambience of the accommodation. This varies from the small, informal and intimate to the large, rule-bound and impersonal. The few very large refuges do not, as a rule, provide an atmosphere that is conducive to good chat. Often they are mostly full of substantial groups who may only wish to talk to each other. However, we have had sociable occasions in large refuges, notably the Refugio d'Estós, as recorded above. Generally, in *gîtes* and refuges, the communal meals have always been a highlight for us and we have met some fantastic people at mealtimes.

Be ready to accept all comers, from local bergers to fellow trekkers. There is always something to discover, and I have already told of the camaraderie that may build when several trekkers are, by chance, following the same itinerary for a few days.

The annual fiesta at Tavascan in the near-eastern Pyrenees (always on August 5, see Chapter 8)

Check out the village fêtes (fiestas) that you might come across, where knowing a few dance steps can sometimes help especially the middle-aged trekker.

There are also times, however, when you will feel a sense of isolation. We have stayed in run-down hotels and other accommodation in the Basque Country, where we have been the only guests. We have also stayed in places where there is no shared experience with the other guests, again usually in hotels. Conviviality in a hotel is often difficult anyway, because the dinner tables are for small numbers and you have to ask for tables to be joined together so that a larger group may sit together, but that presupposes you know already the members that might form the larger group. We asked for the tables to be put together to accommodate 12 of us at the Hostal dels Trabucayres in Las Illas, September 2013, but by then we had already bonded with our ten French friends (see above).

Giving yourself private space

When all is said and done, however, you might want to isolate yourself (or selves) from time to time. Generally speaking, even if you have made friends you are meeting each night, you will not be walking with them. This has always been the case with us and I think that helps moderate the intensity of engagements through keeping everything just a little at arm's length. I have known some people, however, to team up and walk together. Once this was for the very obvious reason that the mist was down and they wanted safety in numbers.

There are many personal reasons why you may want to be either by yourself or only with your travelling companion(s). You want, at least for one night now and then, some privacy and independence. More basically, you simply want your own food even if it is a dried food ready-meal, rather than what the refuge or *gîte* will provide, excellent though this may be. You don't want to be in a dormitory yet again. You have come across an idyllic spot where it is possible to camp and want to stay there rather than hurry to the accommodation still an hour or more away.

The trump card of carrying a tent, stove and food is that you have the built-in flexibility to be able to choose. Just remember, however, that extra load (Chapter 3) and that you are taking the risk that the lodging is not full when you do need 'proper' accommodation. At the other end of the accommodation spectrum, hotels are usually anonymous places, where you may avoid everyone else, apart from grunting Good Morning, or *Bonjour, Buenos dias, Bon dia* (Catalan) or *Guten Morgen.*

If you are up in the high mountains where there are no hotels (or you can't stand the places or can't afford them) and don't have the wherewithal for camping and food, you might at least want to be able to create some private space in the *gîte* or refuge where you are staying. Some *gîtes* have private rooms, at a price, but even on shared platform beds if you simply climb into your liner and pull a blanket over you, read a Kindle or whatever, you will be left alone. The same applies if you have your nose in a book or Kindle in the common room. You need only the ability to switch yourself off from the noise around you.

Finally, there is nothing wrong with you if you want privacy from time to time. It is inevitable if you are to be away for a significant period. Even the most gregarious people need their own space. There is no single strategy for dealing with it and we are all different, but hopefully some of the above will at least make you aware. Sociability and privacy are a matter of balance.

Top tips from Chapter 5

1. Be socially aware. This includes, but is more than, treading lightly in an environmental sense. It includes an awareness of history, politics, economy, culture and the human condition around you, where livelihoods are forged in these mountains.

2. Do not make harsh judgements about blemishes on the landscape, such as ski resorts, new roads and apartments, and hydro-electric power, without first taking the trouble to understand them in human terms. Also try to understand the dynamics of ongoing depopulation in the Pyrenees. There are no completely right or wrong answers to the dilemmas that are raised. There is, however, a trade-off between environmental footprint and the regional economy.

3. Your experience of the traverse will be much enriched if you allow yourself the time and energy to be sociable with others – with people who live and work in the mountains, those who run the various forms of accommodation, and above all fellow trekkers.

4. Nevertheless, do not attempt to force sociability, but be prepared to be sociable because it will spring naturally from the shared experience of the mountains. You have at least that much in common and in the Pyrenees this shared experience counts for a good deal.

5. Sociability is also helped when other conditions are right and it is you who are able to create the right conditions. Plan your daily treks so that they are only rarely more than nine hours in total, and you then have the time and energy to engage with people you meet. Try to gain some basic knowledge of the region and its history so that you can ask sensible questions. Being able to speak some French or Spanish definitely helps, and is in itself enriching, but English is used in many multi-national conversations. The communal dinner in *gîtes* and refuges is the most usual place to engage with others.

6. When they happen, sociable occasions enable a very, very satisfying discovery of other lives, but do not expect too much of the friendships that are formed. They may be intense, but such friendships rarely extend beyond that time in the Pyrenees together.

7. At some point you are almost bound to want some privacy and don't feel at all sociable. This is normal and it's quite easy to send signals that you wish to be left alone without offending anybody. The simplest is to put your nose in a book (or, in our case a Kindle or iPad mini), or to sit and sketch, knit or sew!

6

Across the Basque Country to the high mountains

From Hendaye to La Pierre St Martin in ten days

This and the following three chapters describe the daily routesof the traverse, including variations, from dipping toes in the waters of the Atlantic to doing likewise in the Mediterranean. Angharad and I have walked virtually all of these routes between 2001 and 2015, often more than once. I will tell you the very few occasions when we haven't.

While these chapters provide directional information, they also aim to provide the fullest flavour possible of the route each day: the highs and lows; the terrain; the weather; the inspirational and breathtaking moments; the quirks of the accommodation; and, of course, a taste of the social life. You will recognise several experiences that are mentioned. I have described them, usually in more detail, in previous chapters. In chapters 6-9, however, it is their combined contribution to each day that matters most.

Together, chapters 6-9 should provide plenty of options to help you devise your own route in Chapter 10. They do much more, however, in that together they create a story that was true for us. Your story of the traverse will inevitably be different in its detail, but I am confident that the underlying forces and fables will be pretty much the same.

This chapter covers the first ten days, from Hendaye on the Atlantic coast to La Pierre St Martin and the gateway to the *Hautes Pyréneés*. Firstly, however, a brief overview based on our 2012/2013 traverse, followed by a few organisational notes.

The traverse of 2012 and 2013

The following table provides a quick, basic comparison of our traverse in 2012 and 2013, and the conventional routes as described in the current HRP, GR10 and GR11 guidebooks.

	Our route	HRP (Joosten guidebook)	GR10 (Lucia guidebook)	GR11 (Johnson guidebook)
Days	51	45	50	45
Distance (km)	773	800	866	820
Ascent (m)	38,000	40,000	48,000	46,000

I suspect that the main reason for the shorter distance and ascent for our route compared with the others is that it does not include the few occasions on which we have been assisted by various forms of transport (see Chapter 4). On the other hand, our overall time for the traverse is greater than the guidebook times, including six days (13 per cent) more than the Joosten guidebook time for the HRP. This is due primarily to fewer long days, and the inclusion of several short ones in our total, the latter being in lieu of complete rest days.

Organisation of route descriptions chapters 6-9

These are provided on a daily basis. Sometimes two routes are given for the day – the preferred route and a variant (usually for bad weather or mist). Occasionally, I also provide an alternative itinerary lasting 2-4 days. Overview line maps are provided to accompany the text, each covering 3-6 days of the traverse. Should you require more detail, I recommend the Google overview maps that are available on my web site[1].

The daily routes start with some baseline information, followed by a description. Most of the baseline information is self-explanatory, but:

Google overview map is a link to my web page where, as indicated above, a further link will take you to the route that is superimposed on Google Maps. You may do several things with these maps in addition to examining them for the routes, of which probably the most useful are to:

---

[1] www.trekthepyrenees.com

Magnify sections of the route. Where the satellite image resolution is good and the way is obvious on the ground, you may magnify to the extent that you can actually see the path.

Toggle between the satellite view and a basic map of the route.

Note that you may already have come across my website and the maps. They are free for anybody to use. You might have seen them and then been persuaded to buy this accompanying book as a result!

Via provides the essential directions, sufficient to be able to trace it onto a paper trekking map. This is always useful to do, but especially so if you are not using a directional guidebook, or the particular route is not included in any of them.

Guidebooks refer to the French and English directional guidebooks for the HRP, GR10 and GR11 where they coincide with most, or all, of our route. *Also relevant* refers to those guidebooks that cover at least part of the route. The guidebooks that Angharad and I have used are:

Georges Véron, *Haute Randonnée Pyrénéenne,* RANDO Éditions 2003. (Abbreviated below as *Véron HRP)*

Ton Joosten, *Pyrenean Haute Route*, Cicerone 2009. (Abbreviated below as *Joosten HRP)*

Paul Lucia, *The GR10 Trail through the French Pyrenees*, Cicerone 2004. (Abbreviated below as *Lucia GR10).*

Brian Johnson, *The GR11 Trail: The Spanish Pyrenees – La Senda.* (Abbreviated below as *Johnson GR11).*

From Hendaye to La Pierre St Martin in ten days

This is a gradual introduction to the rigours of mountain hiking. You start by dipping your toes into the Atantic Ocean and you gradually climb higher and higher into the mountain air. Grass predominates in the early days through the Basque Country. Without the obvious sharp features of the mountains, valleys and lakes of the *Hautes-Pyrénées* and with sometimes a profusion of dirt roads and other tracks, route-finding is potentially a challenge. It actually proves generally to be easy, however, as there are enough distinguishing features (passes and tops) by which to gain bearings and maps are largely accurate. Also, for a significant part of the early days, you are on the way marked GR10/GR11. After eight days you enter karst (limestone) country, which accompanies you to La Pierre St Martin.

Chalets d'Iraty at the end of Day 7 is a useful point to break the trek, in addition to La Pierre St Martin.

Key to text overview maps

————————— Main route

------------- Side routes to overnight stops

—————— ⌈
—————— ⌋ Route variants

—————— ⌈
—————— ⌋

○—— Recommended overnight stops

●—— Significant features (passes, villages etc)

△— Significant peaks (not necessarily on route)

France

....

Spain National frontier

|————————| Progression eastwards

0   2km

Days 1 to 5 Hendaye-Roncesvalles

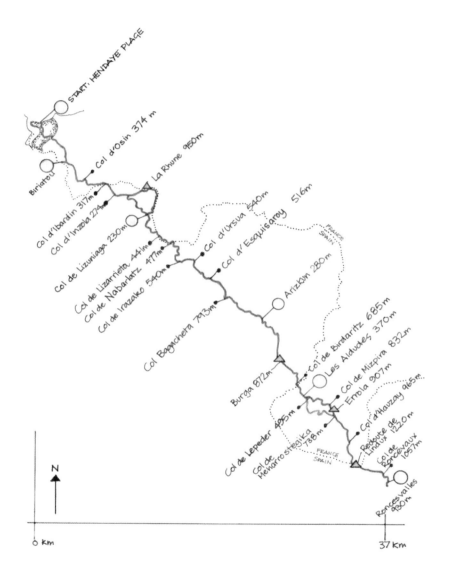

START, HENDAYE PLAGE

Col d'Osin 374 m

La Rhune 950m

Biriatou

Col d'Ibardin 317m

Col d'Inzola 274m

Col de Lizuniaga 230m

Col de Lizarrieta 441m

Col de Nabarlatz 477m

Col de Irazako 540m

Col d'Ursua 540m

Col d'Esquisaroy 516m

Ariz Km 280m

Col Bagicheta 793m

FRANCE / SPAIN

Col de Biralaritz 685m

Les Aldudes 370m

Burga 872m

Col de Mizpira 832m

Errola 907m

Col d'Hauzay 965m.

Redoute de Lindux 1220m

Col de Lepeder 495m

Col de Meharrosteguika 738m

FRANCE / SPAIN

Col de Roncevaux 1057m

Roncesvalles 950m

N

0 Km

37 Km

143

Day 1 Hendaye to Biriatou (50m)

Google overview map: trekthepyrenees.com – Days 1-5 Hendaye to Roncesvalles

Trekking map: Rando Carte de Randonnées, 1:50,000, 1 Pays Basque Ouest

Via: GR10 and underpass of A63 highway

Guidebooks: Joosten HRP, Véron HRP, Lucia GR10

Recognised trails: GR10 and HRP are the same today

Approximate distance: 10 km (includes from the train station to the beach)

Climbing: 52m

Time taken, including breakfast, shopping in the pâtisserie and eating a picnic: four hours.

If you arrive early morning on the night train from Paris, it's a couple of kilometres to the beach and the official start of the GR10, where further preliminaries before setting off through the streets of Hendaye might include paddling in the Atlantic Ocean, having breakfast and buying food for a picnic. Once out of the built-up area of the town, following the waymarks of the GR10 to Biriatou is easy.

For a luxurious start to the traverse, the Hôtel Les Jardins de Bakea[2] in Biriatou is to be recommended, with its fine cuisine, and proves an excellent place to celebrate birthdays en route. Sit outside if it's warm enough. If you arrive early, wander into the centre of the village and have a drink at a bar overlooking the obligatory Basque village *pelota* court. It's also useful when you stay in a town or village to walk to the far end to check the exit the following day. It saves time scratching your head the next morning.

It's very tempting with this very light introduction to combine it with Day 2 and give yourself a real long tramp. Personally, I don't recommend it. The attractions of Les Jardins de Bakea are too great and I like to give myself time to adjust to life on the trail.

---

[2] http://www.bakea.fr/uk/index.php

Day 2 Biriatou to Col de Lizuniaga (230m)

Google overview map:
trekthepyrenees.com –
Days 1-5 Hendaye to
Roncesvalles

Trekking map: Rando
Carte de Randonnées,
1:50,000, 1 Pays
Basque Ouest

Via: GR10/HRP to
Col d'Ibardin, then
HRP and La Rhune
(900m)

The train arrives at the summit of La Rhune

Guidebooks: Joosten

HRP, Véron HRP. *Also relevant:* Lucia GR10

Recognised trails: GR10/HRP & HRP

Approximate distance: 19 km

Climbing: 1,300m

Descending: 1,070m

Total time: 8.5 hours (includes lingering for an hour on La Rhune)

This is an easy walk, much of it on dirt roads until descending from La Rhune, over grassy hills and ridges. The route follows the GR10 to the Col d'Ibardin, with its frontier tacky shopping experience (Chapter 2), although it's a good place for coffee or other snack at one of the many cafés, bars and restaurants. Then, at the eastern end of the main drag, where the GR10 goes left, turn right into Spain to take the HRP route. This passes over an unnamed col (340m), the Col d'Inzola (274m) and another unnamed col (370m). Take note of this last col, which is at a junction of routes (see variant below) and may be reached by car. Carry on, climbing steadily to the summit of La Rhune before descending, never far from the frontier, to the Col de Lizuniaga. Keep your eyes open on this delightful (in clear weather) descent because at one or two places you have to make the correct decision. Generally head south, with deviations both slightly west and especially slightly east. The path has occasional fading yellow and/or white waymarks, also bright blue and at one point red/orange. Thus, from La Rhune summit head down to find in succession border stones (BS) 25, 26 and 27. After BS27 there's a sharp descent, at the end of which arrive at a junction. Don't follow the clear yellow waymark straight on (that path appears to bend east eventually into France), but turn counter-intuitively right on a path which if anything ascends for a few metres before turning left in the correct general direction.

La Rhune dominates the surroundings for much of this walk, being significantly higher and bulkier than anywhere else. The all-round view from the summit is impressive, there's a choice of cafés in which to refresh yourself, and you may join in the excitement of seeing the little train come and go as it winds its way up from the Col de St Ignace, a few French kilometres north-west of the peak. On our ascent in 2014 we saw two eagles with huge wingspans, swooping and diving.

At the frontier Col de Lizuniaga, a bar-restaurant[3] has a few overnight rooms. Alas, when we tried to book two months in advance of our last visit in 2012, it was full, as was other local Spanish accommodation, because of a *fiesta*. Instead, we found a hotel in Sare, the village several kilometres down the road on the French side of the col. As we walked, we hitched, soon being offered a lift from a French-Basque doctor.

If you do end up there, you will find that Sare appears a busy but charming place. Sitting outside a café on a sunny summer afternoon, you have to be careful not to fall in love with it too much. You might never leave. Check out its accommodation options on an internet search, but remember that you need to get back to the Col de Lizuniaga the following morning to resume the trek.

Variant in bad weather or mist

There's little fun in ascending La Rhune if this is the case, and the descent from it might prove tricky in terms of route-finding. Instead, at the aforementioned unnamed col at 370m, turn right, back on yourself, to follow a dirt road, which soon turns into a concrete road and then a tarmac minor road into the valley to the south. At a T-junction in the valley, turn east for the short climb on the road that links the Spanish village of Vera de Bidasoa to the Col de Lizuniaga.

Check out this road on your map – it is indicated by a solid black line, until it turns into a 'proper' tarmac road. It is 4-5 km shorter, involves considerably less ascent, and probably saves about three hours compared with going via La Rhune (two hours if you resist the temptation to savour the attractions of the summit).

---

[3] http://tinyurl.com/Lizuniaga

Day 3 Col de Lizuniaga to Arizkun (280m)

Google overview map: trekthepyrenees.com
– Days 1-5 Hendaye to Roncesvalles

Trekking maps: Rando Carte de
Randonnées, 1:50,000, 1 Pays Basque
Ouest to Collado Esquisaroy; then
Editorial Alpina, 1:40,000, Alduides
Baztan (note that this map does not label
the HRP, although its route is marked).

Via: HRP to where GR11 joins, then
generally south on the GR11/HRP over
the Col de Lizzarrietta, Collado de
Nabalatz, Collado de Irazaco, Collado de
Esquisaroy, and Pausutxar. This last is
named Col Bagacheta by both Joosten
and Véron, also Col de Bagatxeta by
Véron, and the name Bagatxeta is on the
Editorial Alpina map, appearing to

**Confusing signs in the Basque
Country**

describe the environs.It's an important spot, because you leave the GR11
here (which continues south to the village of Elizondo, a Véron HRP
alternative), to go to Arizkun..

Guidebooks: Joosten HRP. *Also relevant:* Johnson GR11, Véron HRP.

Recognised trails: HRP, GR11

Approximately: 29 km

Climbing: 600m

Descending: 650m

Total time: 8.75 hours

For anyone used to tramping distances in the English Pennines or mid-Wales,
this is similar, the toughness being in the distance covered rather than the
nature of the terrain. As with the previous day, dirt roads, grassy hills and
ridges make up the menu. In distance it is our joint-longest (equal with the
final Day 51) day trek on the traverse.

The GR11 joins after a couple of kilometres, and then it's a matter of
following its waymarks for a few hours over the many easy cols (some crossed
by small roads). There's a café on the Col de Lizzarrietta about 90 minutes into
the walk. Both Joosten and Véron warn that it might be closed, but when we
passed this way it was open. Without ever having discussed it, we seem to have

adopted an unwritten rule for the traverse of never passing by a place that sells refreshments. There in 2012 we met a solo English guy who had just embarked on the HRP. He indicated that his rucksack was too heavy and he did not look happy. We never saw him again.

Shortly after the café, at the Col de Usategi, a signpost indicates a confusing set of directions, including two routes for the GR11. We followed the one that corresponded to the map, on a dirt road.

Several cols later, Pausutxar on the map (see the section on maps in Chapter 4 for the confusing plethora of names) marks the parting of the ways with the GR11. At this point you can clearly see in good weather the large valley below, in which sit Arizkun and other villages, but the junction is not that obvious on the ground. That is, if you do not notice that your route, which initially goes northeast, swings round to an obvious ridge running north-south. The ridge and the path are clearly indicated on the Editorial Alpina 1:40,000 Alduides Baztan map. Once on the ridge, simply follow the path, including where it goes down to the left at a small pass to meet a dirt road that swings round below the end of the ridge.

Arizkun has accommodation at a basic inn catering for trekkers, and the bar doubles as a small shop. The village itself is made up of a number of imposing Basque houses and a *pelota* court. Everything about the place has the musty air of being a few decades behind the rest of Europe. We were surprised on both of our stays (2006 and 2012) that the locals did not point at us as we entered, and left the next day.

The inn is the Fonda Exteberria[4]. In 2012, as we checked in, a young, HRP-bound, American guy was stocking up before walking on a few kilometres to pitch his tent. We started our dinner alone in the large empty restaurant, every table immaculately set. We were about half way through when a large group of male farmers came in for a communal dinner. They were shortly followed by the returning American, who had taken the wrong turning out of the village. He had now pitched his tent in the garden of a house opposite. We plied him with a modest amount of alcohol. It seems that he heard about the Pyrenees and traversing it a year earlier while at college. This was his first visit to Europe, today represented by Arizkun. He hoped to complete the HRP several days faster than indicated in the guidebooks. A nice man but, as with the English HRP trekker earlier in the day, we never saw him again either.

---

[4] www.baztanetxeberria.com

Day 4 Arizkun to Les Aldudes (370m)

Google overview map:
trekthepyrenees.com – Days 1-5
Hendaye to Roncesvalles

Trekking map: Editorial Alpina,
1:40000, Alduides Baztan.

Via: a) Roughly south from
Arizkun on PR4 path shown on
map, on the west side below
Larregaña (374m)

b) East to near San Kristobal
church (not necessarily seen)

c) South and east to below
Mendigain (471m)

d) South to Burga (872m)

Look out for cromlechs en route

e) Generally southeast to Les Aldudes, via Basagarko Borda (Col Basabar in
Joosten and Véron HRP) and Berderizko Lepoa (Col de Berdaritz in Joosten
and Véron HRP)

Guidebooks: Joosten HRP. *Also relevant:* Véron HRP

Recognised trail: HRP (although the map doesn't label it)

Approximate distance: 16 km

Climbing: 800m

Descending: 500m

Total time: six hours

You need to consult the map periodically for negotiating the paths out of
Arizkun, some of the route being through trees. Higher up on more open
ground, don't jump with alarm if you hear a gun being fired as you pass an old
wartime pill box. It's probably the starting gun for a trail bike race on another
ridge. It's not all olde-worlde peace and quiet in these parts.

Then you climb Burga (872m) – although, being at the edge of a forest you
have to pass through, it does not feel like a summit. It is a good spot for a
picnic, however, as long as you face south. The forest hides any view north.
When we were last there, a young man arrived, the only trekker we had seen
that day. *'Bon appétit,'* he said as we acknowledged him. Even from two words,
we recognised the accent. He was British, another HRP trekker who planned
to complete it in 28 days (cf Joosten 45 days and Véron 41 days). It seemed to

us that every HRP trekker we met was in need of being able to say 'job done' as soon as possible. Nevertheless he had style, settling down to brew a hot drink. Angharad found him 'dashing' – in both senses of the word!

The journey from Burga to Les Aldudes includes an area of cromlechs (megalithic standing stones), which an information board previews, and you pass into France at Berderizko Lepoa (Col de Berdaritz). The village of Les Aldudes boasts a *gîte d'étape*, a hotel (Hotel Baillea[5]), a petrol station with a small food shop – and nothing else apart from a fancy local meat shop complete with 'happy' pigs strolling around, two kilometres outside the village and open every day. A faded sign shows that an *épicerie* once existed. The *gîte d'étape* does not serve dinner and the petrol station food shop closes on Sundays. The hotel lodging is grubby and a little dysfunctional.

With no real alternative, we have stayed twice at the hotel. The second time it was in the process of being renovated – amateurishly. The proprietor and his wife took dinner at the same time as us at the next table. We chatted with them a little. The proprietor was doing the renovation himself – slowly. We were in the only habitable room. He had been born and raised at the hotel, and the lineage of family ownership went back to his great grandparents. As we ate, the dashing Brit called by. He was staying at the *gîte* and was looking for dinner, but our hosts were unable to feed him.

The next morning at breakfast we learned that Bradley Wiggins had won the Tour de France. We paid our bill to the proprietesse, interrupting her viewing of fashion clothes on the Internet. It was all a little sad.

---

[5] http://tinyurl.com/Hotel-Baillea

Day 5 Les Aldudes to Roncesvalles (930m)

Google overview map: trekthepyrenees.com – Days 1-5 Hendaye to Roncesvalles

Trekking map: Editorial Alpina, 1:40000, Alduides Baztan.

Via: a) Col Lepeder (495m)

b) Minor road: turn left and then right at a junction

c) Straight on, ascending east towards Otsamunho

Les Aldudes

d) Turn right (south) at a flattish grassy area

e) Follow path south as it crosses a stream, turns generally east, and then to the Col de Mizpira (832m) followed by Errola summit (907m) and Meharroztegika Lepoa (738m) where you cross a minor road.

f) Southeast through forest to rejoin the same minor road

g) Generally south on the road keeping right at first junction to second junction at Col d'Hauzi

h) Generally southeast towards Lindux and Burdinkurutxeko Lepoa

i) Leave the road to climb Redoute de Lindux (1,220m)

j) Reach the road again at Lindusko Lepoa and walk to Puerto de Ibañeta (Col de Roncesvalles/Roncevaux), joining the GR11 heading south to Roncesvalles

(Note that 'Lepoa' on the maps is the Basque word for 'Col' in this context; also the Joosten and Véron HRP guides spell the names of the cols differently from, but mostly recognisably similar to, the map names given here).

Guidebooks: Joosten HRP. *Also relevant:* Véron HRP

Recognised trails: HRP (although the map doesn't label it)

Approximate distance: 21 km

Climbing: 1,000m   *Descending:* 400m

Total time: 7.75 hours

The first two-and-a-quarter hours of this walk to the Meharroztegika Lepoa are replete with beautiful Basque mountain scenery and on our journey in 2014 we saw both eagles and vultures. It is, however, complicated, not so much on the paths themselves, which are usually obvious on the ground, but because at several junctions the route to take is not always clear. Hopefully the 'via' instructions above will keep you on the correct course.

After crossing the minor road at Meharroztegika Lepoa, a short-cut through the forest ahead returns you to it. From here route-finding is easy, much of it being on minor roads. As a bonus, forest provides shade and there are water points at regular intervals.

The steep grassy climb to the Redoute (summit) de Lindux takes you above 1,000m for the first time. When we climbed it, company on the summit comprised a silent birdwatcher and the Brit about to dash off again. Looking west you may spot La Rhune. Your eyes will linger more on the eastern aspect, however, for in the far distance are the distinctive shapes of real mountains, including the Pic d'Anie, the most westerly peak over 2,500m.

We met the dashing Brit for the last time at the frontier Puerto de Ibañeta (or de Roncesvalles) or Col de Roncevaux. As we turned south on the path to Spanish Roncesvalles, he was turning north down the road towards the French town of Saint-Jean-Pied-de-Port to spend a night or two with his girlfriend, time which we presumed was not counted among his 28 days.

With its imposing monastery, Roncesvalles is a resting point for pilgrims trekking from Saint-Jean-Pied-de-Port to Santiago Compostella[6]. It has clean hotels (Casa Sabina[7] and La Posada[8]) and spacious apartments (Casa de Beneficados[9]), and if you reserve in the latter you book to eat anyway in the former. These hotel restaurants are jumping with pilgrims who tend to regard anybody doing anything else as curiosities. Without the anchor of shared experience, conversation over dinner tends to be stilted but that hardly matters as all three courses are served and the tables re-set for a second sitting within 40 minutes. I had never thought of pilgrimages as 'industrialised activities' before this experience.

Variant in bad weather or mist

Take the D948 south from Hotel Baillea in Les Aldudes for about 2 km. Turn left on minor road to Meharroztegika Lepoa, then the route as above. This

---

[6] http://en.wikipedia.org/wiki/French_Way
[7] http://www.casasabina.es/
[8] http://www.laposadaderoncesvalles.com/
[9] http://www.casadebeneficiados.com/

route avoids the navigation complications during the first two hours or so of the above. While being over 1 km longer, it is 45 minutes shorter as you stride out along the roads.

Days 6 to 10 Roncesvalles to La Pierre St Martin

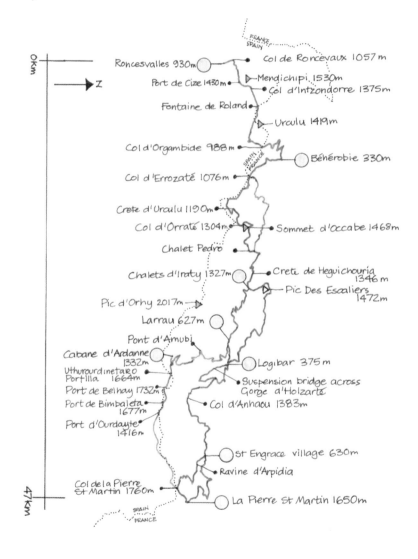

Day 6 Roncesvalles to Béhérobie (330m)

Google overview map: trekthepyrenees.com – Days 6-10 Roncesvalles to La Pierre St Martin

Trekking maps: Editorial Alpina, 1:40,000, Alduides Baztan from Roncesvalles to 2 km along the road heading northeast from Puerto de Ibañeta/Col de Roncevaux/Roncesvalles;

Looking into Spain from the GR11

IGN, 1:25,000 Saint-Jean-Pied-de-Port, from Roncesvalles to Col d'Orgambidé

Rando Carte de Randonnées, 1:50,000, 2 Pays Basque Est from Mendi Chipi to Col d'Errozaté and the road to Béhérobie

(Note that the 1:25,000 IGN map overlaps with the other maps at either end. You require only a few kilometres of it in the region of Mendi Chipi to bridge them. Unfortunately, this 'bridge' is on Spanish territory, and so the detail is missing on the IGN 1:25,000 map, which is French. However, you are following the waymarks of the GR11 at this point so route-finding should not be a problem.)

Via: a) GR11 to Puerto de Ibañeta (Col de Roncesvalles/Roncevaux)

b) GR11 northeast to Port de Cize Roncesvalles/Col de Lepœder (not marked on IGN 1:25,000 map)

c) GR11 northeast, where Mendi Chipi (1530m) is the bulky height on the left. Arrive at Fontaine de Roland (marked on IGN 1:25,000 map), just after the dirt road you are walking along turns north, carrying the pilgrims with it

d) Leave the dirt road to continue on the GR11 east along the frontier to Col d'Arnostéguy

e) GR11 southeast, then HRP northeast to Col d'Orgambidé and France (final two or so kilometres on road; the HRP leaves the GR11 shortly before reaching the road)

f) Minor road and long descent to Béhérobie

Guidebooks: Joosten HRP. *Also relevant:* Johnson GR11

Recognised trails: GR11 and HRP (only the Pays Basque Est map labels the HRP)

Approximate distance: 24 km

Climbing: 800m   *Descending:* 1,300m

Total time: seven hours

While still predominantly grassy, the surrounding hills are steeper and just that bit wilder today, and there is plenty of up and down, although nothing too taxing.

For the first half of the walk you are likely to have the company of scores of pilgrims most of them traipsing towards you, and some not looking too happy with their ordeal. After parting company at the Fontaine de Roland, you will see barely a soul.

The several kilometres of descent from the Col d'Orgambidé to Béhérobie on the minor road are long and tortuous. You might think about hitching a lift from the occasional vehicle that passes as you walk. We did this in 2012, and the first vehicle stopped when we were about halfway down. It still saved 4-5 km of tramp under a merciless sun.

The hotel at Béhérobie (there's virtually nothing else there) is called Les Sources de La Nive[10]. You possibly won't be allowed into your room until 1700, but it has a small open-air swimming pool if you have to wait. At dinner you are shown to a table bearing the same number as your room.

The other guests tend to be respectable middle-aged couples or equally respectable families with children. The hotel is certainly old-fashioned in its code of conduct, but in an unassuming pleasant way, and not at all like the other old-fashioned experiences at Arizkun and Les Aldudes, of dirty and untidy rooms, beds falling down and dining rooms that have seen better days. It also has bags more charm than the set-up at Roncesvalles. In a strange way you might be a little reluctant to depart the next day. We were!

---

[10] http://www.hotelsourcesdelanive.com/

Day 7 Béhérobie to Chalets d'Iraty (1,327m)

Google overview map: trekthepyrenees.com – Days 6-10 Roncesvalles to La Pierre St Martin

Trekking map: Rando Carte de Randonnées, 1:50000, 2 Pays Basque Est.

Via: a) South, along east bank of the Nive

b) Col d'Errozaté (1,076m)

c) Southeast on minor road to frontier (BS224) and road junction

d) South on minor road to Cabanes d'Egurgi, joining the GR12

The upper Nive valley

e) GR12 round south side of the southwest summit of Urcula (1,248m) to col (1,190m) between it and the central summit.

f) Continue on GR12 round the north side of Urcula north-east summit (1,334m) and then east to Col Curutche (1,287m) and Col d'Oraaté (1,304m) where a road ends

g) North on dirt road (GRT9) round west flank of Occabé (1,468m)

h) Join GR10 near Cromlechs of Occabé and follow to Chalet Pedro and D18

i) North short distance on D18, then right fork on D19 for few metres

j) Turn right off the road to follow GR10 to Chalets d'Iraty on the Col Bagargui (1,327m)

Guidebooks: Véron HRP. *Also relevant:* Joosten HRP and Lucia GR10.

Recognised trails: HRP/GR12/ GRT9/GR10

Approximate distance: 22 km

Climbing: 1,650m

Descending: 650m

Total time: nine hours

Not catering specifically for walkers, hotels tend to serve breakfast later than ideal when one has a long trek ahead. *Les Sources de la Nive* is no exception, so expect heat quite early on this trek.

Ascending the sleek, steep-sided valley from the hotel has a mountainous feel to it. Once at BS224, the Joosten guidebook has you turning east-southeast off the road to climb round the northern flank of the southwest summit of Urcula and reach the col between it and the central summit. This is more direct than the route I describe above, but is pathless and you will certainly have problems in mist. I prefer our route, which picks up the waymarked GR12.

The cromlechs are somewhat underwhelming, but from here you are on the excellently waymarked GR10 all the way to your destination.

The *gîte d'étape* at the Chalets d'Iraty[11] is only one building in a complex, which comprises a number of chalets, a campsite, a restaurant and a shop. When we arrived in 2012, it was being cleaned with power gear and heavy-duty chemicals. The cleaners were wearing protective clothing. I was impressed, Angharad suspicious. Meanwhile, a van turned up outside and the driver dumped two suitcases in the porch. Angharad speculated idly that perhaps you could have baggage carried for you along the GR10. She turned out to be correct.

A while later, we met Marie and Sandrine for the first time, the two French women who sparked the socialising of the following nights (see Chapters 1, 2, 3 and 5). We were sitting at the picnic table outside the *gîte*, moving our hand-washed clothes from shade to sun, as the latter fell lower in the sky. They appeared from their day trekking along the GR10 with a bottle of wine and the self-heating dinner described in Chapter 3, both of which they had bought from the shop.

Our dinner that night was a tough steak in the restaurant. The best thing about the place is the picture-book view east to the Pic d'Anie and its cirque of high mountains beneath a large smiley moon and starry sky. They still require a further three days' walk, but are now a distinct beckoning presence in that night sky.

Variant in bad weather or mist

From the Col d'Errozaté, take the minor road climbing in zig-zags generally north, then east to where the D301 joins; then generally northeast to where the GR10 joins the road which turns southeast. Much of this is through a vast landscape with no shade. Turn left (east) at a road junction, just after passing a stream, parting company here with the GR10. Tramp generally east (by this time you might be tempted to hitch a lift, that is, if there's any traffic) through

---

[11] http://tinyurl.com/chalets-iraty

Bois d'Astaquieta to Iratika Etchola to pick up the GR10 again. Chalet Pedro (see above) is a short detour to the right. Now continue on the GR10 as in the preferred route to the Chalets d'Iraty.

Day 8 Chalets d'Iraty to Logibar (375m)

Google overview map: trekthepyrenees.com – Days 6-10 Roncesvalles to La Pierre St Martin

Trekking map: Editoria Rando Carte de Randonnées, 1:50,000, 2 Pays Basque Est

Via: GR10 heading generally north initially, before turning east and finally southeast

Guidebook: Lucia GR10

Recognised trail: GR10

Approximate distance: 19 km

Climbing: 424m

Descending: 1,376m

Total time: 8.5 hours

Entente cordiale with new-found French friends (2012) at Logibar

Although still largely grassy, there's even more of a feel of being among mountains on leaving the Chalets d'Iraty early morning in a pleasant cool shade. A little later, the walk along the bilberry-topped ridge from the Pic d'Escaliers is a delight. Further on, cattle may be found wrecking the path, but are docile enough.

The GR10 crosses a (very) minor road at one point, where a tree provides sufficient shade for a picnic. When we picnicked there in 2012 complete silence reigned apart from the low hum of insects until, suddenly, an interruption – seemingly from nowhere – as a middle-aged couple appeared with a large basketful of mushrooms. From their ruddy looks and tanned faces, they were definitely outside types. From their tattered and torn attire – her frock and his shirt and breeches – they were almost certainly local. Visitors, even trekkers, usually try to maintain some standard of appearance. Also, from the battered and bruised appearance they shared, they appeared to have been in the wars. She was sporting a sling, supporting her right arm and wrist, while he had a makeshift bandage round his forehead, only partially covering up a large graze and the initial signs of a black eye. They seemed completely oblivious to their physical state, but very interested in showing off their grand haul of fresh mushrooms. Then they vanished as quickly as they had arrived. Angharad speculated that they were selling the mushrooms, possibly to the smart hotel with its fine dining reputation, in the village of Larrau (see Days 8-10 alternative itinerary).

From there, the GR10 winds its way high above a valley, with a bird's eye view of Larrau. All shade vanishes. Be careful when descending steeply on loose stones in places; they may start to behave like ball bearings. I bent a leg rather more than I would have liked when this happened to me and it took a further two days to recover completely (although it did not interrupt the traverse).

Logibar comprises an *auberge*[12] with *gîte d'étape* attached, and a few scattered dwellings. When we arrived we were met by a round of applause. Marie, Sandrine plus two other couples from Chalets d'Iraty were sitting together under the sunshade having a drink, having taken the variant route (below). They had also acquired two young men who turned out to be Air France employees trekking the GR10.

We had booked into a room in the *auberge* (old-fashioned, saggy mattress, not en suite, but clean), the others into the *gîte*. We met for *apéritifs* and had a hearty dinner together outside in the warm air. We realised that we could get on with these people. I barely felt my left leg stiffening.

Variant in bad weather or mist

Simply walk down the road to Larrau and then down the valley to Logibar.

---

[12] http://www.auberge-logibar.com/

Day 9 Logibar to St Engrâce (630m)

Google overview map: trekthepyrenees.com – Days 6-10 Roncesvalles to La Pierre St Martin

Trekking map: Editoria Rando Carte de Randonnées, 1:50,000, 2 Pays Basque Est.

Via: a) GR10 along the Holzaté and Olhadubi gorges

b) Plateau d'Ardakhotchia (980m)

c) West side of the Gorges de Kakouéta (which is not clearly seen)

d) D113 road and generally east to St Engrâce village

Guidebook: Lucia GR10

Recognised trail: GR10

Approximate distance: 21 km

Climbing: 1,187m

Descending: 932m

Total time: nine hours

The Holzaté Gorge and suspension bridge

Today you are in karst (limestone) country, starting with a walk up the impressive Holzaté Gorge. The path is straightforward but be careful when the rocks are wet – limestone is slippery. The suspension footbridge that crosses the confluence of the Holzaté and Olhadubi gorges dates from the 1920s, according to local knowledge. It used to have no sides, and only the cables to hold on to. That must have been hairy, especially when it sways. Again, according to local knowledge, it was renovated around 2010 and when we crossed in 2014 it not only had new-looking cables but also a wire fence had been installed along each side. Nevertheless, it was still very impressive, but not for vertigo sufferers.

As with Logibar, the *gîte* is attached to an *auberge*[13] where you take meals. When we stayed there in 2012 there was a bed bug problem that had been strongly

---

[13] http://tinyurl.com/st-engrace

hinted at when we arrived at Chalets d'Iraty. Most sojourners were unaffected but one young woman was attacked badly.

Bed bugs notwithstanding, dinner in the *auberge* was excellent. With our French chums it was also a riot, large quantities of wine being consumed. Marie had also roped into our group three young Scandinavian men, who were cycling towards the Atlantic. I confess to not remembering much about the details of the conversation, except at one point our friends raised the subject of British humour. They referred to 'Mont-ip-paton', to which we initially looked blank. Then one mentioned *La Vie de Brian*. 'Ah, Monty Python' Angharad and I chorused, and everybody broke into Always Look on the Bright Side of Life… or death.

Then we staggered into the tiny road outside the *gîte*, swapping anecdotes. Nobody was in a hurry to enter the dormitory. Perhaps the whole evening was an escape to banish thoughts of bed bugs, so we talked and laughed loudly at things that would seem extremely unfunny out of context. It was still light – just. We watched the moon and stars rise over the mountain.

Variant to avoid Holzaté and Olhadubi gorges and the suspension bridge

Ignore the 'GR10 not this way' waymark at the start and take a path that goes generally east before turning south on a dirt road to the Plateau d'Ardakhotchia to join the route described above. This also saves a good hour, but misses the drama of the two gorges. It was once the official route but is now the return part of a circular tour from Logibar, the first two thirds of which being the two gorges on the present official GR10. It is waymarked yellow, although you might spot a few of the original red and white GR10 flashes.

A further variant marked on the map follows the east side of the Gorges de Kakoueta. It clearly adds distance, but saves much of the final walk along the D113.

Day 10 Sainte-Engrâce to La Pierre St Martin (1,650m)

Google overview map: trekthepyrenees.com – Days 6-10 Roncesvalles to La Pierre St Martin

Trekking map: Editoria Rando Carte de Randonnées, 1:50,000, 2 Pays Basque Est

Via: GR10 (no profusion of variants marked on the map today)

A grotesque rock carving oversees a water trough on the GR10 today

Guidebook: Lucia GR10

Recognised trail: GR10

Approximate distance: 13 km

Climbing: 1,185m

Descending: 165m

Total time: five hours

After leaving the village you walk up a pleasant limestone gorge, climbing left out of it steeply near its head through a forest. Higher up you cross a dirt road several times, occasionally after walking a few metres along it. Keep alert for the GR10 signs. Shortly after emerging from the forest be careful at the Cabane d'Escuret de Bas to turn right, and southwest before following the waymarks again generally south, then east-southeast to the Col de la Pierre-St-Martin (1,760m). From here take the road down to the unlovely La Pierre St Martin, about which I have waxed lyrical elsewhere (Chapter 2).

Angharad and I have stayed at the *gîte* – Refuge Jeandel[14] – twice. The first time was in 2008 when the *guardien* – an ex-rugby player – and his wife persuaded Angharad as we were about to leave at 0800 to sing the Welsh national anthem because they loved, via the television, to hear it sung at the

---

[14] http://www.refuge-jeandel.com/

Millennium Stadium in Cardiff before international matches. Thus, outside the refuge in a thick mist, Angharad duly obliged with *Hen Wlad Fy Nhadau* (Land of my Fathers) and promptly burst into tears as the applause started at the end.

The second time, in 2012, however, stern instructions awaited our arrival. Everybody had to hang sleeping bag liners on an outside line and only take into the *gîte* that which was strictly needed for the night. Rucksacks and boots were to be deposited in an outhouse. The *guardien* appeared, looking as if he had just returned from the moon and had not had time to change into earthly clothes. He was only too aware, he explained, of the bed bug problem further west and along the pilgrims' Santiago de Compostella route, and he was doing his damnedest to ensure that it did not spread to the Refuge Jeandel.

The *guardien's* 24-year-old daughter was in residence, helping for the season. She spent most of her time silently doing craft embroidery. Angharad showed an interest and immediately was given a tour of the artefacts. I, meanwhile, grew concerned that we would come away with an additional load in our rucksacks.

Variant in bad weather or mist

This GR10 variant is marked on the Lucia guidebook overview map, but not on the Pays Basque Est map. You simply follow the road route to the Col de Suscousse, Soum de Saudet (1,542m) and La Pierre St Martin.

Days 8-10 Alternative Itinerary

Google overview map: trekthepyrenees.com – Days 6-10 Roncesvalles to La Pierre St Martin

Trekking maps: Editoria Rando Carte de Randonnées, 1:50,000, 2 Pays Basque Est. Covering Days 9 and 10 where route-finding is less easy - IGN 1446 ET Tardets-Sorholos, 1:25,000

Guidebook: Véron HRP; also relevant Joosten (HRP)

Recognised trail: HRP

This alternative itinerary for Days 8-10 would rival the preferred itinerary were it not for substantial road sections at the start and end and a night in an unstaffed *cabane*. In between lies a splendid ridge walk.

Day 8 Chalets d'Iraty to Larrau (627m)

Via: D19 road ESE to Larrau

Approximate distance: 9 km

Climbing: Almost zero

Descending: 700m

Total time: three hours

This is an easy day, which I prefer to take rather than a rest day unless there are good practical reasons for the latter. Walk down the D19 road, taking short-cuts where available. The first 2,000m mountain, the Pic d'Orhy, is very close. In fact, the 'official' HRP of Véron and Joosten heads over this peak directly from Chalets d'Iraty before continuing southeast and arriving at the Cabane d'Ardané a day early. We, however, prefer an easy day after a week of mostly substantial hikes

Of the two hotels in Larrau, we have only stayed at the Etchimaité[15]. That we have done so on four occasions is testament to its excellent cuisine.

Day 9 Larrau to Cabane/Abri d'Ardané (1,332m)

Via: Pont d.Aubi/d'Amubi and Cabane de Pista Ganekoa

Approximate distance: 19 km

Climbing: 900m

Descending: 200m

Total time: seven hours

Leave Larrau near the campsite, heading southeast on a small road that turns into a dirt road. The Pont d'Amubi crosses the head of the Holzaté Gorge, although you won't be aware of its drama here. Shortly after, turn left, heading east then south past the Cabane de Pista Ganekoa. Eventually arrive at another dirt road, which takes you left, then bends right to the Cabane d'Ardané. The 1:25,000 map is useful because it names the Cabane. On the 1:50,000 map it's a black speck southwest of and a short distance from the 1,312m spot height. You pass a shepherds' summer residence about 300 metres before it, and if you are lucky you will see the practice of transhumance in full swing as we did in 2008. It's basic, with eight-12 bunk beds, but had recently been cleaned by the shepherds when we stayed.

Day 10 Cabane d'Ardané to La Pierre St Martin (1,650m)

Via: Col Uthu (1664m), Port de Belhay (1,732m), Port de Bimbaleta (1,677m), Port d'Ourdayté (1,416m), Refugio de Belagua (shut down in 2012), road to Col de la Pierre-St-Martin (1,760m) and down to La Pierre St Martin

Approximate distance: 25 km

Climbing: 900m

---

[15] http://www.hotel-etchemaite.fr/

Descending: 650m

Total time: ten hours

This is a long walk. Generally taking you east-southeast to the (closed in 2012) Belagua refuge and the road, it's also complicated, passing over four cols. But it's also very beautiful, with scenery on a grand scale. There is little shade to be found from a potentially scorching sun and probably no water. The route either follows the frontier or is close to it. In parts the path is at best sketchy on the ground and route-finding will be difficult in mist. See also Chapter 4, which mentions a possible alternative path along one section of the route.

Top tips from Chapter 6

1. If you end a day in a village or town, try to check the exit route for the following day. Generally be prepared to check the map frequently in the Basque Country.

2. If road variants are available, consider them seriously when misty on otherwise complicated sections of the route.

3. Beware loose stones under your feet when descending.

4. Hopefully the bed bug problem is now no more. Do be aware of the signs of something not being quite right at accommodation, such as heavy duty cleaning taking place when you arrive.

7
Across the Hautes-Pyrénées Occidentales and Centrales
From La Pierre St Martin to Refugi de la Restanca in 20 days (11-30)

You enter the grandeur of the Hautes-Pyrénées on Day 11 and remain in them throughout. You might cover only a few kilometres some days, but don't be lulled into a false sense of security by this information. The paths are rugged and steep. Even Day 11 requires the use of hands at one point. Progress is often very slow. You are no longer tramping but watching every step.

The trekking is also within national parks much of the time. On fine days, at least, you will always meet others on the paths and some particularly beautiful sections will almost feel crowded, although not if you have experienced the Alps. Don't expect to be alone for long. Most nights, when staying in mountain refuges or small inns, you will probably need to pay by cash. ATMs on the route may be found in Gavarnie and Benasque. Unless otherwise stated, the refuges to which I refer are all staffed, so offer meals as well as accommodation.

I have chosen Refugi de la Restanca, at the eastern end of the Pyrénées-Centrales to end this chapter because here the first choice must be made about how you are going to negotiate the following six days, which are the subject of Chapter 8. If you wish to break your journey at the Refugi de la Restanca, however, you will have to walk out, and you will likely walk out to Arties or Salardu in the valley below, a hike that is covered by day 31 in Chapter 8.

Useful points to break the trek en route to Refugi de la Restanca, without having to walk out, are:

Lescun, at the end of Day 11 (refuge, *gîte d'étape, chambres d'hôte*)

Candanchu, at the end of Day 13 (interchangeably called a *gîte* or refuge)

Gavarnie, at the end of Day 20 (hotels, *gîte d'étape*)

Parzan, at the end of Day 24 (hotel, *casa rurale*)

Benasque, at the end of Day 27 (hotels)

Vielha, at the end of Day 29 (hotels)

Days 11 to 16 La Pierre St Martin to Refuge d'Arrémoulit

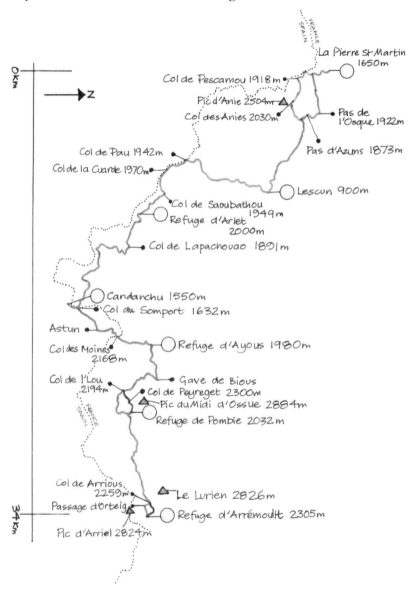

Day 11 La Pierre St Martin to Lescun (900m)

Google overview map: trekthepyrenees.com –
Days 11-16 La Pierre St Martin to Refuge
d'Arrémoulit

Trekking map: Rando Carte de Randonnées,
1:50,000, 3 Béarn

Via: GR10 via Pas de L'Osque (1,922m), Pas
d'Azuns (1,873m) and Refuge de Labérouat

Guidebook: Lucia GR10

Recognised trail: GR10

Approximate distance: 16 km

Climbing: 340m

Descending: 1,090m

Total time: 8.25 hours

Pas de l'Osque

The climb to the Pas de L'Osque is over limestone. It's impressive as the path winds its way through the maze of white-grey rocks riven by sink-holes and tiny valleys. Keep your eyes on the GR10 waymarks, which are sufficient also to guide you even in mist, as happened to us on one of the two occasions that we have passed this way. As recently as 2012, when I was 66, we found the final metres of scramble to reach the top of the pass a piece of cake. The reward in fine weather is the first spectacular close-up of the 2,504m Pic D'Anie and its satellites, their limestone outlines harshly defined by the bright sunshine. This is a seminal moment as you enter the *hautes montagnes*, always remembered. Although narrow, the Pas is comfortable enough to sit down on, have a snack and take in the view.

The slanting path north from the Pas de l'Osque is straightforward. At the Pas d'Azuns an even better close-up view unfolds, yet what really catches the eye is the distant eastern panorama, with the distinctive Pic du Midi d'Ossue conspicuous.

From the Pas d'Azuns descend to the Cabane du Cap de la Baitch and to a predominantly grassy area, where you are likely to have to pass through a flock of sheep guarded by a watchful *patou* dog on a rock above. When we did this in 2012, having checked that we were simply passing through and not sheep rustlers, the *patou* turned its head disdainfully away. Shortly afterwards, we walked into the mist that had hung in the valley all day, and into a forest. As the conifer gave way to beech, we heard voices coming towards us, owned by two casually attired women not observing the usual continental, pert dress code. 'Are you English?' Angharad asked as they passed by. 'How did you know? Did you hear us discussing Keats,' was the unconventional response. 'No,' said Angharad, 'I recognised the brands on your rucksacks.'

Cue laughter and we chatted awhile about the mist, reassuring them that all would be in perfect sunshine once they reached the upper edge of the forest. Given their preoccupation at that moment with mist and John Keats, we could only surmise that they had been discussing the following lines from his 1795 poem To Autumn, even though we were at that moment in high summer...

> *Season of mists and mellow fruitfulness,*
> *Close bosom-friend of the maturing sun;*
> *Conspiring with him how to load and bless*
> *With fruit the vines that round the thatch-eves run...*

This descent through the forest passes the Refuge de Labérouat from where a small road goes down to Lescun, although the GR10 avoids most of it. Then at last you arrive – at the quintessential Pyrenean village of Lescun, above the quintessential Vallée d'Aspe, facing the quintessential Cirque de Lescun and the quintessential Pic d'Anie. The Pic d'Anie Chambres d'Hôte, previously a hotel, are clean and en suite and we stayed there in 2012, but our French friends stayed in one of two *gîtes* and there is also a refuge. The Chambres d'Hôte, gîtes and refuge are under the same ownership[1]. For us, happily there were no signs of heavy-duty cleaning. Perhaps the start of the *haute montagne* had halted any further migration of bed bugs east.

Variant via the HRP

This variant goes from La Pierre St Martin a little further south along the frontier before turning east to cross the Col d'Anies (2,030m) at the foot of the climb to the Pic. It then descends to join the GR10 at the Cabane du Cap de la Baitch. Having not walked it, I cannot comment on its virtues.

---

1 http://hebergement-picdanie.fr/

Day 12 Lescun to Refuge d'Arlet (2,000m)

Google overview map: trekthepyrenees.com – Days 11-16 La Pierre St Martin to Refuge d'Arrémoulit

Trekking map: Rando Carte de Randonnées, 1:50,000, 3 Béarn

Via: HRP via the Cols de Pau (1,942m), Cuarde (1,970m) and Saoubathou (1,949m)

Guidebook: Joosten HRP; also relevant Véron HRP

Recognised trail: HRP

Approximate distance: 19 km

Climbing: 1,300m

Descending: 200m

Total time: 8.75 hours

The Cirque de Lescun

Note that, if you plan to buy a picnic from the small shop in Lescun, it does not open until 0930, which means a late start. It's a long, tough climb to the Col de Pau, from where it's relatively easy going along or close to the frontier ridge, with fine open views, to the Refuge d'Arlet. The paths are generally obvious on the ground. When we passed this way, red graffiti on rocks on the pass proclaimed a happening on February 10 and 11, 1944, but we have never discovered what it was.

You at last reach 2,000m above sea level at the Refuge d'Arlet[2] (unless you took the Pic d'Orhy variant on Day 8). It's a smallish refuge, with outside 'washroom', but has a nice feel to it. Sometimes people hire a mule in the valley and walk up using it to carry their belongings and/or small children.

---

2 http://tinyurl.com/refugearlet

Day 13 Refuge d'Arlet to Candanchu (1,550m)

Google overview map: trekthepyrenees.com – Days 11-16 La Pierre St Martin to Refuge d'Arrémoulit

Trekking map: Rando Carte de Randonnées, 1:50,000, 3 Béarn

Via: HRP via the Col de Lapachouno (1,891m), Cabane d'Escuret, Peyrenère, Col du Somport (1,632m)

Philosophy over dinner in Candanchu

Guidebook: Véron HRP; also relevant Joosten HRP

Recognised trail: HRP

Approximate distance: 19 km

Climbing: 700m

Descending: 1,100m

Total time: 7.25 hours

A pleasant, easier day, giving time to admire the pudding rocks – a conglomerate including coarse pebbles – early in the hike, and subsequently the various domesticated animals en route, including sheep, pigs and horses. From Peyrenère it's about 3 km to Candanchu, climbing the N134 road to the Col du Somport, then turning right down the minor road into the village. Since a road tunnel under the Col du Somport was opened in 2003, the N134 has little traffic, but you might wish to walk and hitch along it. An infrequent bus service stops at the top and will take you down to the village. Check the timetable at the bus stop. By the way, the creation of the road tunnel under the Col du Somport[3] met with significant and persistent opposition from conservationists.

Candanchu is primarily a ski resort so not much happens there in summer. When we stayed the night in 2012, the *gîte* (Albergue El Aguila[4]) was clean and

---

3 http://en.wikipedia.org/wiki/Somport
4 http://tinyurl.com/albergueaguila

friendly and we had a whole dormitory to ourselves. The only other people staying were two middle-aged French guys from the Ariège, with whom we discussed Plato over dinner, and the representation of the Pyrenees as mountains of hope and freedom (see Chapter 6).

Variant avoiding the road walk from Peyrenère

A short distance south of the spot height 1,349m on the 1:50,000 Béarn map turn off the path heading towards Peyrenère and head generally south, over the Pas de l'Échelle and down the other side to join the GR11 southeast of the Lac d'Estaëns. Follow the GR11 east, then south, then east again to Candanchu. We have not walked this variant.

Days 12-13 Alternative Itinerary

Google overview map: trekthepyrenees.com – Days 11-16 La Pierre St Martin to Refuge d'Arrémoulit

Trekking map: Rando Carte de Randonnées, 1:50,000, 3 Béarn

Guidebook: Lucia GR10

Recognised trail: GR10

This is useful primarily if you need an ATM, or to buy provisions, or want to 'save' a day reaching the Refuge d'Ayous. It takes you away from the highest mountains, however, and lacks the excitement of the preferred route.

Day 12 Lescun to Etsaut (597m)

Via: GR10 via the Col de Barrancq (1601m) and the village of Borce

Approximate distance: 16 km

Climbing: 790m

Descending: 1,090m

Total time: 8.25 hours

While relatively gentle to the Plateau de Lhers, the ensuing toil to the Col de Barrancq is steep and tiring. Nearer the top, a forest tempers the heat with welcome shade. The descent to Borce in the Vallée d'Aspe is unremittingly steep.

When we stayed there in 2012, the *gîte* in Etsaut[5] was the last place we saw our French friends together as one group. Then, after dinner, we had a last drink

---

5 http://www.garbure.net/

with the first of these friends – Marie and Sandrine – because before dawn we would go our separate ways. We have never seen nor heard from Marie since, but we did meet with Sandrine again eight days later at the end of our trek – at her house just outside Luz-Saint-Sauveur, where she and her husband took us to a municipal *fête* (Chapter 2).

Day 13 Etsaut to Candanchu (1,550m)

The main reason we went to Etsaut in 2012 was that the Refuge d'Arlet was fully booked when we tried to reserve it a few weeks beforehand – I presume that a large party was staying. Another, more pressing reason turned out to be that we needed several hundred euros to see us through the following days of refuges. Thus we took the SNCF (French Railway) bus down the valley several kilometres to the ATM in the village of Bedous. When we returned a few hours later we carried on to the Col du Somport (it goes through the tunnel, first to Canfranc, in Spain, and then turns back on itself to climb to the Col du Somport). If you're likely to need it, check out the bus[6], clicking on the line Oloron-Bedous-Canfranc and noting that there are different timetables for winter (*hiver*) and summer (*été*).

We were about to foot it from the Col du Somport when a group of Spanish hikers told us that another bus was due that would take us into Candanchu village centre.

This was, therefore, an enforced rest day. It's worth noting, that if you're in a hurry, and have no need of an ATM, you may continue on the GR10 from Etsaut to Refuge d'Ayous and thereby 'save' a day. Part of the way is along the Napoleonic *Chemin de la Mâture* – a passage cut into the rock for carrying trees destined for the French Navy. It is, however, distant from the highest mountains until closer to the Refuge d'Ayous.

---

6 http://tinyurl.com/bus-bedous-somport

Day 14 Astun ski station (above Candanchu) to Refuge d'Ayous (1,980m)

Google overview map: trekthepyrenees.com – Days 11-16 La Pierre St Martin to Refuge d'Arrémoulit

Trekking map: Rando Carte de Randonnées, 1:50,000, 3 Béarn

Via: a) HRP via Col des Moines (2,168m) to a junction where HRP turns east.

b) Carry straight on at this junction (north) to Lac Bersau and Refuge d'Ayous

Guidebooks: Joosten HRP, Véron HRP

Recognised trail: HRP

Approximate distance: 8 km

Climbing: 740m

Descending: 300m

Total time: 5.25 hours

On the Col des Moines

Check out the local bus service Canfranc-Candanchu village-Astun[7] ski station. In 2012 it conveniently left the village a few metres from the *gîte* at 0900. It saved us, and several other hikers, an hour of walking along the road (see also Chapter 2).

From Astun, the HRP to the Col des Moines is a steady climb. In 2012 it was made interesting by the sight on the far side of the valley of scores of vultures queuing patiently to take their pick from some poor dead beast. We also temporarily left our rucksacks at the Col to climb the Pic des Moines.

You will meet plenty of fellow hikers in this popular area, and even more on reaching Lac Bersau, a good spot for a picnic and only 2-3 km from the Refuge d'Ayous[8]. This is mostly day-hiker territory, where the path is rough

---

7 http://tinyurl.com/Astunbus
8 http://tinyurl.com/refugeayous

but easy and the lakes beautiful, while over all towers the Pic du Midi d'Ossue (2,884m).

Walking on from the picnic spot in 2012, we met and chatted to a middle-aged British couple. Then, as we left them, we found ourselves walking towards the smiling faces of *les deux Parisiens*, now with their young man of a son. We had last seen them with our other French friends at Lescun, which felt like an age ago. A further long chat and catch-up and we made our final farewells. There's something very satisfying about meeting people that you thought you would never see again, by chance among such scenery.

Despite distractions such as these, you should still reach the Refuge d'Ayous by mid-afternoon. It can be busy, even full, so it's advisable to reserve in the high season.

Day 15 Refuge d'Ayous to Refuge de Pombie (2,032m)

Google overview map: trekthepyrenees.com – Days 11-16 La Pierre St Martin to Refuge d'Arrémoulit

Trekking map: Rando Carte de Randonnées, 1:50,000, 3 Béarn

Via: Lac de Bious-Artigues, Lac de Peyreget, Col de L'Lou (2,194m)

Guidebooks: Véron HRP, Joosten HRP

Recognised trail: GR10 and HRP

Approximate distance: 13 km

Pic du Midi d'Ossue from the Lac de Peyreget

Climbing: 783m   *Descending:* 731m   *Total time:* six hours

I always find it a slight irritation when a day in the mountains starts with a significant descent before climbing. In 2012, however, we couldn't get down fast enough on the GR10 to the foot of the Pic du Midi d'Ossue, and close to where we had started this whole Pyrenean escapade in 2001, at the Lac de Bious Artigues. The signpost, the footbridge over the wide, swiftly flowing stream – the moments came flooding back, except now we were better prepared for what lay ahead over the coming days. We strode up to the valley head and also made light work of the ensuing steep climb to the small Peyreget lake. There, amid the debris of rocks, we ate our picnic and contemplated the final part of the route ahead.

You should do the same from this wild spot, with the naked rock of the Pic du Midi d'Ossue soaring above. You may then take the direct route to the Refuge de Pombie over a boulder field (Chapter 4) and across steep terrain on both sides of the Col de Peyreget (2,300m), which we did in 2001. Alternatively you may take the easy, albeit longer in distance, variant round the south side of Pic Peyreget via the Col de L'Lou which, with the benefit of our previous experience, we did in 2012.

Note that the Refuge de Pombie[9] doesn't provide picnics for the following day, or at least it didn't in 2001 and 2012. It does have crisps and chocolate to sell.

Day 16 Refuge de Pombie to Refuge d'Arrémoulit (2,305m)

Google overview map: trekthepyrenees.com – Days 11-16 La Pierre St Martin to Refuge d'Arrémoulit

Trekking map: Rando Carte de Randonnées, 1:50,000, 3 Béarn.

Via: Gave de Brousset, across the D934 road, Col d'Arrious (2,259m), Passage d'Orteig

Early morning above the clouds at the Refuge de Pombie

Guidebooks: Joosten HRP, Véron HRP

Recognised trail: HRP

Approximate distance: 13 km

Climbing: 1,000m   *Descending:* 730m   *Total time:* 7.25 hours

The panorama of mountains looking east from the Refuge de Pombie is impressive. It is even more impressive just before the sun rises from behind them, when their outlines are dark and clearly defined. When they are sitting on top of cloud that fills the valleys below, you can but stop and stare. This simplicity of form from afar, however, is beguiling. Within 24 hours, you will be trekking through the heart of them – Le Lurie (2,826m), Palas (2,974m) and the first of the 3,000m peaks, Balaïtous (3,144m) – where everything is much more complicated and not only the devil, but also the beauty, fascination and wonder lies in their detail.

---

9 http://refugedepombie.ffcam.fr/

From the Pombie, the path descends about 650m to the valley, along which runs a minor road to and over the frontier Col du Pourtalet. Even in mist, the route-finding is relatively easy.

Climbing steadily the other side and arriving at last at the Col d'Arrious, turn right where the path forks and walk to the Passage d'Orteig via the Lac d'Arrious. This is a ledge along a cliff face above an abyss. It is secured with a cable to hold (see Chapter 4). After a few minutes you arrive at the far side, breath a sigh of relief and continue on rough ground east to the Refuge d'Arrémoulit[10].

This refuge, like the Arlet, has an outside washroom, comprising a stone sink at the back, with permanent cold running water and a mirror attached to the wall where you may wash, shave, brush teeth and generally smarten yourselves for dinner and social encounters inside. It also boasts a drop-toilet in a shed over rough ground about 20 metres away. I have described in Chapter 3 its simple but effective system for warning would-be users that it is already occupied.

The refuge is also cramped, but it stands in amazing surroundings and we love it. This is partly due to the stylish staff being able to serve 'kir' as an aperitif in a variety of fruits, and produce a dish of olives with them (Chapter 3). Dinner lighting is by oil lamp, breakfast by candlelight.

Variant that avoids the Passage d'Orteig

This variant is for vertigo sufferers and if the rocks are likely to be wet and slippery. From the Col d'Arrious descend steeply northeast along an obvious path towards the Lac d'Artouste, picking up the path south-southeast to the Refuge. It adds about a kilometre and 170m to the total climb – and no adrenalin hit.

---

10 http://refugedarremoulit.ffcam.fr/

Days 17 to 20 Refuge d'Arrémoulit to Gavarnie

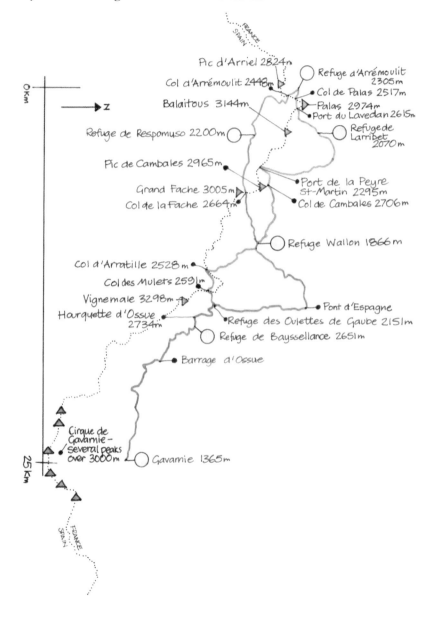

Day 17 Refuge d'Arrémoulit to Refugio de Respomuso (2,200m)

Google overview map: trekthepyrenees.com – Days 17-20 Refuge d'Arrémoulit to Gavarnie

Trekking map: Rando Carte de Randonnées, 1:50000, 3 Béarn

Via: a) Col d'Arrémoulit (2,448m) and Lacs d'Arriel

b) Southeast (path marked HRP Variante Sud on map) high above Rio Aguas Limpias

c) Embalse de Respomuso

Guidebooks: Joosten HRP, Véron HRP

Recognised trails: HRP, GR11

Approximate distance: 10 km

Climbing: 273m   *Descending:* 378m   *Total time:* 6.5 hours

Above one of the Lacs d'Arriel

The Col d'Arrémoulit is only 148m above the refuge. It's an easy ascent despite there being no definitive path through the rocks, although there are some guiding cairns. The descent to the Lacs d'Arriel, in Spain, is steep, while the boulder field at the bottom adds to the fun (Chapter 4).

More dramatic scenery accompanies you alongside and between the Lacs d'Arriel, until at last the *chemin empierré* (a 'made' path) is reached, which, despite an unfortunate start where it has caved in probably as a result of a rock fall, provides an undulating journey high above the Rio Aguas Limpias to the Embalse de Respomuso dam. There, join the GR11 along its northern side to the Refugio de Respomuso[11].

The *refugio* is large (105 places). With small dormitories containing bunk, as opposed to platform, beds and each attached to an exclusive bathroom housing toilet, hot water and shower, it has a hint of comparative luxury. Downstairs, however, is somewhat soulless, comprising a large, cavernous room with dining tables and chairs, and a bar at one end. Dinner may also be soulless (Chapter 3). When it hosted us in 2012, it seemed that most of our

---

11 http://tinyurl.com/refugiorespomuso

fellow Spanish sojourners were intending to hold, with French counterparts, a Catholic mass on the Col de la Fache the following day (a Sunday no less), which was also to be our high point en route to Refuge Wallon.

Dinner is served from a hatch, all three courses at once on individual trays – school dinner style. As with the dinner at Roncesvalles 12 days earlier we felt a little out of place and subdued.

Day 18 Refugio de Respomuso to Refuge Wallon (1,866m)

East from the Col de la Fache, after the storm of the previous night

Google overview map: trekthepyrenees.com – Days 17-20 Refuge d'Arrémoulit to Gavarnie

Trekking map: Rando Carte de Randonnées, 1:50000, 3 Béarn

Via: Col de la Fache (2,664m)

Guidebooks: Joosten HRP, Véron HRP

Recognised trails: GR11/HRP to just east of the Embalse de Respomuso, then HRP

Approximate distance: 13 km

Climbing: 464m   *Descending:* 798m   *Total time:* 7.75 hours

Our sleep at the Respomuso in 2012 was interrupted by a spectacular storm. Come morning, menacing cloud hung over the mountain tops, although, straining our eyes up the valley from the *refugio*, it appeared that our high point for the day, the Col de la Fache, was just clear.

The GR11 turns south at the eastern end of the Embalse de Respomuso, while your route, the HRP *Variante Sud* (HRP southern variant), continues east. The next lake of any substance – the Embalse de Campoplano – soon appears, sporting its half-finished dam, a project now abandoned judging by the air of decay. The lake is joined to the main stream flowing down the valley by a short tributary at the eastern end. Both have to be crossed. The main stream especially is difficult to cross to its south side when in spate.

This was the case for us in 2012 after the storm. We managed to cross the tributary stream – the outflow from the lake – only with the helping hands of the leader of a Spanish group. They too were going to Refuge Wallon but via a more circuitous route, and so we were left to our own devices to negotiate the main stream tumbling down from the Lacs de la Fache high above. We wandered up and down beside the raging torrent, scarcely able to believe that in 2001, when we were last at this spot, it had probably been no more than 3cm deep. In the marshy surroundings we came across a depressing pile of detritus from camping. It lay in a tiny pond, where 11 years ago we had seen frogs. Thankfully such sightings are extremely rare. Eventually we decided we had to wade across at the only likely place – off came the boots and we made it, albeit with Angharad complaining bitterly.

All in all we lost 30 minutes negotiating the inflow stream, but at least we had dry boots and socks. This wasn't the outcome for Angharad higher up, unfortunately, when crossing a side stream. She slipped on a wet rock and filled a boot with water.

Climbing higher, we met participants of the Mass (see previous day) on their way down. Then we had to negotiate a tiny patch of snow before the final climb to the pass, on steep scree. On reaching it, a few ominous claps of thunder greeted us, but then faded.

To find the route off the Col de la Fache, go north along the ridge for a few metres from where you join it. Then the path down is obvious.

It is a long, long descent to the Refuge Wallon. While still rough, compared with the ascent the path is relatively well made. Lower down there are several long zig-zags. We more or less located the spot where I suffered a black eye in 2001 after a stupid stumble and I duly exorcised the ghost.

You might be allocated a two-bunk room to yourselves at the Refuge Wallon[12], which is a blessing, but overall it was a dilapidated place in 2012, with paint peeling off everywhere and generally in need of tender loving care. It was there that we met the shepherd who entered to escape the pouring rain (Chapter 1). We also talked to a British couple about the same age as us. They were camping by the stream and were concerned about the rising waters.

---

12 http://www.refuge-wallon.net/

Day 19 Refuge Wallon to Refuge de Bayssellance (2,651m)

Google overview map: trekthepyrenees.com – Days 17-20 Refuge d'Arrémoulit to Gavarnie

Trekking map: Rando Carte de Randonnées, 1:50000, 3 Béarn

Via: a) Pont d'Espagne

b) Lac de Gaube and Refuge des Oulettes de Gaube

c) Hourquette d'Ossue (2,734m)

Vignemale from the climb to the Hourquette d'Ossue

Guidebooks: Joosten HRP, Véron HRP. *Also relevant:* Lucia GR10

Recognised trails: GR10 and GR10/HRP

Approximate distance: 20 km

Climbing: 1,234m   *Descending:* 449m   *Total time:* 9.25 hours

The Refuge Wallon is also called the Refuge du Marcadau, after the valley in which it is situated. In the absence of mist, the valley is reputed to be a beautiful spot, but when we departed down it in 2012 there was mist aplenty, although it wasn't actually raining.

The route down to Pont d'Espagne and then up the GR10 variant to the Hourquette d'Ossue is straightforward. I have described elsewhere taking the chair lift from Pont d'Espagne to save 250 metres of climbing (Chapter 4). I have also described our eventual arrival at the Refuge de Bayssellance and the special pleading I made to a deputy *guardien* for bottom bunks, and the Canadian couple we socialised with over dinner (Chapter 3). Between all these happenings on a single day in 2012, we watched the weather improve.

The staffed Refuge des Oulettes de Gaube lies conveniently at the foot of the steep climb to the Hourquette d'Ossue, with the highest mountain on the frontier ridge, the Vignemale (3,298m) almost literally in your face. It's possible to stay here rather than at the Bayssellance on the far side of the pass and still reach Gavarnie in time for supper the next day. In any case, it's a good spot to eat a picnic while admiring the ice blue glacier on the north face of the mountain. If you do rest awhile here, keep an eye on the time – it's easy to become transfixed.by the sight.

The climb to the Hourquette d'Ossue is well waymarked on a good path. On the final zig-zags through scree, you might exchange cordial curses in French. Compared with the eroded scree slope to the Col de la Fache the previous day, however, it is easy. From the top, the view opens to the south, the Cirque de Gavarnie and its array of 3,000m peaks, and the huge gap through it, leading to Spain – the Brèche de Roland. Sweetest of all is the sight of the highest and oldest staffed refuge in the Pyrenees – the Bayssellance[13] – only 83m below.

Days 17-19 Alternative Itinerary

Google overview map: trekthepyrenees.com – Days 17-20 Refuge d'Arrémoulit to Gavarnie.

Trekking map: Rando Carte de Randonnées, 1:50,000, 3 Béarn

Guidebooks: Joosten HRP, Véron HRP

Recognised trail: HRP

Our preferred itinerary described above for these three days is magnificent but tough. This alternative is if anything even more magnificent and certainly tougher. Snowfields may impede progress either side of the Col du Palas and Port du Lavédan (Day 17), and the Col de Cambales (Day 18)

Day 17 Refuge d'Arrémoulit to Refuge de Larribet (2,070m)

Via: HRP via the Col du Palas (2,517m) and the Port du Lavédan (2,615m)

Approximate distance: 6.5 km

Climbing: 310m

Descending: 545m

Total time: seven hours

When we did this route back in 2001, I recorded that I had never hiked so slowly in my life. I could hardly believe that it had taken so long to cover such a short distance.

The way up and over the far side of the Col du Palas for a brief communion in Spain is rough, but the fun really starts from that point. Palas mountain (2,974m) towers above, its frontier ridges appearing impenetrable. Suddenly, however, a weakness may be discerned in the wall of rock. It might also be recognised because trekkers are slithering down towards you. It is the route to the Port du Lavédan, which requires climbing very large boulders poised at

---

13 http://tinyurl.com/refugebayssellance

awkward angles. I record the less than glorifying experience of propelling ourselves upwards in Chapter 4.

Scratched in the rock hemming you in at the top are the welcome words 'Port du Lavédan'. You are in the right place – albeit on a near-knife-edge.

Now back in France, every step on the way down feels like a hazard. You will be relieved to reach the Refuge de Larribet,[14] which boasts a shower! It was while enjoying a couple of beers late afternoon outside that, in 2001, the British SAS (retired) arrived, starting the unforgettable two-day encounter I describe in Chapter 5.

Day 18 Refuge de Larribet to Refuge Wallon (1,866m)

Via: HRP via the Port de la Peyre-St-Martin (2,295m) and the Col de Cambales (2,706m)

Approximate distance: 18 km

Climbing: 1,200m

Descending: 1,350m

Total time: ten hours

The initial walk down to the head of the Vallée d'Arrens is simple. Even more simple is the trek, much of it on dirt road, back up to the Port de la Peyre St-Martin. You may, if you wish, drop down from here about 100m on easy grass slopes to the Embalse de Camoplano and so pick up our preferred itinerary from the Refugio de Respomuso, described above.

The standard HRP route involves doubling back from the Port for a rough, tough, steep climb over the Col de Cambales. Its string of lakes at the far side provides a wonderful spectacle.

Day 19 Refuge Wallon to Refuge de Bayssellance (2,651m)

Via: HRP via the Cols d'Arratille (2,528m) and des Mulets (2,591m), Refuge des Oulettes de Gaube and Hourquette d'Ossue (2,734m)

Approximate distance: 13.5 km

Climbing: 1,400m

Descending: 615m

Total time: 9.5 hours

---

14 http://refugedelarribet.ffcam.fr/

This route turns off the preferred itinerary for Day 19 a short distance down the Marcedau valley from the Refuge Wallon, where a footbridge across the river leads into the Gave d'Arratille. Once over the Cols d'Arratille and des Mulets, descend to the Refuge des Oulettes de Gaube, joining the GR10 preferred itinerary to the Refuge de Bayssellance.

Overall, it is significantly shorter in distance than the preferred itinerary and involves more climbing, although much less descent. It takes about the same time, mainly owing to rougher terrain. It is a fine weather route.

Day 20 Refuge de Bayssellance to Gavarnie (1,365m)

Google overview map: trekthepyrenees.com – Days 17-20 Refuge d'Arrémoulit to Gavarnie

Trekking maps: Rando Editions Mapa Excursionista with the Institut Cartogràfic de Catalunya, 1:50,000, 24 Gavarnie-Ordesa. Note that the 1:50,000 Béarn map of previous days may be used for most of the route. You could take a tiny section of the Gavarnie-Ordesa map for the final descent to Gavarnie and ascent to the Refuge des Espuguettes (Day 21)

Looking towards the Cirque de Gavarnie on the descent from the Refuge de Bayssellance

Via: HRP/GR10 and the Barrage d'Ossue

Guidebooks: Joosten HRP, Véron HRP. *Also relevant:* Lucia GR10

Recognised trails: GR10/HRP

Approximate distance: 16.5 km (via GR10 from Barrage d'Ossue)

Climbing: Virtually none   *Descending:* 1,251m

Total time: eight hours

This is a real trek out, downhill and more downhill (apart from one short, slightly exposed ascent), with the Cirque de Gavarnie and its associated peaks composed perfectly appearing closer and closer. You might even meet one of the deputy *guardiennes* from the Bayssellance already on her way back from Gavarnie with a rucksack full of bread, having set off at 0630.

As well as being the highest mountain on the frontier ridge, the southeast face of Vignemale boasts the largest glacier in the Pyrenees, a vast expanse of ice, which must be crossed by those aspiring to reach the peak. You can see the guided parties above, tiny specks walking slowly and deliberately with their ice axes and crampons.

At last you reach the plain and the Barrage d'Ossue, a dam holding back a small lake. If you dip your feet into the inflow Ossue stream, you will find it unsurprisingly ice cold – it issues straight from the glacier above.

The Barrage d'Ossue, which also marks the end of a vehicle track from Gavarnie, holds a special memory for us. In 2001, we reached the parking area 30 minutes before a prearranged pick-up by Pyrenean Mountain Tours. On booking our six-day itinerary via this company, Angharad had noticed in the small print the name of one of the two directors. Her best friend at high school 35 years previously had gone by this name, but Angharad had moved away, changed schools and they had lost touch. As we were being briefed by the guide at the start of this trek, Angharad asked about her and was told that she was due to arrive within the next two days and would still be around as we finished.

We sat on a rock and watched the occupants of the cars in the parking area return from their hikes and drive off. It was clouding over rapidly. We felt a few drops of rain and heard thunder rumble in the distance. An hour passed, the vehicles and their occupants had all departed, and our pick-up was now 30 minutes late. We started walking down the dirt road towards Gavarnie. It was, after all, the only road that a vehicle could take.

About 15 minutes later a Landrover appeared in the distance, climbing slowly towards us. We carried on walking. As it drew closer we could make out the words, Pyrenean Mountain Tours, on the side. It stopped by us. Angharad looked and a broad smile lit her face. Her words – 'It's Jessica' – seemed almost an under-statement. The driver jumped out and said, equally dead-pan, 'Hello Angharad', and shook hands. Then the hugs, tears and laughter started as 35 years were crowded into one emotional moment in the *Hautes-Pyrénées*.

The GR10 route to Gavarnie from the Barrage d'Ossue follows the far side of the valley to the road. It's easy and beautiful, but is significantly longer than walking (or walking and hitching) along the road. Gavarnie has hotels and other tourist trappings. It also has a fine *gîte d'étape*, Le Gypaete[15].

---

15 http://legypaete.pagesperso-orange.fr/

Days 21 to 25 Gavarnie to Refugio de Viados

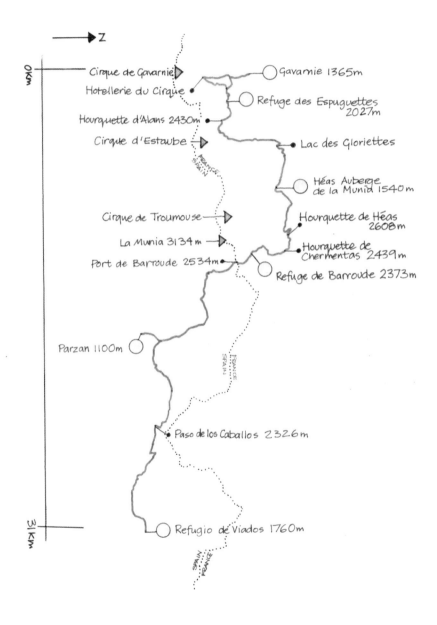

Day 21 Gavarnie to Refuge des Espuguettes (2,027m)

Google overview map: trekthepyrenees.com – Days 21-25 Gavarnie to Refugio de Viados

Trekking map: Rando Editions Mapa Excursionista with the Institut Cartogràfic de Catalunya, 1:50,000, 24 Gavarnie-Ordesa.

Via: HRP

Guidebooks: Joosten HRP, Véron HRP

Recognised trail: HRP

Approximate distance: 5 km

Climbing: 662m   *Descending:* Practically none   *Total time:* Two hours

Above Gavarnie

Simply follow the road that leads into the cirque from the village and turn left at the signpost for the footpath that climbs without difficulty to the Refuge des Espuguettes. The retrospective views to the Cirque de Gavarnie and Vignemale are impressive, even more so if you have special effects such as clouds drifting over the peaks and along the valleys, accompanied by the occasional thunder clap.

This is intended to be an easy day. Also, if you have broken your journey at Gavarnie, it acts as a gentle reintroduction when you resume days, weeks, months or a year later. You may, of course, if you wish to save a day, walk straight past the Refuge des Espuguettes and carry on to Héas, still arriving in time for dinner, but that's a long day.

When we first visited in 2002, the Refuge des Espuguettes[16] was a bit of a dump run by a group of young men who liked to listen to heavy metal while preparing dinner. By the time of our next visit in 2013, however, it had been substantially renovated and was run by a pleasant and enthusiastic young couple. We approved.

Variant if you want to visit the Cirque

Walk from the village, joining the procession of *tout le monde* and their hired mules to the Hotel du Cirque. Then you leave the crowds, circling back on a

---

16 http://refuge-des-espuguettes.blogspot.co.uk/

path that leads nicely to the refuge. This variant is about 8 km and takes a leisurely four hours.

Day 22 Refuge des Espuguettes to Héas (1,540m)

Google overview map: trekthepyrenees.com – Days 21-25 Gavarnie to Refugio de Viados

Leaving the Refuge des Espuguettes

Trekking map: Rando Editions Mapa Excursionista with the Institut Cartogràfic de Catalunya, 1:50,000, 23 Aneto-Posets

Via: HRP to the Hourquette d'Alans (2,430m) and Lac des Gloriettes, then along the road

Guidebooks: Joosten HRP, Véron HRP

Recognised trails: HRP

Approximate distance: 15 km

Climbing: 488m   *Descending:* 1,000m   *Total time:* 7.75 hours

The ascent to the Hourquette d'Alans provides further retrospective views to the Cirque de Gavarnie. Once over it, forward your sights to the Cirque d'Estaube with its fine array of peaks. The Hourquette itself is a neat pass. Sometimes you might encounter snow either side and the descent is steep initially. Generally, however, this is an easy traverse. Lower down it might become quite crowded on a hot summer's day, with groups of people near the stream.

The tarmac from the Gloriettes dam is a slog, compounded by the false dawn of the sign indicating that you are entering Héas. The 'village' is, in fact, a collection of well strung-out houses, with the Auberge de la Munia[17] at the far end. When we stayed in 2013, it proved a good, clean, basic place and our room was en suite. Wi-Fi was free but, because of the thick stone walls throughout, the signal was only available in certain rooms and near the reception.

---

17 http://www.aubergedelamunia.com/

Before dinner we met the young, HRP-bound, Belgian couple (Chapters 3 and 5) for the first time, having a drink before pitching their tent on grass about 100 metres away. Over dinner we also met English-Irish Dave who was traversing east-west and who had tales of much snow lying ahead of us (Chapter 3). Happy Birthday was sung to a young French child whose family was having dinner on the next table. Within minutes of informing our hostess that it was also Angharad's birthday, a lighted candle appeared and with it a reprise of the ditty.

Day 23 Héas to Refuge de Barroude (2,373m)

Google overview map: trekthepyrenees.com – Days 21-25 Gavarnie to Refugio de Viados

Trekking map: Rando Editions Mapa Excursionista with the Institut Cartogràfic de Catalunya, 1:50,000, 23 Aneto-Posets

Via: HRP to the Hourquettes de Héas (2,608m) and Chermentas (2,439m). Then generally south below the Pic de la Géla and the Barroude Wall

Vignemale from the path to the Hourquette de Héas

Guidebooks: Joosten HRP, Véron HRP

Recognised trails: HRP

Approximate distance: 13 km

Climbing: 1,320m   *Descending:* 447m   *Total time:* 7.75 hours

This is a fine, beautiful hike that is straightforward in fine weather and as long as you are not hampered by snow. The Hourquette de Héas is an exciting, airy place to be. The path off it, right for a few metres down an easy gradient of slanting rock, then zig-zagging left through scree, is steep. Just take a little care on it. The views of the Cirque de Troumouse to the south are excellent.

The Hourquette de Chementas, in contrast, is broad and fairly grassy. A little way down on the far side you turn right onto the path that passes below the Pic de la Géla and the Barroude Wall – literally a solid wall of rock above you. It is a delightful path, again without difficulty as long as you don't encounter snow at the head of a couple of gulleys.

We have been this way three times. On the first two occasions we encountered no snow. On the third we did and I have told in Chapter 2 of the harrowing experience that lost us a day and drove us to buy instep crampons.

With this story in mind and taking sensible precautions (which we had not done), you should make it to the Refuge de Barroude[18]. The two times we stayed there, the food was fantastic. In fact, in 2004 when we arrived with two female friends from Britain, one of them commented about having to walk almost eight hours for the best meal of her life.

Stop Press: Alas the refuge was destroyed by fire in October 2014. Hopefully it will have been rebuilt by the time you read this. Otherwise, it's a very long day from Héas to Parzan. Including stops, it's likely to take 13-14 hours.

Day 24 Refuge de Barroude to Parzan (1,100m)

Google overview map: trekthepyrenees.com – Days 21-25 Gavarnie to Refugio de Viados

Trekking map: Rando Editions Mapa Excursionista with the Institut Cartogràfic de Catalunya, 1:50,000, 23 Aneto-Posets

Via: Port de Barroude (2,534m), Rio de Barrosa, south along the A138 road

Guidebooks: Joosten HRP, Véron HRP

Recognised trail: HRP

Approximate distance: 15 km

Recognised trail: HRP

Approximate distance: 15 km

Meson la Fuen Parzan: with our Belgian friends

Climbing: 161m   *Descending:* 1,434m   *Total time:* seven hours

It's a short easy climb of 162m from the refuge to the frontier Port de Barroude. The broad, grassy *port* is in stark contrast with the surrounding mountains, although the nicely graded zig-zags going down into Spain need a touch of concentration to locate at the start. Overall this is a lonely descent into Spain, in wild surroundings. Lonely that is, until much lower down, where you are likely to meet families enjoying themselves on the banks of the Rio de

---

18 http://www.refuge-barroude.fr/

Barrosa. For the final stretch you have no option but to tramp about 5 km along the A138 road which is usually fairly quiet with respect to motor traffic.

The Meson la Fuen[19] in Parzan is an unspectacular hotel alongside the main road, almost opposite a petrol station, but which at least feeds you and is clean. When we last stayed there in 2013, it was along with the young Belgians (Day 22) and a British couple now living in Australia whose European 'fix' each summer was to do some of the GR11.

The dinner menu was in an unrecognisable language that was neither Spanish nor French (possibly it was Aragonese). We worked most of it out between us, but the two young waitresses proceeded to mime laying eggs, complete with sound effects, when we asked for clarification about one item. No, it wasn't eggs, but chicken.

Day 25 Parzan to Refugio de Viados (1,760m)

Google overview map: trekthepyrenees.com – Days 21-25 Gavarnie to Refugio de Viados

Trekking map: Rando Editions Mapa Excursionista with the Institut Cartogràfic de Catalunya, 1:50,000, 23 Aneto-Posets

Via: North on A138 and right before Central Electrica del Barrosa (about 1.5 km); then over the Paso de los Caballos (2,326m)

Guidebooks: Joosten HRP, Véron HRP, Johnson GR11

Recognised trails: GR11/HRP

Approximate distance: 20 km

Climbing: 1,500m   *Descending:* 860m   *Total time:* 8.5 hours

Today is long but easy, following the GR11 waymarks all the way. From the A138 highway it's a substantial tramp on dirt road with forest providing shade until past the Urdiceto hydro-electric station, and then a path to the Paso de los Caballos (the dirt road will also get you there). In contrast, the descent on a good footpath is delightful and very Pyrenean, with the Posets massif

---

19 http://www.lafuen.com/

impressive across the Valle de Gistain. Lower down you are on dirt roads, or short-cutting across their zig-zags – keep your eyes on the GR11 waymarks. The Refugio de Viados[20] (or Biados) is privately run, very cosy and friendly.

Days 26 to 30 Refugio de Viados to Refugi de la Restanca

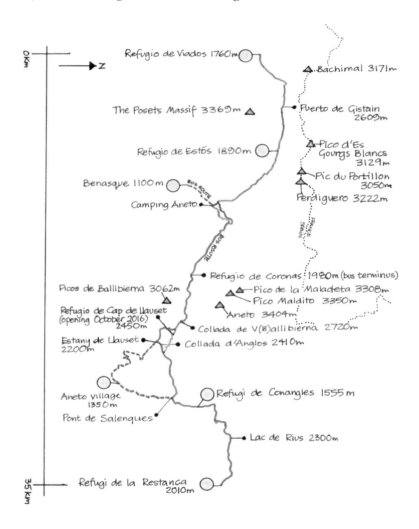

---

20 http://www.viados.es/

Day 26 Refugio de Viados to Refugio de Estós (1,890m)

Google overview map: trekthepyrenees.com – Days 26-30 Refugio de Viados to Refugio de la Restanca

Looking towards the head of the Valle de Estós

Trekking map: Rando Editions Mapa, Excursionista with the Institut Cartogràfic de Catalunya: 1:50,000, 23 Aneto-Posets

Via: Puerto de Gistain (2,609m)

Guidebooks: Joosten HRP, Johnson GR11

Recognised trails: GR11/HRP North to confluence of streams, then GR11 east

Approximate distance: 11 km

Climbing: 800m   *Descending:* 670m   *Total time:* 8.75 hours

Along the first stretch you have to cross several small, but slightly tricky, ravines. Then there's a more tricky crossing at the confluence of streams at the foot of the long ascent to the Puerto de Gistain. Also, when we went this way in 2013 (but not on a previous occasion in 2004), there were some large snowfields to cross either side of the Puerto, although now we had our six-spike instep mini-crampons (Chapter 4), which held perfectly. A mercifully brief storm added further to the excitement. Otherwise, this is a straightforward hike along the GR11.

Sitting with beers in 2013, under a late afternoon sun outside the *refugio*, we watched, along with almost everyone else, a helicopter swoop and pick up a man with a broken leg on the other side of the valley – his misfortune, our salutary warning.

Mention must also be made of the tea brewed for us on this trek, in hot sunshine just the far side of the confluence of streams, by the Anglo-Australian couple that we had first met at Parzan. It was delicious and it was a shame that they overtook us soon after, never to be seen again. We also had a fine after-dinner conversation with a young Spanish man at the Refugio d'Estós, described in Chapter 5.

Overall, the Refugio de Estós[21], while still large and a little dilapidated (though much better than the Refuge Wallon) left a good impression. It was certainly better than on our previous visit in 2004.

Day 27 Refugio de Estós to Camping Aneto (1,250m), then ride to Benasque

Google overview map: trekthepyrenees.com – Days 26-30 Refugio de Viados to Refugio de la Restanca

Trekking map: Rando Editions Mapa Excursionista with the Institut Cartogràfic de Catalunya, 1:50,000, 23 Aneto-Posets

Via: GR11 alongside the Rio Estós

Valle de Estós

Guidebook: Johnson GR11

Recognised trail: GR11

Approximate distance: 9.5 km to Camping Aneto

Climbing: Almost nil   *Descending:* 640m   *Total time:* 3.25 hours

This is an easy walk down the Valle de Estós. On reaching the main valley road, turn right for Camping Aneto[22] which has a café/restaurant – useful for coffee and/or early lunch – and also some rooms that may be available for a night's stay. You could also turn left for Camping Ixeia[23] a few minutes away on the GR11, which has a bar-restaurant and bunkhouse.

Two bus services – from La Beserta and Vallibierna – link Camping Aneto/Ixeia and Benasque[24]. To the casual eye the village is pretty and smart. It has hotels, restaurants and shops, including a post office if you wish to send

---

21 http://www.refugiodeestos.com/web/index.html
22 http://tinyurl.com/campinganeto
23 http://tinyurl.com/campingixeia
24 La Besurta to Benasque and vice versa: http://tinyurl.com/busbenasque-besurtaVallibierna to Benasque and vice versa: http://tinyurl.com/busbenasque-vallibiernal

anything home. Check its opening and closing times. It is used to dealing with trekkers who need to get rid of surplus gear. We have always stayed at the Hotel Ciria,[25] which has good rooms.

Note that from Camping Aneto you may continue along the GR11 to the start of Day 28's trek, but then you will have to stay at the unstaffed Refugio de Coronas and produce your own food. Another possibility is to go left to the head of the valley and ascend to the Refugio de la Renclusa, and next day join Day 29 of the alternative itinerary that is described below. For me, however, the fleshpots of Benasque are more inviting, especially as there is an early morning bus service up the Vallibierna (see link above) to the start of tomorrow's trek.

Day 28 Bus from Benasque to Refugio de Coronas (1,980m) then trek to Aneto village (1,350m)

Special note: This, and that described for the following Day 29, comprise the preferred itinerary until the summer of 2017 when a new staffed refuge on the main GR11 route is expected to be open. See below

Google overview map: trekthepyrenees.com – Days 26-30 Refugio de Viados to Refugio de la Restanca

The GR11 junction for the Embalse de Llauset

Trekking map: Rando Editions Mapa Excursionista with the Institut Cartogràfic de Catalunya, 1:50,000, 23 Aneto-Posets

Via: Collada de Vallibierna (2,720m) and the Embalse de Llauset

Guidebooks: Joosten HRP, Johnson GR11

Recognised trails: GR11/(HRP variant)

Approximate distance: 21 km from Refugio de Coronas to Aneto village

Climbing: 900m from Refugio de Coronas to Aneto village

Descending: 1,400m from Refugio de Coronas to Aneto village

Total time: 9.5 hours from Refugio de Coronas to Aneto village

Note that the spellings Vallibierna and Ballibierna are interchangeable.

---

25 http://www.hotelciria.com/home

The 0715 hikers' and climbers' bus up the Vallibierna (see Day 27 entry above for website) to the unstaffed Refugio de Coronas takes almost an hour and saves the trekker significant time and effort. Much of it is on a winding dirt road, precipitous on one side.

From the Refugio de Coronas the route is exactly as you would expect on the south side of Aneto, at 3,404m the highest mountain in the Pyrenees. It's rough and tough with boulder fields and a brief scramble. The HRP guidebook combines today and tomorrow into a single day, but when we did that in 2005 it took over 12 hours and I remember declaring it afterwards to have been the hardest hike of my life. Life in the Pyrenees never stands still, however, and by the summer of 2017, a new staffed refuge – the Refugio de Cap de Llauset[26] – is expected to be open, splitting this direct route into two days and thus making it completely feasible. You will see from the website link that its planned completion date is October 2016. Meanwhile and until the Refugio de Cap de Llauset becomes a reality, breaking the trek by descending to Aneto village takes you out of the way a little, but to Angharad and me feels so much more civilised.

Back to the trek itself, the boulder fields and brief scramble above the Ibones de Vallibierna greet you on the ascent to the Collada of the same name. Then it's an equally rough, steep descent until you reach a signpost indicating the path on your right to the Estany de Llauset, which you take. (If you carry straight on, bearing left initially, you will be on the route that combines days 28 and 29 into one trek, but note the paragraph above, which tells of the new refuge on this route that is currently being built). Signposts are fashionable in these parts, so ensure that you turn right at this signpost and not at any that may or may not appear beforehand and which indicate different destinations.

The walk south alongside the Estany de Bozornàs, then over a small pass and down to the Estany de Llauset is easy compared with what has gone before. At the signpost above the Estany, follow the GR11 waymarks rather than cutting straight down. They bring you to a serviceable but crude bridge over the inflow stream. You will then come across a *via ferrata* cable for a short distance as you walk east-southeast above the northern shore. It's not really necessary. At the far end (outflow) there is a parking area. The GR11 now follows the rough road down to Aneto village with some indicated variations and short-cuts. The road is about 10 km and will take 2.5 hours or more depending on whether or not you have a break. It goes first through a 2 km tunnel with lighting that is reminiscent of what might appear on a spooky digital game, but check the official GR11 route from the parking area which avoids it. You may decide to hitch down the road.

---

26 http://tinyurl.com/capdellauset

The Hostel Rurale Casa Moline[27] is a thoroughly charming, old-fashioned (but en suite) small hotel on one side of the village square. A few hikers come this way and some also spend the night, but Aneto village is truly off the beaten track. In 2013 we spent two of the most contented evenings of our trek there, and it didn't disappoint when we returned in 2014. Dinner is not until 2100, in true Spanish style, but who cares? The atmosphere, the larger-than-life characters of our hosts Mario, Pilar and their daughters, the home-cooked food with home-grown salad – we could have stayed for ever, forgetting and being forgotten.

Day 29 Ride from Aneto village to Estany de Llauset then trek to to Pont de Salenques (1,430m) and Refugi de Conangles (1,555m)

Google overview map: trekthepyrenees.com – Days 26-30 Refugio de Viados to Refugio de la Restanca

Trekking map: Rando Editions Mapa Excursionista with the Institut Cartogràfic de Catalunya, 1:50,000, 23 Aneto-Posets

Via: Collada d'Anglos (2,410m) and the Ibones d'Anglos

Guidebooks: Joosten HRP, Johnson GR11

Estany Gran and the Refugio d'Anglos

Recognised trails: GR11/(HRP variant)

Approximate distance: 7.5 km to Pont de Salenques; 9.5 km to Refugi de Conangles

Climbing: 220m   *Descending:* 1,000m

Total time: 5.25 hours to Pont de Salenques

If you are happy to spend a second night at the Casa Moline, Mario will offer a cheap taxi service to:

• The Estany de Llauset (2,200m) to resume the trek;

• Pick you up from the Pont de Salenques at the end of the hike (likely to be mid-afternoon or slightly earlier);

---

27 http://www.casamoline.com/

- Take you the following day to the Hospital de Vielha, a few kilometres north of the Pont de Salenques, where the road emerges from a tunnel.

Almost every moment of the hike from the Estany de Llauset to Pont de Salenques is a delight. The path over the Collada d'Anglos is a little exposed at times on the ascent, but it picks its way nicely through the rocky terrain, with the help of *via ferrata* along one short section. Down the other side, near the unstaffed Refugio d'Anglos and by the Ibones d'Anglos, you join the direct route from the Collada de Vallibierna.

The descent from here to the Pont de Salenques is long and rough, but a revelation compared with having to hurry down after over nine hours on the march (which was the case for us in 2005 when we did not break the journey at Aneto village). I would even go so far to say that it is relatively enjoyable on a path with many zig-zags. Following its south (right) bank, the Riu de Salenques provides an impressive show of raw water power as it makes its way down to the lake and the road.

If you are not being picked up to spend a second night at Casa Moline (see above), note that the aforementioned Hospital de Vielha refuge at the start of tomorrow's trek was closed in 2014 and had been for a few years. It's possible to stay at the Refugi de Conangles[28] a kilometre or so south from Hospital de Vielha, back towards the Pont de Salenques, but you should check it out beforehand. Given that the area where the tunnel emerges is quite a mess, I recommend returning to the Casa Moline and using Mario's taxi service as above.

Days 26-29 Alternative Itinerary

This route from the Refugio de Viados to the Hospital de Vielha, covered above, is part of what Joosten describes as an 'easy' variant of the HRP, being on the GR11 all of the way (see also Chapter 4). It is only perhaps easy, however, in comparison to the alternative – the standard HRP route described by Joosten and Véron. We have never attempted this latter itinerary, and have no intention of doing so. Only a brief account is produced here – enough to trace it on the map.

Day 26 Refugio de Viados to Refuge de la Soula (1,690m)

From the confluence of streams described in our preferred itinerary for Day 26 above, leave the GR11 and head north-northeast followed by northwest to

---

28 http://www.refugiconangles.com/

ascend the Port d'Aygues Tortes (2,683m). The way continues north for a while, then east before swinging northwest again to the Refuge de la Soula[29].

Day 27 Refuge de la Soula to Refuge du Portillon (2,571m)

The way is generally southeast over the Col des Gourgs Blancs (2,877m) and the Tusse de Montarqué (2,889m). Georges Véron declares that the region through which this route passes is one of the most beautiful of all the Pyrenees. He also states, however, that you enter a glacial region that demands experience of the high mountains and serious kit, such as an ice axe, crampons and rope. Ton Joosten declares that the final section before reaching the Refuge du Portillon[30] is 'very difficult and dangerous in bad weather'. You can't say that you haven't been warned if you choose to go this way. Possible snowfields will make it worse.

Day 28 Refuge du Portillon to Refugio de la Renclusa (2,140m)

Again there may be snowfields on the route. Go east at first to traverse the Col Inférieur de Litérole (2,983m) – the highest pass of all on the 'standard' HRP. Joosten describes the descent from this pass as very steep, Véron as quite steep. From here the direction is generally southeast (although you go east then north at one point!) to the road near the Hospital de Benasque. From here you may follow the road a few kilometres to the foot of the easy climb to the Refugio de la Renclusa.

Joosten repeats the warning of Day 27 so be warned again. The Refugio de la Renclusa[31] is the base refuge for the ascent of Aneto. You might wish to take a day out to do this, but you should hire a guide.

Day 29 Refugio de la Renclusa to Refugi de Conangles (1,555m)

First, retrace your steps a short distance to a junction at 1,980m where you turn right, and later right again to follow the generally southeasterly direction of the day's route via the HRP's second highest pass – the Coll de Mulleres (2,928m). The initial descent from here is difficult. You first have to scramble north along the ridge until you find the way off, very steeply. Véron advises you not to hesitate to rope up if you're in need of reassurance. If a substantial amount of snow remains, this initial descent is, in the words of Joosten, 'precarious', and we have read about at least one death here in recent years in such conditions. The warnings for the previous two days apply.

---

29 http://www.refuge-lasoula.com/
30 http://refugeduportillon.ffcam.fr/
31 http://tinyurl.com/refugiorenclusa

Day 30 Refugi de Conangles (in lieu of Hospital de Vielha) to Refugi de la Restanca (2,010m)

Google overview map: trekthepyrenees.com – Days 26-30 Refugio de Viados to Refugio de la Restanca

Estany de Rius and the Encantats

Trekking map: Rando Editions Mapa Excursionista with the Institut Cartogràfic de Catalunya, 1:50,000, 22 Pica d'Estats-Aneto

Via: a) Port de Rius (2,320m) and Estany de Rius (HRP/GR11)

b) Rius/Arties Valley (GR11)

c) Fork southeast before Basses de Rius which are marked on map.

Guidebooks: Joosten HRP, Véron HRP, Johnson GR11

Recognised trails: GR11 (also HRP to Estany de Rius)

Approximate distance: 13 km

Climbing: 770m   *Descending:* 390m   *Total time:* Seven hours

On the long but straightforward climb via the GR11 to the Port de Rius, note to turn right where the path straight ahead goes towards Lac Redon. Then, from the Port, walk along the northern shore of the Estany (Lac) de Rius with the Encantats massive as backdrop – a magical setting. At the lake outflow take the nicely graded GR11 path descending the Rius/Arties valley (east), perhaps avoiding the occasional snowfield.

The final section from near the Basses de Rius (about 1,950m) leaves the GR11 that is marked on the map and takes a path southeast that is indicated on the 1:50000 map as a black pecked line. On the ground it is in fact marked with the red and white paint flashes of the GR11. It contains a short, awkward section of boulders where Angharad tripped badly in 2013 (Chapter 2). The final 150m climb to the Estany de la Restanca is steep, but at the top the destination is in your sights and not far away, across the dam.

While quite large (80 places), the Refugio de la Restanca[32] has a friendly international atmosphere

---

Variant via the HRP loop

Both Joosten and Véron find that the Encantats so completely live up to their name – enchanting – that they extend the middle section of Day 30. From the eastern end (outflow) of the Estany (Lac) de Rius, turn right to go southeast, past the Estany Tort de Rius and over the Collada d'Estany de Mar to the lake after which it is named. Here, turn northeast, past the Estany, eventually arriving at the Refugi de la Restanca. Both Joosten and Véron reckon it adds about 2.5 hours (without stops) to the journey.

Top tips from Chapter 7

1. Remember that you need a large sum of euros to cover paying in the mountain refuges.

2. Check on the Internet for local bus timetables. You might save yourself an hour or more of road walking at the start (or end) of a day.

3. In the *Hautes-Montagnes* be prepared for days occasionally when you cover less than two kilometres per hour.

4. Be on your guard when you relax. Accidents are rare but can happen.

5. If you have the time, leave the rucksack(s) and climb the Petit Vignemale (3,032m) from the Hourquette d'Ossue. It's straightforward and takes about 90 minutes there and back.

6. People trekking in the opposite direction are a useful source of information about conditions ahead.

7. Be prepared for snow in the *Hautes-Montagnes* and be suitably equipped (see Chapter 4). You can always post mini-crampons and ice axe home once you are sure that you will have no further need.

8
Take your pick: into the heart of the near-eastern Pyrenees

From Refugi de la Restanca to Refugi Vallferrera in six to seven days (31-36+)

The near-eastern Pyrenees are hard! Although slightly lower in altitude than their counterparts to the west, paths are often little trodden and there is a feeling of real isolation – on some days you might be lucky to see a single person. When you consider too the roughness of the terrain, you'll understand why these mountains take no prisoners.

But the rewards are also great. To have the sense of being in the heart of a vast landscape, with range upon range of mountains extending in both directions, is both humbling and uplifting. It is as close to a wilderness as you will find on the traverse. You may be forgiven if you forget that you are travelling from one coast to another. It is here that I fell in love with the Pyrenees and it is to here that I am pulled on every subsequent visit. The more I get to know the area, the more I want to know every bit of it

The peak of Mont Roig (Mont Rouch in French) – the Red Mountain – provides a particular challenge. Its main peak stands at 2,868m and forms the culmination of a stretch of the frontier ridge that has stupendous views. Mont Roig, however, has several ridges emanating from it, meaning that the Pyrenean traverse can't avoid some kind of difficult encounter with the mountain without a long detour, even if none of the routes pass over the actual summit.

This chapter, therefore, covers a relatively short section of the traverse but with five possible routes, each with its own rewards and challenges. Four of the routes do not diverge until past Montgarri, on Day 33. The fifth diverges immediately at the Refugi de la Restanca.

Useful points at which to break the trek are:

Salau, end of Day 33 for the Red Route;

Vall d'Aneau (Villages of Alós d'Isil, Isil, Esterri d'Aneau and La Guingueta), end of Day 33 for Purple, Orange and Green routes;

Tavascan, end of Day 35 all routes except Brown Route (Day 36).

POINTS OF INTEREST DAYS 31-36
-REFER TO MAP OPPOSITE
RED ROUTE
1. Arties 1050m
2. Borda de Perosa
3 Port de Salau 2087m
4 Col de Crusous 2217m
5 Cabane de Marterat
6 Port de Marterat/Tavascan 2217m
7 Western end of Pla de Boavi
8 Col de Sellente/Baborte 2487m

PURPLE ROUTE
9 Palenca de la Peña
10 Col de la Cornella/de Coronas 2485m
11 Coll de Curios 2428m
12 Coll de Calberanté 2610m
13 Coll de Certascan 2605 m

ORANGE ROUTE
14 Isil
15 Esterri d'Aneau
16 Col de Mascarida -about 2520m

BROWN ROUTE
17 Couflens
18 Col de la Serre du Clot 1540m

GREEN ROUTE
19 Col de Crestada/Goielli crestada 2475m
20 Port de Caldes 2570m
21 Port de Ratera 2534m
22 Jou
23 Dorvé
24 Coll de Calvo 2207m
25 Coll de Lleret 1830m
26 Lleret
27 Aineto
28 Boldis Sobira
29 Coll de Tudela 2243m

PEAKS ▲
(A) Montardo 2833m
(B) Gran Tuc de Colomers 2933m
(C) Gran Encantat 2745m
(D) Pics de Bassiero 2887m
(E) Tuc de Barlonguera 2802m
(F) Campirme summit 2631m
(G) Mont Rouch (Mont Roig) 2857m
(H) Tuc de Certescan 2853m
(I) Pic de Baborte 2938m
(J) Pic de Sottlo 3072m
(K) Pic d'Estats 3143m
(L) Pic de Montcalm 3077m

Days 31 to 36 Refugi de la Restanca to Refugi Vallferrera

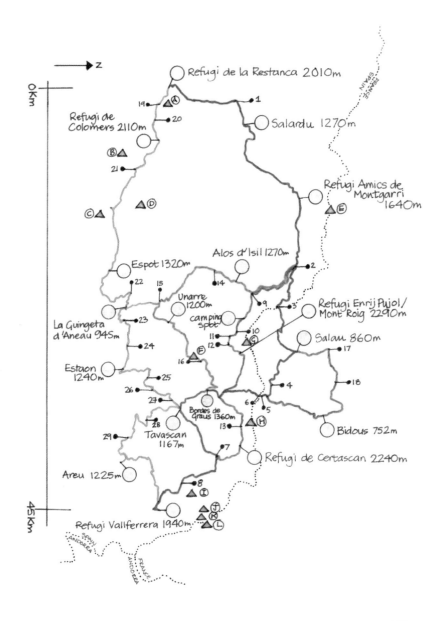

The connoisseurs' trans-frontier Red Route

Google overview map: trekthepyrenees.com – Days 31-36 Refugi de la Restanca to Refugi Vallferrera

Trekking maps: Rando Editions Mapa Excursionista with the Institut Cartogràfic de Catalunya, 1:50,000, 22 Pica d'Estats-Aneto

IGN 2048 OT 1:25000 Aulus Les Bains/Mont Valier (French side of the frontier Days 33 and 34)

Editorial Alpina 1:25,000 E-25 Pica d'Estats Mont Roig (Spanish side of the frontier from day 35)

The Red Route is my preferred way. It and its Brown extension below are the only two routes that circumvent Mont Roig/Rouch on its northern side. They avoid the worst horrors of the purple route underfoot (also below) and take you to accommodation with meals at the end of each day. You remain, however, part of the high mountains and the hours are long. Some of the distances are long too, but on those days a significant number of kilometres are on dirt or tarmac roads where good time may be made. The main difficulty is route-finding on an intermittent path on Day 34.

Two easy days start the Red Route. Then the challenges begin.

Day 31 Refugi de la Restanca to Arties village, then taxi to Salardu (1,270m)

Via: Pontet de Rius, and the Riu de Vallarties

Guidebooks: Joosten (HRP) and Véron (HRP) cover the variant described below

Recognised trail: GR11 variant to part-way down the Riu de Vallarties

Approximate distance: 13 km

Climbing: Virtually none

Descending: 900m

Total time: 4.25 hours to Arties

On reaching the valley floor after the steep descent from the Refugi de la Restanca

This is the direct descent to the upper Garonne valley, or the Garona as it is known in Spain. Cross over the dam of the Restanca lake, turn right, then left and north down the steep path through the forest to arrive at the valley floor at the Pontet de Rius. Turn right and follow the dirt road (becoming tarmac towards the end) down the valley to Arties. In 2013 we had to wade where it crosses the *Riu* by a parking area and shortly after the GR11 variant turns off to the right, because the road and its bridge had been washed away (Chapter 2). More spectacular storm damage and another road diversion greeted us just above the village of Arties. Hopefully, all will have been restored when you come to do this hike.

The central plaza of Arties has a delightful tapas bar, which is too good to miss at lunchtime. You may call a taxi from the plaza to take you the short distance up the valley to Salardu. If you're being a purist, walk along the main road – but it won't be a pleasant experience. Salardu offers various forms of accommodation, restaurants and a shop. We have always stayed at the Hotel Deth Pais[1], basic but clean.

Variant via the Refugi de Colomers

Walk to the Refugi de Colomers as described for day 31 on the Green Route, except go to the old building that overlooks the Estany Major de Colomers rather than the replacement refuge. Without crossing the dam, leave the GR11 and head generally north, descending eventually to Salardu. This variant is obviously longer and more difficult than the preferred route above and it misses the tapas bar in Arties. It does, however, stay in the mountains for a few hours before descending and avoids the main road into Salardu (apart from having to cross it to gain access to the village at the end).

Day 32 Salardu to Refugio Amics de Montgarri (1,640m)

Via: a) Path to Bagergue

b) Solid black line track marked on map, generally southeast out of Bagergue to join dirt road

c) Southeast and finally northeast on dirt road (tarmacked later) to Plan de Beret and car park

Above Montgarri

d) Path from northwest end of car park, heading north-northeast up the valley, swinging round to northeast in later stages to Montgarri.

---

1 http://www.hoteldethpais.com/en/

Guidebooks: Joosten HRP and Véron HRP as far as the Plan de Beret

Recognised trail: HRP

Approximate distance: 18 km

Climbing: 600m   *Descending:* 200m   *Total time:* five hours

This is another easy day. From the Plan de Beret car park you may take the dirt road all the way to Montgarri (and beyond), but with fine weather and plenty of time to admire the view, it would be a shame not to take instead the good footpath on the west side of the Noguera Pallaresa valley.

On the final descent, the church of Montgarri, below, appears serene and very much at home in the landscape. I am far from being a religious person (references to churches in this book are few and far between), but I did once join Angharad in looking round this one. It forms one side of the square that fronts the Refugio Amics de Montgarri[2] which, as the name suggests, was itself once a religious building that has been restored by 'friends'. Many day-trippers descend on it in summer, when it offers a bar and lunch in a restaurant. Very few stay overnight, however, and dinner is usually a quiet affair. We have always had a dormitory to ourselves and it is the only refuge in which we have stayed, where we have been offered towels.

Day 33 Refugio Amics de Montgarri to Salau (860m)

Via: Borda de Perosa and Port de Salau (2,087m)

Recognised trail: Trans-frontier (old HRP variant)

Approximate distance: 27 km

Climbing: 600m

Descending: 1,200m

Total time: ten hours

Mont Roig massif from below Port de Salau

Take the dirt road that runs to Alós d'Isil (along with the Orange and Purple Routes below) as far as Borda de Perosa (9 km). This is where the dirt road turns southeast from its previous easterly direction and the valley widens a

---

2 http://www.montgarri.com/refugio/

little. I confess that when Angharad and I were last on this route – in 2013 – we accepted a lift from the guardian at the *refugio*, which he had offered while we were talking the previous afternoon.

There's an orientation board at Borda de Perosa describing the refugee flows from France during World War 2 (chapters 1 and 2), and a signpost indicates those trans-frontier trails that start here. You take the trail to the Port de Salau, which begins on a broad grassy track heading east. The general direction, however, is southeast as the track winds its way gently up the mountainside, ignoring the path that goes off left to the Port d'Aulan.

The broad track finally gives up about 45 minutes from the Port de Salau, but with little climbing still to be done on a path that follows the contours around the mountainside. It is indistinct in places but try to follow the occasional yellow or white waymarks.

The Port is adorned with the extensive remains of old mine buildings and wood-hauling machinery, while a plaque commemorates the flight of Spanish Civil War refugees in 1938 and of World War 2 refugees in the opposite direction in 1944. Yes, you are on a *Chemin de la Liberté* (Chapter 1). In 2013 there was also a shepherd talking on his mobile phone and hundreds of sheep, which needed significant warding-off as we tried to have a brief picnic. In equal measure they showed little respect for either the national frontier or the legitimate property rights concerning our food.

The steep descent is hampered at the start by the plethora of paths, some being old mine tracks, others short-cuts worn by hikers, while significant erosion by the elements adds to the confusion. Follow the red and white marks around the zig-zags as far as possible. Many of these waymarks are on metal screwed in the rock, but some are already coming adrift. After the first unstaffed *cabane*, the path improves, being mainly grassy and going down in nice zig-zags until a double crossing of an eroded gully. Then it deteriorates again, and we also had in 2013 to avoid some very low snowfields covered in soil, before reaching a well-made path below the second unstaffed *cabane* marked on the map (it looked half-demolished in 2013). This path leads inexorably down through lovely woods to the parking area above Salau.

Overall this should be a marvellous trek in fine weather, with Mont Roig and its satellites impressively in your face throughout the descent. Hundreds of sheep, a shepherd on his mobile and history – from war refugees to the remains of (and a museum in Salau devoted to) old mine workings – all play their part in stoking the imagination. In 2013 our minds were almost blown apart by the time we reached the end of this trek.

Salau has a hotel/*auberge* – Les Myrtilles[3] (The Bilberries) and *gîte d'étape*[4] that is run by the local Commune (France's smallest governmental unit). You need to request meals in advance at the latter.

Day 34 Salau to Bordes de Graus (1,360m)

Via: Col de Crusous (2,217m) and Port de Marterat/Tavascan (2,217m)

Recognised trail: old HRP variant and Trans-frontier Trail.

Approximate distance: 21 km

Life is only a long dream, which leads to death!

Climbing: 1,660m   *Descending:* 1,160m   *Total time:* 11 hours

You may wish to hitch as you walk 4 km up the minor road to the abandoned buildings of the tungsten mine, now adorned with interesting graffiti. Don't turn right on the path to the Cirque d'Anglade but head generally east-southeast through woods at the far end of the buildings. The route has yellow waymarks to the Col de Crusous and beyond, but they are intermittent, especially higher up, where you need them most. Don't count on meeting anybody to ask the way.

Cross the stream on a footbridge and climb out of the woods and up to the Cabane de Saubé, which is used by shepherds. From behind the *cabane* the path goes steeply up grass generally east-southeast to arrive at a vague ridge (1,900m) with a short descent to a depression beyond. From here the Col de Crusous is in full view ahead. Don't head straight towards it by going down to the depression, but turn right along the ridge to a yellow waymark that turns you east towards the Col, while keeping to slightly higher ground.

Take time to admire the view forwards and backwards from the Col de Crusous and locate the yellow waymark leading you off. After a relatively short descent, the path turns right to the south side of the valley before heading east

---

3 http://tinyurl.com/lesmyrtilles

4 http://tinyurl.com/salaugite (Note that you should scroll down the page to 'gîte d'étape', the 'd'étape' bit being important for locating the correct place).

again. As the Cabane de Crusous comes into sight, still some distance below, locate a small col above and to the south of it (half-right from where you are standing). Try to maintain height as you head for this col and pass a pool of water, the Laquet de Cabarère, which is labelled in appropriately tiny print on the 1:25,000 IGN map.

From here a better path descends initially south-southeast then south-southwest to meet the Brown Route at the trans-frontier trail ascending from the French hamlet of Bidous, to the north. Turn right and follow this good path with red and white waymarks (and some superfluous yellow ones) to the frontier Port de Marterat/ Tavascan, passing on the way the Cabane de Marterat. If you have had enough trekking for one day and possess some food, you might consider staying the night at this clean and well-appointed (including bunk beds for seven, plus blankets) *cabane* that is run by the local commune. The nearest water source (instructions for finding it are in the *cabane*) is a few hundred metres away, however, so you should fill your bottles as you cross the stream about 20 minutes beforehand. It is labelled *Source de Mariole* on the IGN 1:25,000 map.

Assuming you are continuing, veer right from the Port at the start of the descent into Spain and pick up a path that goes down in zig-zags towards the Estany del Port below. You have to cross some rough, mainly wet, grassy ground before you reach the *estany*, where the path is indistinct in places but it doesn't really matter if you miss some of the red and white marks. A good path goes along the eastern shore of the Estany del Port and its little sibling – Estany Xic – before descending again with some wonderful long zig-zags to the parking area at the end of a dirt road.

The parking area is another designated place of remembrance for refugee crossings. From it you may take the waymarked trans-frontier trail to Noarre and then to Bordes de Graus. Its only difficulty is the occasional fallen tree blocking the path.

Faster and shorter is to go down the dirt road. There's another turn-off for Noarre signposted below (by a few hundred metres) the spot where the Purple Route descending from Refugi Enrij Pujol joins. A further option (although possibly no faster) is to continue on the dirt road to where it meets the road descending from the Pleta del Prat ski station (Orange Route) at Quanca. Turn left along the road and it's barely 2 km to Bordes de Graus.

A favourite place for us, Bordes de Graus[5] is pleasantly situated where accommodation comprises a relaxed, unregimented campsite, a *refugi* (with a private room at an extra price) and an apartment to let. It also has a bar and

5 http://tinyurl.com/bordesdegraus

restaurant-café, showers, toilets, a washing machine, and a children's games room in a nearby barn. The family that owns it is very friendly.

Day 35 Bordes de Graus to Tavascan (1,167m)

Via: The Riu de Tavascan

Recognised trail: Trans-frontier Trail

Approximate distance: 5 km

Climbing: Very little

Descending: 350m

Total time: 2.25 hours

Improvised gateway and field boundaries en route

This is a leisurely, 'restful' day and I am fairly confident that you will need it. If you walked the previous day via Noarre you will have crossed the Riu de Tavascan by a footbridge to enter Bordes de Graus. To start today, return to the Noarre path but turn right downstream following its east bank.

When you reach the road descending towards Tavascan, go to the picnic area on the opposite side a little to your right. Now take the path that climbs above the west bank of the Riu, rounding one minor buttress with the aid of a *via ferrata* (hardly necessary). The path carries on, eventually descending and crossing to the east bank again (not shown on the map) for the final section through a lovely gorge to the village.

The main road ascending the Vall de Cardós ends at Tavascan and gives the village a kind of 'wild west' air as cars and tractors mingle. It is here that the hotels (Marxant[6], and Estanys Blaus and Lacs de Cardós[7]), taxi service, small tourist information centre and shop (at the southern end) are located. To the side of the main road, however, the old village is delightful. If you have timed things well you will arrive on August 5, the annual fiesta day, which culminates with a dance in the village square.

---

6 http://www.hotelmarxant.com/
7 http://www.llacscardos.com/

Day 36 Tavascan to Refugi Vallferrera (1,940m)

Via: Pla de Boavi and the Coll de Sellente (2,487m)

Guidebook: Veron HRP

Recognised trail: HRP variant

Approximate distance: 20 km

Climbing: 1,200m

Descending: 600m

Pla de Boavi

Total time: 9.25 hours

The main Vall de Cardós divides at Tavascan. The Riu de Tavascan runs south-southeast past Bordes de Graus to the village, while flowing southwest through the Pla de Boavi to join it is the Noguera de Lladorre.

The dirt road ascending alongside the latter to the parking area at the western end of the Pla de Boavi is a tramp of 6 km. If tempted to book the Tavascan taxi the previous afternoon, my advice is to go for it, thus turning a 20 km trek into 14 km overall. Then walk the 2 km to the eastern end, where you cross the Riu de Sellente by the footbridge. Count yourselves as lucky, for when we first walked here in 2005 you had to crawl above the torrent by means of a felled, slippery tree trunk.

The path now climbs the west side of the Riu, but passes from one side to the other more than once as it progresses in a generally southerly direction. It is well marked and leads unerringly to the Coll de Sellente. From here the path descends to the unstaffed Refugi de Baborte, which will be clearly seen in clear weather. Turn right and after a short distance you are along the eastern side of the Estany de Baborte. The path now goes down to the Cabana de Bassello and soon after swings generally southeast to join eventually the GR11 and dirt road (Green Route) at the Pont de la Molinas. Go up the valley on the dirt road a short distance until you reach the signpost pointing left to the Refugi Vallferrera[8].

---

8 http://tinyurl.com/refugivallferrera

When we were last there in 2013 the *refugi* had recently been renovated and was very smart, while sacrificing nothing of its previous atmosphere. The washroom and showers are in a separate building.

A memorial board tells of republican connections from the Spanish Civil War. We engaged with a fell-running couple – a Swedish guy, who lived near Barcelona, and a South African woman, who lived in Andorra. We each had plenty to say about the burning issue of Catalan independence, the relative welcomes that one receives in French and Spanish refuges, and much more besides. Meanwhile, the *guardiens* warned that tomorrow was forecast to be very hot and that, if we wanted to reach Andorra, an early start was essential. Our fell-running chums planned such a start anyway as they wanted jog to Tavascan in time for a pizza lunch! We also set our alarms accordingly.

The Cabane de Marterat on the Red Route

The Brown Route extension to the Red Route

Google overview map: trekthepyrenees.com – Days 31-36 Refugi de la Restanca to Refugi Vallferrera

Trekking maps: Rando Editions Mapa Excursionista with the Institut Cartogràfic de Catalunya, 1:50,000, 22 Pica d'Estats-Aneto

IGN 2048 OT 1:25000 Aulus Les Bains/Mont Valier (French side of the frontier Days 34 and 35)

Editorial Alpina 1:25,000 E-25 Pica d'Estats Mont Roig (Spanish side of the frontier Day 35)

Guidebook: Lucia GR10 (day 34 only)

Recognised trails: GR10 and Trans-frontier Trail.

This is a two-day variant of the Red Route Day 34 from Salau to Bordes de Graus and is recommended if visibility is likely to be poor. It uses minor roads and the GR10 to Bidous, from where the well marked trans-frontier trail leads all the way, up to and over the Port de Marterat/Tavascan and down the other side to Bordes de Graus. It rejoins the Red Route about 2 km before the Port de Marterat/Tavascan.

If you do not want to lose a day through using the Brown Route you could hitch round to Bidous on arriving at Salau. Other permutations are possible. For example, on one occasion we hitched from Salau (the first vehicle stopping) to Pont de La Taule (9.5 km) and stayed in the *auberge* – Les Deux Rivières[9]. Apart from the *auberge*, Pont de la Taule comprises a road junction for driving to the roadhead parking at Ossèse beyond Bidous the following morning, which we did by ordering a taxi to pick us up from the nearby small town of Seix.

Day 34 Salau to Bidous (752m)

Via: Couflens, Col de la Serra du Cot (1,540m), St Lizier, Bidous

Approximate distance: 17 km

Climbing: 876m

Descending: 986m

Total time: 6.5 hours

Walk north on the road down the valley to Couflens (4 km) and turn east along the GR10, which takes you over the Col de la Serra du Cot and on to St Lizier in the Commune of Ustou. Leave the GR10 here to take the small road south up the valley to Bidous where the wonderful Gîte d'étape l'Escolan[10] awaits.

Day 35 Bidous to Bordes de Graus (1,360m)

Via: Port de Marterat/Tavascan (2,217m)

Approximate distance: 18 km

Climbing: 1,740m

Descending: 1100m

Total time: 9.5 hours

Look out for the *Chemin d'Espagne* trail leaving to the right of the road a few minutes from the Gîte l'Escolan. It nicely cuts out the bends of the road as you walk up the valley for 2-3 km as far as the roadhead (small parking area) at

---

9 http://tinyurl.com/deuxrivieres
10 http://lescolan.com/index_en.html

Ossèse. Now it's a matter of following the red and white (also yellow) marks of the trans-frontier trail and a long but beautiful and varied ascent to the Port de Marterat/Tavascan.

No superlatives can do this trek justice – you are given everything apart from a rock climb. There is a point where the mountains ahead appear impenetrable but the path is magical and ingenious as it winds its way around buttresses and snowfields, avoiding all difficulties. It climbs steeply through trees to hanging valleys full of wild flowers, and crosses cascading streams.

At around 1,600m, however, there is a sobering moment as you pass below the rusting Croix de la Portière (Cross of the Gateway) commemorating death by avalanche during World War II (photograph Chapter 1)..

Higher still you look back to views of a distant plain. And what a fantastic surprise it is on rounding what turns out to be the final corner: the Cabane de Marterat in front with sometimes in early summer a small, very easy snowfield (no crampons needed) to cross, and a short 70m climb to the Port behind. Before then, however, you will have been joined by the Red Route, so follow its directions (Red Route Day 34) for the way down from the Port.

After we had completed the route all the way to Bordes de Graus in 2013 we declared it to be one of the top half dozen hikes of our lives. That was despite much energy spent trying to anticipate the route and potential hazards ahead as we climbed. We each had 'watershed' moments when we questioned whether we would ever do anything like this again – but we did, two years later.

The sylvan start to the trans-frontier trail from the roadhead beyond Bidous

Google overview map: trekthepyrenees.com – Days 31-36 Refugi de la Restanca to Refugi Vallferrera

Trekking maps: Rando Editions Mapa Excursionista with the Institut Cartogràfic de Catalunya, 1:50,000, 22 Pica d'Estats-Aneto

From the Col de la Cornella on day 34: Editorial Alpina 1:25,000 E-25 Pica d'Estats Mont Roig

Guidebooks: Joosten HRP and Véron HRP

Recognised trail: HRP

This route is worthy of both positive and negative superlatives, especially with respect to Days 34 and 35. Yes, you are immersed among the high mountains. Yes, the sights may be awesome. Yes, it is wild and lonely. Yes, you will gain a sense of real achievement on completion.

But: there are several hard days in succession, the path under your feet may be marked only with a few cairns at times; it is very rough, you have numerous passes to ascend and descend, and you have nasty boulder fields to cross. A vicious descent from the first of the three high cols on Day 34, and later a large area of huge glaciated boulders to negotiate, might constitute a particular shock to the system. There may be two snowfields to cross at the end of Day 35. On top of that you will camp wild at the end of Day 33 and find yourself at an unstaffed refuge at the end of Day 34.

Given that cairns are essential to show the way on significant sections of this route I always add stones to them. Now read on:

Day 31 Refugi de la Restanca to Arties village, then taxi to Salardu (1,270m)

Day 32 Salardu to Refugio Amics de Montgarri (1,640m)

On both these days follow the Red Route described above. Easy so far!

Day 33 Refugio Amics de Montgarri to Comamela Valley Head (1,900m)

Via: Palanca de la Piña

Approximate distance: 22 km

Climbing: 530m

Descending: 350m

Total time: eight hours

Follow the Red Route on the dirt road east as far as Borda de Perosa (9 km). Here, carry on along the dirt road as it swings southeast towards Alós d'Isil.

Pass the Refugi del Fornet (open only in winter) and turn off the road (now tarmac) at Palanca de la Peña (or Piña), crossing a bridge over the Noguera Pallaresa. Just over the bridge, we once peered inside the lower building, finding only a bed and a stack of empty whisky bottles – the sad sight contrasting vividly with the serene surroundings outside.

Take the path behind the higher building to climb through trees up the Comamela valley. Emerging from the trees, continue to ascend to the valley head and the confluence of two streams. Ahead is a scree path ascending Mont Roig (but you will not take it). Spend the night here. The stars are magnificent if you have to get up in the early hours.

Note that, instead of wild-camping, you could continue down the road a kilometre or so from Palanca de la Piña to Alós d'Isil, where there is now a staffed *refugi* (see Orange Route below). This course of action, however, is likely to add two and half to three hours onto what is already a long day tomorrow.

Day 34 Comamela Valley Head to Refugi Enrij Pujol/Mont Roig (2,290m)

Via: Cols de la Cornella (2,485m), Curios (2,428m) and Calberante (2,610m)

Approximate distance: 13 km

Climbing: 900m.

Descending: 400m

Total time: 10.5 hours

Cross the stream and head south, uphill to a tiny lake, then turn east towards the Col de la Cornella. As previously noted in Chapter 4, you cross two hanging valleys – one above the other – which are quaintly described as 'false cols' in the Joosten and Véron guidebooks. Both are filled with boulders that have to be negotiated before the faint path zig-zags up scree to the narrow pass. It is also known as the Col de Coronas, but the 1:25,000 map fails to mention it by any name. The map does indicate a gap in the ridge at 2,481m, which must be the spot.

The way to the Estanys de Tatera far below appears uninviting and appearances prove not to deceive. Note that it is a direct line, more or less, and the path that is marked on the 1:25,000 map as following the contours round to the northeast to the Basses de Tartera does not appear to exist. Firstly from the col, however, bear left for a few metres, then right to cross a gulley head. The step across would be easy but for the unstable ground where you land the other side. Then head down very carefully on the very steep mix of grass and scree.

Between the Estanys, pick up the path that leads southeast to the Col de Curios, which is a simple slog – a relief even. The path crosses a little to the north of the pass, turning east and climbing gently to a small tarn – the Bassa de Curios – before continuing to climb, now more steeply, to the final Col de Calberante.

The path then takes you above and round the west side of the highest of the Gallina lakes (the Estany Major), before turning east to the north of it and by some subsidiary large pools. When you arrive at the outflow from the Estany Major you will see the Refugi Enric Pujol far below, a tiny speck of metal glinting in the sun (you hope). It is just to the east of the lowest Gallina lake. Cross the Estany Major outflow and descend roughly north towards the *refugi*, passing the two intermediate Gallina lakes on the way. I say 'roughly north' because you have to pick a way through the huge brown boulders that were long ago polished smooth by a melting glacier, where a confusing array of cairns does not help (described in Chapter 4). This is an amazing landscape, but not so good to have to find your way through at the end of a hard day.

At last you reach the lowest lake and are heading along its eastern shore towards the *refugi*. Then comes the *coup de grâce*. To reach the refugi a rocky buttress must first be negotiated, beyond which you cross the lake outflow just before it enters a ravine (again described in Chapter 4). Once safely over, it's a short easy climb to your destination. What a pity that it's unstaffed, that you have to return to the outflow for water and you now have to prepare food. But do try to appreciate the evening glow on the surroundings. Even allow your emotions to show as you do so.

Day 35 Refugi Enrij Pujol to Refugi de Certascan (2,240m)

Via: Noarre (1,600m) and the Col de Certascan (2,605m)

Approximate distance: 17 km

Climbing: 1,050m

Descending: 1,100m

Total time: 10.5 hours

This is another long day, made psychologically worse because the first few hours are spent descending to the dirt road at Plana del Falo (indicated on the 1:25,000 map), where you join the Red Route briefly. Then, after a few hundred metres along the road, a further slight descent on a path going east brings you to picturesque Noarre. From the Refugi Enrij Pujol you will have descended about 700m.

You cannot break the journey at Noarre unless you happen to own one of the holiday homes, which are the only houses in use. It's amazing that they exist at all as there is no vehicle access to the hamlet. You could, however, take the Red Route path to Bordes de Graus (about 45 minutes) or even Tavascan (a further two hours from Bordes de Graus) and break your journey there. We once spent a good 30 minutes debating these options after we had stopped to eat our picnic at Noarre, before deciding to carry on to the Refugi de Certascan.

It's a long ascent from Noarre of over 1,000m to the Col de Certascan, not helped by the fact that it will now be around the middle of the day with the sun high in the sky. At one point there's a short scramble up rocks to the tiny lake on the Pleta Vella, but otherwise the climb is toil pure and simple, albeit with grand views. The way down from the Col is initially steep and don't be lulled. There may be two snowfields to cross lower down that are not seen from the top. Once the gradient eases, however, it's a pleasant hike to the refuge, which does not reveal itself just beyond the Estany de Certascan until the final minutes.

Being staffed, the Refugi de Certascan[11] represents civilisation after the trials and tribulations over the previous two days. While it is one of our favourite refuges, the inside circulation space is wanting and it can be crowded because the guardian has created two round-trip itineraries (chapters 1, 2 and 10) that include this and other refuges. The popular *Porta del Cel* takes in both Bordes de Graus and the Refugi Vallferrera, as well as climbing the 3,143m Pica D'Estats. The other – the more recent *Muntanyes de Libertat* – includes Bidous and the Brown/Red route trans-frontier trail to Bordes de Graus.

Day 36 Refugi de Certascan to Refugi Vall Ferrera (1,940m)

Via: Pla de Boavi and the Coll de Sellente (2,485m)

Approximate distance: 21 km

Climbing: 1,200m

Descending: 600m

Total time: 12 hours

Like the previous day, this also involves an initial long descent before starting to climb. It is, however, a beautiful descent, and typically Pyrenean.

Walk east from the Refugi de Certascan along the northern side of a tiny lake. Continue east following the good path as it swings round to the south. Ignore the turn right (west) that goes down to the dirt road at the foot of the conspicuous waterfall, Canalada, and a few metres beyond ignore also the less obvious path climbing east. This latter path is the first part of an HRP variant

---

11 http://www.certascan.com/angles/index.htm

that crosses the frontier at the Port de l'Artiga, and goes over a large boulder field before the long descent to Mounicou, above the main Ariège valley.

Instead, carry straight on. After a short climb, the path skirts small buttresses, some of which give momentary feelings of exposure, before arriving at the dirt road you will have seen below, making its way from Canalada to the Estany Romedo de Baix.

Cross the dirt road and pick up the path which, after an initial turn west, then south and east, heads generally south to the Pleta de Llurri. Beyond, it enters trees and descends to arrive eventually at the western end of the Pla de Boavi, close to the buildings of Pla de la Borda. This section from Pleta de Lluri is on a wonderfully graded old 'made' path. You might almost forget that you are on a steep descent and have a substantial climb ahead.

Once at the Pla de Boavi, turn left (east) along the Red Route (Day 36) from Tavascan to Refugi Vallferrera.

Evening glow, looking east from the Refugi Enrij Pujol

The pioneers' Orange Route

Google overview map: trekthepyrenees.com – Days 31-36 Refugi de la Restanca to Refugi Vallferrera

Trekking maps: Rando Editions Mapa Excursionista with the Institut Cartogràfic de Catalunya, 1:50,000, 22 Pica d'Estats-Aneto

From Day 35: Editorial Alpina 1:25,000 E-25 Pica d'Estats Mont Roig

None of the guidebooks cover the Orange Route, which takes a southerly tack but is much closer to the high mountains than the Green Route GR11 described below. Much of Day 35 – the heart of the route – is over pathless terrain and should only be attempted in fine weather. Nevertheless, and despite climbing to the highest point of the five traverses of Days 31-36, it avoids the difficulties underfoot of its cousin – the Purple Route a little to the north.

You may, however, join the Purple Route on Day 35 by walking north from Unarre to the village of Cerbi, where the tarmac ends (3.5 km). Then there are two options. (i) Follow the dirt road from the north-west corner of the village to its end below the Estany de la Gola, where a path will take you alongside the Estany and up to the Col de Curios. (ii) Turn left off the dirt road about 10 minutes after leaving Cerbi and just before a hydro-electric building. Follow the footpath, delightful at first, but becoming indistinct in it higher stages to the same destination. Both routes save having to go over the Col de la Cornella – the most difficult pass of the Purple Route. Both routes are also about the same distance (7 km) from Cerbi. Following the footpath is much slower (3.5 compared to 2.5 hours along the dirt road) but also much more interesting.

Note that if you are not averse to hitching as you walk, you may combine Days 33 and 34 of the Orange Route. Another option, to achieve the same end, would be to arrive at Esterri d'Aneu on Day 33 by walking/hitching, and then book a taxi to Unarre (or even further to Gavas where the path starts) immediately after breakfast on Day 34.

Day 31 Refugi de la Restanca to Arties village, then taxi to Salardu (1,270m)

Day 32 Salardu to Refugio Amics de Montgarri (1,640m)

As with the Purple Route, follow the Red Route description for these easy days (see above).

Day 33 Refugio Amics de Montgarri to Alós d'Isil (1,270m)

Approximate distance: 20 km

Climbing: Practically zero

Descending: 350m

Total time: 5.5 hours

Today is an easy tramp. Follow the dirt road that runs below the frontier ridge, and which is never far from the Noguera Pallaressa. It is the same as the Red Route as far as Borda de Perosa, and the Purple Route as far as Palanca de la Peña but, instead of turning to cross the Noguera Pallaressa at the latter, continue along the now tarmac road to Alós d'Isil. The Refugi d'Alós[12] opened in the village in 2014. At the bottom of the web page you may click for an English translation from Catalan. It appears to offer no dining, although there is a kitchen to cook your own (stock up in Salardu) and a bar. It's worthwhile contacting the refuge directly to ask about food. Other accommodation options are located further down the Vall d'Aneau, at Isil village (Casa Sastres[13] – but check it out) and Esterri d'Aneau (plenty of accommodation – booking.com lists 19 for example – so do your own search).

I digress at this point into a commentary on a little guidebook history. The dirt road from Mongarri to Alós d'Isil (becoming tarmac in its later stage) was described in the early editions of Véron HRP guidebooks as an alternative HRP route, especially useful in bad weather. Then early this century the first edition of the Joosten HRP guidebook appeared, which dismissed the dirt road as 'too easy', and now fails to mention it at all. The Joosten preferred option is to turn southeast at the start of the Plan de Beret (see Red Route Day 32) to Baqeira-Beret and then through the Baciver-Marimanya massif to Alós d'Isil. It takes two days, including a night in an unstaffed refuge. Véron also describes this route.

Personally, I don't think that anything can be 'too easy' on the HRP and if you come across a route that is a simple stride and where you don't even have to consult anything to find the way, count it as a rare blessing not a sin. Moreover a walk along a river valley such as the Noguera Pallaressa has its own pleasures and fascination, making it a pleasant change from mountain bashing.

Here is what Véron had to say about the dirt road to Alós d'Isil in his (early) 1981 edition: 'This easy way is not without charm, passing through a beautiful valley with a rich and interesting vegetation that includes, in particular, wild

---

12 http://refugidalos.cat/
13 http://tinyurl.com/casasastres

raspberries, strawberries and even gooseberries.' We testify that it also has wonderful butterflies.

Day 34 Alós d'Isil to Unarre (1,200m)

Via: Esterri d'Aneu

Approximate distance: 15 km

Climbing: 230m

Descending: 300m

Total time: five hours

This is another tramp on minor roads, first down the Vall d'Aneu to Esterri d'Aneu, then climbing up a side valley to your destination. Unarre is small, pretty, and has a café-restaurant – Casa Tonya[14] – that may also provide accommodation, but it must be confirmed in advance.

Day 35 Unarre to Bordes de Graus (1,360m)

Via: Gavas, Campirme (2,631m) and the Pleta del Prat ski station

Approximate distance: 19 km

Climbing: 1,450m

Descending: 475m

Total time: nine hours

After two hikes of comparative ease, today you return to commune with the mountains and you even climb one. From this side they are lonely mountains too, as overgrown old tracks, and often no discernable path at all, testify. As we left Gavas with a friend in 2014, a cheery local woman waved at us shouting 'Campirme, Campirme', referring to the mountain of that name, towards which we were heading. After Gavas, you are unlikely to encounter anyone until well down the far side.

This is how the day unfolds:

Take the road 3 km to Gavas (turn right at the junction, not left towards Cerbi). From here to the Pleta del Prat ski station you should use the 1:25,000 map listed at the start of the Orange Route. References below are to this map.

From the far end of the village try to keep on the sometimes overgrown, graded old path that ascends the Serra de Vivalles. You eventually arrive at a sheepfold at about 2,050m that is just discernable on the map. In 2014 we made our own way from here more or less directly to the summit of

---

14 http://www.casatonya.info/

Campirme, most of it toiling up steep grassy slopes. With benefit of that exact science – hindsight – it might be a better idea to stay on the path, which doubles back south from the sheepfold and then follow a broad ridge roughly east to the main ridge and a minor summit marked at 2,551m. Here turn left along the ridge to Campirme, on which stands an 'official' observation point.

The summit panorama is fantastic. To the southwest the shapely Encantats dominate, and it's possible to make out the snow slopes of Aneto in the far west. To the north the view is more circumscribed by Mont Roig (2,868m) and its satellites on the frontier, and mighty impressive they look, while to the east the full height of the Pic (Tuc) de Certascan (2,853m) is revealed, with the Pic d'Estats (3,143m) beyond. Below, a bird's eye view of the Estanys de Soliguera completes the pleasing scene.

Getting off the mountain onto the right ridge and col for descent proves challenging even in good weather, the area to the north of the summit being broad and grassy, almost a plateau. There are some intermittent wooden poles painted yellow at the top.

Head slightly east of north at first, then turn east to meet a path coming up from the Estanys de Soliguera (now to the south of you). Don't descend to the *Estanys* (wrong valley!) and don't follow the path to the obvious pass ahead, from where there's a nasty pathless scree descent to the ski road coming from Pleta del Prat. Instead turn left, now fairly close to the edge (slightly west of north) climbing a little to another pass – the Pala de Montareny on the 1:25,000 map. From here your immediate objective, the Estang (lake) de Mascarida is in full view below (in clear weather!) and an obvious path zig-zags down to it. It was near the *estang* in 2014 that we met a person for the first time since leaving Gavas over four hours previously – a shepherd with his *patou* (Chapters 1 and 2) and flock of sheep.

Follow the now obvious path down to the Pleta del Prat ski station. Quite early in the descent pass the derelict remnants of a Spanish civil war outpost. About half way down you may cross over to the ski road, which is brutal but allows a faster descent if you're tired. Otherwise stay on the path, allowing yourself to be distracted – if you have the time – by the patches of bilberries. This path, linking the ski station, the Estang de Mascarida and, a short distance beyond, the intriguingly named Estang del Diable (lake of the devil), which has no outflow, is a popular day walk, especially at weekends. Late in the afternoon of a weekday in 2014, however, we met only two French backpackers preparing their overnight camp.

The main building of the ski station calls itself a *refugi*, but it appears to offer accommodation only in the ski season. It houses a café that is open on summer weekends and possibly during the week too. We arrived just after 5pm and it was closed. The ski station and area are small – too small, and with insufficient reliable snow to be economic, according to one hotel proprietor in Tavascan below. You may walk down the road from here to Bordes de Graus, about 5.5 km. Note the significant short-cuts that are marked as a path on the map that will save a kilometre.

See the Red Route, end of Day 34, for information about accommodation and services at Bordes de Graus.

Days 36 and 36+1

Follow the Purple Route (Days 35 and 36) via the Refugi de Certascan or the Red Route (Days 35 and 36) via Tavascan to Refugi Vallferrera.

The lakes
below
Campirme

The Green Route along the GR11

Google overview map: trekthepyrenees.com – Days 31-36 Refugi de la Restanca to Refugi Vallferrera

Trekking map: Rando Editions Mapa Excursionista with the Institut Cartogràfic de Catalunya, 1:50,000, 22 Pica d'Estats-Aneto

Guidebook: Johnson GR11

The GR11 will take you all the way from the Refugi de la Restanca to Refugi Vallferrera over seven days – hence the short descriptions below. It is the most southerly of the five routes and the easiest, being on good waymarked paths throughout and not reaching the same altitudes of the others despite some stiff ascents. Although much of the walking is both charming and interesting, I have the nagging sense along this section of the GR11 that I have forsaken the high mountains after the second day. You see them plainly enough to the north, but are not part of them. There are points, however, where the GR11 converges with one or more of the other routes and at these you may make the choice to continue along them instead.

Day 31 Refugi de la Restanca to Refugi de Colomers (2,110m)

Via: Port de Güellicrestada (2,475m) and Port de Caldes (2,570m)

Approximate distance: 9 km

Climbing: 670m

Descending: 564m

Total time: 5.5 hours

This is an understandably popular hike, bejewelled with lakes and over two high passes. The way can be rough in the second half, but it is a mercifully short day, yet still in the high mountains. A new Refugi de Colomers[15] replaced the old one in 2008.

Day 32 Refugi de Colomers to Espot (1,320m)

Via: Port de Ratera de Colomers (2,534m) and the Estany de Sant Maurici

Approximate distance: 20 km

Climbing: 500m

Descending: 1,295m

Total time: nine hours

Another beautiful hike, up and down sylvan valleys that are again adorned with lakes, turning to rugged grandeur and possibly snowfields either side of the Port de Ratera de Colomers. For the final section, from Estany de Sant Maurici to Espot, the GR11 follows the road some of the way, but also avoids it to one side or the other. Espot is a sizeable village with various tourist trappings, including hotels and restaurants. For accommodation, try the Casa Rural Alba d'Esteve[16], or the Hotels Saurat[17], Or Blanc[18] and El Encantats[19] (but these don't exhaust the possibilities).

---

15 http://refugicolomers.com/en/
16 http://tinyurl.com/albadesteve
17 http://tinyurl.com/hotelsaurat
18 http://www.superespot2000.com/
19 http://hotelencantats.com/

Day 33 Espot to La Guingueta d'Aneau (945m)

Via: Jou

Approximate distance: 10 km

Climbing: 180m

Descending: 550m

Total time: five hours

Today the GR11 takes you away from the high mountains on a mixture of dirt road, ordinary road and path, passing the small village of Jou en route to the Vall d'Aneau and La Guingueta, where there are a couple of hotels – Poldo[20] and Cases[21]. This is an easy day.

From La Guingueta, you may transfer to the wilder Orange Route via a short walk north along the road to Esterri d'Aneau (3-4 km), which has a greater range of facilities.

Day 34 La Guingueta d'Aneau to Estaon (1,240m)

Via: Dorbé and Coll de Calvo (2,207m)

Approximate distance: 14 km

Climbing: 1,375m

Descending: 980m

Total time: eight hours

If it's hot this is a tough day with shade at a premium. Keep your eyes alert for the GR11 waymarks in the scrub above Dorbé early in the walk, and at other points later where the path goes over grass and is not so obvious on the ground.

Situated about 400m above La Guingueta, Dorbé is fascinating. When we passed through, one of the several houses was occupied, the rest being in various stages of dilapidation. The water point in the village square will be welcome on a hot, dusty morning, while nearby is adorned with interesting graffiti concerning 'fascistas'.

Estaon is a pleasant village, but has only four resident families according to the Refugi d'Estaon[22] guardian, the other dwellings being mostly second homes for Barcelonans. When we stayed, the *refugi* offered splendid facilities and was

---

20 http://www.hotelpoldo.com/en/
21 http://www.en.hotelpallarssobira.com/
22 http://refugiestaon.com/

spotlessly clean. You should check it out in advance, however – refuges and other accommodation tend to go as well as come in these parts.

Day 35 Estaon to Tavascan (1,167m)

Via: Bordes de Nibrós and Coll de Llerét (1,830m)

Approximate distance: 14 km

Climbing: 640m

Descending: 795m

Total time: eight hours

This is a relatively easy day, except you need to take a little care crossing one or two exposed small gulley heads when past Llerét village and contouring above the Vall de Cardós. The descent to Aineto village, before Tavascan, is steep.

Tavascan boasts hotels with bars and restaurants and a small shop. For more information see Day 35 of the Red Route. You may, if you wish, transfer to the Red Route here for a mountain walk, to arrive at Refugi Vallferrera on Day 36.

Day 36 Tavascan to Areu (1,225m)

Via: Boldis Sobirà and Collet de Tudela (2,243m)

Approximate distance: 18 km

Climbing: 1,125m

Descending: 1,020m

Total time: nine hours

After a steep start out of Tavascan, the path contours round to the small village of Boldis Sobirà. Keep alert for the GR11 waymarks to arrive at the Collet de Tudela. Descending the far side of the pass through a wood, the path eventually turns into a dirt road, which leads down to the Ferrera valley, just north of Areu. The village has a hotel (Hotel Vall Ferrera[23]), restaurant and shop and possibly other accommodation in houses.

Day 36+1 Areu to Refugi Vallferrera (1,940m)

Via: Pla de la Selva

Approximate distance: 8 km

Climbing: 700m   *Descending:* 80m

Total time: 4.5 hours

---

23 http://www.hotelvallferrera.com/

A walk up the valley mostly on dirt roads and forest paths, with easy gradients. Make sure that you notice when the GR11 turns right off the initially tarmac, but now dirt, road from Areu. This is shortly before the road turns east and a few minutes after you have crossed the Rio Noguera de Vall Ferrera. The path crosses the dirt road a few times as it heads up the valley, joining it again finally before the junction and short climb left to the Refugi Vallferrera[24]. This is an easy day. See the Red Route Day 36 for information about the *refugi*.

Growing
vegetables
near Areu

Top tip from Chapter 8

Take restful, that is short, days, from time to time to recover after strenuous treks, for example, the few kilometres from Bordes to Graus to Tavascan.

---

24 http://tinyurl.com/refugivallferrera

9
Spain, Andorra, France and the Mediterranean in quick succession

From Refugi Vallferrera to Banyuls-sur-Mer in 15 days (37-51)

While still being surrounded by impressive mountains over the first nine days, the path underfoot gradually becomes less rugged, although it has its moments – for example the climb of Canigou on Day 46. In fact, the whole trek is full of contrasts. Obviously this must be the case because you start in the *Hautes-Montagnes* and end with the Mediterranean Sea lapping around your feet. Much also changes, however, from day to day. For example, Day 42 is a long tramp across the broad Tet valley, Day 43 finds you on an exhilarating hike along the frontier ridge at an average height of around 2,700m, while on Day 44 you spend much of the journey on high plateaux. Even the final Day 51 has a steep and rough section before descending through vineyards to the shore.

You are likely to meet more hikers than on the previous wilderness Days 31-36. It won't be crowded, however, except for the ascent of Canigou on a fine weekend.

The traverse of Andorra requires a further note. The staffed accommodation is to be found in the hotels of the villages and towns close to the main east-west highway. This means usually either hitching or hiring a taxi to connect to the valleys and mountains to the north, where the traverse runs. Our strategy has been to hitch down the valley at the end of a day's trek, but to take a pre-booked taxi in the reverse direction to the start of the next day's trek, when the reliability of the transport has felt like a much more important consideration.

Useful points to break this trek are:

Hospitalet-près-l'Andorre, at the end of day 40 (hotel and *gîte d'étape*)

Amélie-les-Bains, at the end of day 47 (hotels)

Days 37 to 41 Refugi Vall Ferrera to Refuge des Bésines

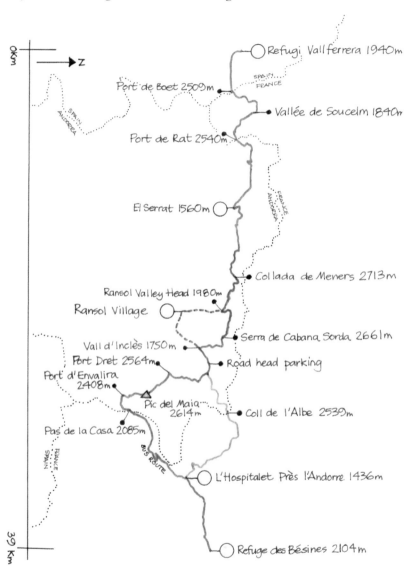

Okm

→ Z

Refugi Vall ferrera 1940m

Port de Boet 2509m

SPAIN
FRANCE

Vallée de Soucelm 1840m

Port de Rat 2540m

SPAIN
ANDORRA

El Serrat 1560m

FRANCE
ANDORRA

Collada de Meners 2713m

Ransol Valley Head 1980m

Ransol Village

Serra de Cabana Sorda 2661m

Vall d'Inclès 1750m

Port Dret 2564m

Road head parking

Port d'Envalira 2408m

Pic del Maia 2614m

Coll de l'Albe 2539m

Pas de la Casa 2085m

FRANCE
SPAIN

BUS ROUTE

L'Hospitalet Près l'Andorre 1436m

39 Km

Refuge des Bésines 2104m

226

Day 37 Refugi Vallferrera to El Serrat (1,560m)

Google overview map: trekthepyrenees.com – Days 37-41 Refugi Vallferrera to Refuge des Bésines

The Medacorba massif on the France-Andorra frontier

Trekking map: Rando Editions Mapa Excursionista, with the Institut Cartogràfic de Catalunya, 1:50000, 21 Andorra-Cadi

Via: a)Port de Boet (2,509m)

b) Etang de la Souceranne (1,900m)

c) Etang de Roumazet

d) Ruisseau de Soulcem (1900m)

e) Port de Rat (2,540m) and the d'Ordino-Arcalís ski station

Guidebook: Véron HRP

Recognised trail: HRP variant (not labelled on the map)

Approximate distance: 28 km (12 km of which are on road after the ski station)

Climbing: 1,209m   *Descending:* 1,600m (930m to the ski station).

Total time: 12 hours (9.5 hours to the ski station)

This trek from Spain to France to Andorra, while being generally in the right direction (east!), includes two *ports*, each involving 600m of ascent.

The waymarking and path on the ground are a little obscure either side of the Port de Boet, but very good as you wind your way up the Port de Rat, amid surroundings of raw, jagged mountains and naked rock. Looking down into Andorra from the Port, the bird's eye view of the ski station d'Ordino-Arcalis, 320m below, changes everything, so be forewarned. In 2013 – our second time on this trek – we were simply glad that the end of the mountainous part was in sight, except there was one final hurdle. Just beyond the Port de Rat lay a classic snowfield. It was not very large but sloped steeply. We found a way around the side.

If you have set your sights on refreshment at the ski station, you need to reach it by about 1600. Then it's a long trek down to El Serrat. In 2005, when we didn't arrive at the ski station until past 1900, we rang our hotel in El Serrat

(Hotel Bringué[1] – make sure you choose the one in El Serrat, there is another listed) to order a taxi. In 2013, at 1700 when people and their cars were still around, we hitched a lift.

As a postscript to our 2013 experience, the previous evening's warning from the *refugi* guardian that this would be 'the hottest day so far' didn't materialise. In fact, the weather was mixed, with large temperature variations. The first minor storm came just 20 minutes into the walk, and thereafter it was a mixture of sun, cloud and showers, some a little thundery. We soon learned that a sudden strong gust of wind portended rain.

Day 38 El Serrat to Refuge to Ransol Valley Head Parking (1,980m)

Google overview map: trekthepyrenees.com – Days 37-41 Refugi Vallferrera to Refuge des Bésines

Trekking Map: Rando Editions Mapa Excursionista, with the Institut Cartogràfic de Catalunya, 1:50,000, 21 Andorra-Cadi

Via: a) Refuge de Sorteny

West from the Collada del Meners

b) Collada del Meners (Coll de la Mina – 2,713m)

c) Riu del Meners

d) Parking area at the Ransol Valley head (not marked on map).

Guidebooks: Joosten HRP, Véron HRP

Recognised trail: HRP

Approximate distance: 14 km

Climbing: 1,050m   *Descending:* 500m

Total time: 7.5 hours (6.5 hours from Refuge de Sorteny)

Today's start involves returning up the road towards the ski station. Turn right at the first hairpin out of the village, alongside the Riu de Rialb, to meet a small

---

[1] http://www.hotelbringue.com/en/

road that ends just before the unstaffed Refuge de Sorteny. Another option is to book a taxi to take you there (the small road turns off the ski station road a little higher than the walking junction), which saves over an hour of trek, mostly on road, and about 300m of ascent.

From the Refuge de Sorteny it's a straightforward trek to the Collada del Meners. In early August 2013 much of it went through a wonderful array of wild flowers (Chapter 2), while an eagle with a huge wingspan soared above. There is just enough room to eat a picnic on the Collada, which gives long views back to snow-covered Aneto and company in the far distance, and forward to Pic Carlit on the eastern horizon. The Collada was our highest point since the Hourquette d'Ossue on Day 19.

The descent is very steep at first, then just plain steep across a landscape studded with small lakes. In 2013 a grand mosaic of snowfields decorated both sides of the Collada but thankfully the path avoided them. We also made friends with a Catalan family from Barcelona (Chapters 2 and 5).

The day's trek ends at the Ransol valley-head parking area (you return here to continue the next day). It's less than 5 km down the minor road to the nearest accommodation – the hotels of Ransol – but we have hitched with ease. We have stayed at the Hotel Segle XX[2] which is clean and offers a fine buffet dinner

Day 39 Ransol Valley Head Parking to Vall d'Inclès (1,750m)

Google overview map: trekthepyrenees.com – Days 37-41 Refugi Vallferrera to Refuge des Bésines

Trekking Map: Rando Editions Mapa Excursionista, with the Institut Cartogràfic de Catalunya, 1:50,000, 21 Andorra-Cadi

Via: a) Refugi de Cóms de Jan(2,220m) and then initially east on waymarked path

Serra de Cabana Sorda

b) Serra de Cabana Sorda (2661m). The waymarked path on the ground appears to cross north of that marked on the map, and a little north of Tosa de Caraup (2,541m)

c) Yellow/red waymarks east and then north (route not marked on map)

d) Estany de Cabana Sorda (2,250m). The *cabana* is on the far (east) bank of the outflow – Riu de Cabana Sorda.

e) Waymarked path (yellow) down west bank of the outflow towards Vall d'Incles (not marked on map until lower down, then as a path crossing from the east bank)

Guidebooks: Joosten HRP, Véron HRP

Recognised trail: HRP

Approximate distance: 14 km

Climbing: 800m   *Descending:* 900m   *Total time:* six hours 20 minutes

This is yet another fine walk. It is steep on the final climb towards the Serra and down the other side, especially the final part of the descent to the Refugi de Cabana Sorda.

In 2013 we took a taxi back to the Ransol valley-head for the start, while, at the other end of the day, we hitched and again the first car stopped for us as we reached the road in the Vall d'Inclès. (Note also that a shuttle bus runs up and down this valley from 0900 until early evening.)

From the Ransol valley-head parking area you should reach the unstaffed Refugi de Cóms de Jan in less than an hour. From there, pick up the red and yellow waymarks going east, before curving south. These waymarks serve you well (much of the route isn't marked on the map), to and over the Serra until some distance down the far side.

Turn right in front of the unstaffed Refugi Cabana Sorda, without crossing the stream. Yellow waymarks then lead down a good path, which delivers you about half way along the Vall d'Inclès. Much of this final descent went through a vast bouquet of stunning wild flowers for the second day in succession when we last did it in 2013, while earlier we saw our second eagle in two days.

There are various villages with hotels, where the Vall d'Inclès joins the main valley and highway. In 2013 we returned to the previous night's Hotel Segle XX, in Ransol (see above), which meant that today we had the relief of carrying only day sacks.

Day 40 Head of Vall d'Inclès to Pas de la Casa (2,085m) – then bus to Hospitalet-près-l'Andorre (1,436m)

Google overview map:
trekthepyrenees.com – Days 37-
41 Refugi Vallferrera to Refuge
des Bésines

Pla del Siscaró

Trekking Map: Rando Editions
Mapa Excursionista, with the
Institut Cartogràfic de Catalunya,
1:50,000, 21 Andorra-Cadi

Via: a) Pla del Siscaró (2,149m)

b) Port Dret (2,564m)

c) Pic del Maia (2,614m, higher if you include its radio mast)

d) Port d'Envalira (2,408m)

Guidebook: Véron HRP

Recognised trail: HRP variant

Approximate distance: 16 km

Climbing: 750m   *Descending:* 600m   *Total time:* six hours to Pas de la Casa

You will need an early taxi to take you back up the valley, as cars are prohibited from around 0830. Then the walk-out from Andorra to France begins. From the roadhead at Camping d'Inclès (parking area but no longer official camping) take the track heading up the valley and turn right at the signpost for the Pla de Siscaro.

This is a rare trek on which you can make good time. From the final high point, the Pic del Maia, the lingering views west to the Pic d'Estats, Mont Roig and, in the very far distance, the snow-covered Aneto and Maladetta, are difficult to turn one's back on. You must do so, however, and ahead the Carlit massif heralds the next stage.

By improvising on dirt track and ski runs to the south, it is possible to avoid much of the highway down from the Port d'Envalira to Pas de la Casa after the initial few hundred metres. The town, with its conspicuous consumption, is likely to be a culture shock, but the tourist office staff will provide the necessary information regarding the bus timetable to l'Hospitalet-près-l'Andorre, and relatively quiet places to drink and eat during the waiting period. See Chapter 2 for more about our Pas de la Casa experience.

The Gîte l'Hospitalité[3] is a great place to spend the night, but check that you are able to be fed there after the bus arrives. If not, you will have to go to the village hotel[4] for an evening meal.

Variant (in good weather only)

You don't have to go to Pas de la Casa. I prefer that way because the route as far as the Pic del Maia is beautiful and, moreover, the terrain that you are crossing allows for time to stop and appreciate it. I confess that I also have an obscure fascination with Pas de la Casa. This variant, however, takes you directly to l'Hospitalet-près-l'Andorre.

Take the path up the valley from Camping d'Inclès but, instead of turning right to the Pla de Siscaro, carry straight on via the Estany de Juclar and the Col d'Albe (2,539m), arriving eventually at L'Hospitalet after a rough, but impressive hike: about 9.5 hours in total.

Day 41 Hospitalet-près-l'Andorre to Refuge des Bésines (2,104m)

Étang des Bésines

Google overview map: trekthepyrenees.com – Days 37-41 Refugi Vallferrera to Refuge des Bésines

Trekking Map: Rando Carte de Randonnées, 1:50,000, 8 Cerdagne-Capcir

Via: Northeast, then east to Étang des Bésines and the refuge beyond

Guidebooks: Joosten HRP, Véron HRP

Recognised trail: HRP

Approximate distance: 10 km

Climbing: 700m   *Descending:* 50m   *Total time:* four hours

L'Hospitalet-près-l'Andorre is not a difficult place to leave. A main road, a hydro-electric power station and a railway line crammed together into a narrow valley combine to make it look… er… functional. I have described in Chapter 3 the Saturday 'shopping train' spectacle as it arrives here.

---

[3] http://www.gitelhospitalite.com/english
[4] http://tinyurl.com/hotelpuymorens

As a pure and simple trekker you soon leave the village and its Saturday morning custom behind for a short, easy day in typical Pyrenean scenery, although the climb out of the village is steep. It is followed by nicely graded zig-zags with long views down the Ariège. The last 2 km to the Étang des Bésines is a level 'made' track, followed by rougher ground along the lake before the short, steep climb to the refuge.

The couple who run the Refuge des Bésines[5] are pleasant, very kind and produce a fine dinner. When we last stayed there in 2013 we were seated with three British men, all solitary walkers. One was doing the HRP, while an older man (about our age) was doing a circuit in the area. The third was much younger, also doing a circuit, but carrying both a chip on his shoulder and a huge weight in his rucksack. At one point, he started having a go at those of us who were retired about our cushy life with pensions that he would never have. The older man put him firmly in his place, with a variation of the dictum of a Dutch man we had met at the Refugi de la Restanca – 'If you don't use it, you lose it' – which he reformulated as 'If you don't fight for it, you will lose sight of it'.

It was also at the Refuge des Bésines that we met the man and woman in their 80s who had trekked there (Chapter 5).

---

[5] http://besines.free.fr/index.htm

Days 42 to 44 Refuge des Bésines to Refugi d'Ull de Ter

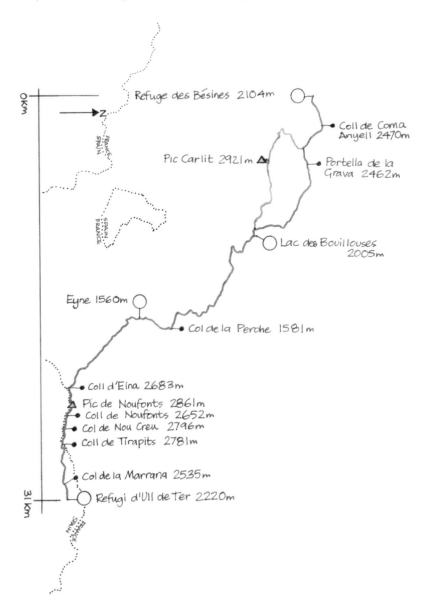

Refuge des Bésines 2104m

Coll de Coma Anyell 2470m

Pic Carlit 2921m

Portella de la Grava 2462m

Lac des Bouillouses 2005m

Eyne 1560m

Col de la Perche 1581m

Coll d'Eina 2683m

Pic de Noufonts 2861m
Coll de Noufonts 2652m
Col de Nou Creu 2796m
Coll de Tirapits 2781m

Col de la Marrana 2535m

Refugi d'Ull de Ter 2220m

0km

31 km

FRANCE SPAIN

SPAIN FRANCE

FRANCE SPAIN

N

Day 42 Refuge des Bésines to Lac des Bouillouses (2,005m)

Google overview map: trekthepyrenees.com – Days 42-44 Refuge des Bésines to Refugi d'Ull de Ter

Trekking Map: Rando Carte de Randonnées, 1:50,000, 8 Cerdagne-Capcir

Via: Coll de Coma Anyell (2,470m) and Portella de la Grava (2,426m) on the GR10

Guidebooks: Lucia GR10, Joosten HRP, Véron HRP.

Coll de Coma Anyell

Recognised trail: GR10

Approximate distance: 22 km

Climbing: 650m   *Descending:* 750m   *Total time:* 7.25 hours

The GR10 ascends to the Refuge des Bésines from the village of Mérens-les-Vals, in the Ariège, and then continues today to the Lac des Bouillouses. This is a classic trek through the Pic Carlit massif, with landscapes on a grand scale. Up to the Coll de Coma d'Anyell, the going is rough and I remember that during our ascent we also had to step aside and wait for a huge flock of sheep that was being driven down the mountain. The climb to the Portella de la Grava is more straightforward. On the far side a sign indicates that you are entering an area of *ours* (bears) and *loups* (wolves) but we saw only a couple of marmots and a few unidentified small brown birds.

It is a long walk down from the Portella de la Grava, as Pyrenean descents always are. Also not unknown is for the sky to cloud over as you descend mid-afternoon, with rumbles of thunder by the end. There are various places to stay at Lac des Bouillouses, including the cosy Auberge du Carlit[6] (which also owns a nearby *gîte*).

Variant via Pic Carlit (2,921m)

This is the 'standard' HRP route and Pic Carlit is the highest mountain in the Pyrénées-Orientales. The HRP leaves the GR10 near the Étang de Lanoux between the Coll de Coma d'Anyell and the Portella de la Grava. The final climb is steep to the pass just below the summit, but the view is wonderful.

---

[6] http://aubergeducarlit.free.fr/

From the summit, return to the pass and turn right down to a ridge, and later through a landscape that is dotted with small lakes before arriving at your destination.

Obviously this variant is both tougher and longer in time than our preferred, very satisfying route via the GR10. Only consider it in settled weather...

Day 43 Lac des Bouillouses to Eyne (1,560m)

Google overview map: trekthepyrenees.com – Days 42-44 Refuge des Bésines to Refugi d'Ull de Ter

Trekking Map: Rando Carte de Randonnées, 1:50,000, 8 Cerdagne-Capcir

Via: Estany Nègre, Estany de la Pradello, Bolquère, and Col de la Perche (1,581m).

Guidebooks: Joosten HRP, Véron HRP

On the road to Eyne

Recognised trail: HRP

Approximate distance: 19 km

Climbing: 100m   *Descending:* 550m   *Total time:* Seven hours

Today's trek crosses the gathering grounds of the Tet valley, which empties into the sea at Perpignan, to the foot of the last of the high Pyrenean ranges (Chapter 2). There are no mountain ridges, no high passes to be crossed. Véron labels it a transition day; Joosten finds it 'unfortunately less interesting' after the first hour.

If you have vivid imaginations like Angharad and me, you will certainly find it different from the usual trek, but still interesting. Agreed, between Superbolquère and (plain old) Bolquère, it degenerates into new forest tracks, tarmac roads and other ski-related development. However, the views back to the Carlit massif and forward to the high ridge of tomorrow are good. If you're very lucky you will have to wait for the 'Yellow Train' to cross the road by the Col de La Perche, providing another moment of minor excitement.

The only place to stay in Eyne is the Gîte Cal Païr[7] (or Gîte Le Presbytère, which is part of the same complex with the same owner). I have described in

---

[7] http://www.gite-calpai.com/

Chapter 5 our bizarre arrival in 2013 where a blackboard with our names on it substituted for a human reception (another sign stated that this was a *gîte d'étape*, not a bar), the fantastic dinner two hours later in banquet style, and the after-dinner conversation in the parlour with another Georges Véron fan who was fascinated that we had used the original French guide to work out our northern passage of Mont Roig on Days 33 and 34 (Chapter 8). In vivid contrast with our arrival, I still picture the scene when the hostess warmly greeted us as we entered the dining room and our eyes alighted on the dinner table where everything was beautiful, from the cloth serviettes to the last candle, and where we took our places among 20-25 others of many nationalities.

Day 44 Eyne to Refugi d'Ull de Ter (2,220m)

Google overview map: trekthepyrenees.com – Days 42-44 Refuge des Bésines to Refugi d'Ull de Ter

The summit of Pic Noufonts

Trekking Map: Rando Carte de Randonnées, 1:50,000, 8 Cerdagne-Capcir

Via: a) Coll d'Eina or Col de Nuria or Col d'Eyne (2,683m)

b) Pic Noufonts (2,861m) and Coll de Noufonts (2,652m) where the GR11 joins

c) Coll de Noucreus (nine crosses – 2,796m)

d) Coll de Tirapits (2,781m)

e) Coll de la Marrana (2,535m)*Guidebooks:* Joosten HRP, Véron HRP. *Also relevant:* Johnson GR11 (from Coll de Noufonts)

Recognised trails: HRP and HRP/GR11

Approximate distance: 24 km

Climbing: 1,700m   *Descending:* 1,050m   *Total time:* ten hours

It would be difficult not to linger and chat over the lavish and fresh breakfast at the Gîte Cal Païs. Among several conversations as we tucked in on a fine morning in September 2013, I have recorded in Chapter 2 the one with two British 'twitchers'. They barely needed to say anything, their joint demeanour telling the story of failed expectations with respect to the migrating autumn birds for which this area is famous.

There's no doubt that you usually move more quickly in the Pyrenées-Orientales than in the high mountains to the west. This also means, however, that you tend to trek for longer distances, as is the case today. Dubbed by Véron as the grand, classic, Catalan stage and Joosten as 'delightful', it involves a climb up to, and an extended traverse along, the consistently high frontier ridge. Views, near and far, unfold either side, until the turn-off at the Coll de Tirapits for the final two to three hours to the Refugi d'Ull de Ter.

You can make good time to the first point on the ridge, the Col d'Eyne, firstly up the deep-cut Vallée d'Eyne, which then opens to a vast landscape before the final steep ascent. While exhilarating throughout, the ridge makes you pay for it with much up-and-down toil, including the ascent of the highest point of our preferred traverse, the Pic Noufonts.

The toil, however, brings other rewards. On our two visits, in 2006 and 2013, changing weather was itself a spectacle when cloud started to form, as were two eagles which appeared very close on both occasions as we reached the Coll de Tirapits (see Chapter 2). The penultimate stretch towards the Coll de la Marrana then provided further delights in the form of a herd of isards (Pyrenean chamois) and numerous marmots.

At the Coll de la Marrana comes the reassuring sight of the ski development of Ull de Ter below, somewhere amid which is the refugi[8] – a relaxed, friendly place but be slightly wary of the shower. In 2013 it gave up as Angharad climbed into it. I called the *guardien*, which led to Angharad shutting herself in the steamed-up shower cubicle to protect her modesty, while he performed repair work outside, calling on her to test it from time to time.

---

[8] http://www.ulldeter.net/en/

Days 45 to 48 Refugi d'Ull de Ter to Amélie-les-Bains

Day 45 Refugi d'Ull de Ter to Refuge de Mariailles (1,710m)

Google overview map: trekthepyrenees.com – Days 45-48 Refugi d'Ull de Ter to Amélie-les-Bains

Trekking Maps: Rando Carte de Randonnées, 1:50,000, 10 Canigou ; From Roc Colom, IGN 2048 OT 1:25000 Massif du Canigou

Via: a) Ski Station de Vall Ter (2,170m)

b) Pla de Coma Amarda

Porteille de Rotja and the start of the Esquerdes de Rotja beyond

c) Porteille de Meurens (2,381m) – not marked on map but it's where the path crosses the frontier

d) Portella del Callau (2,387m) and skirt round north side of Roc Colom

e) Porteille de Rotja (2,377m)

f) Path heading northeast on northwest side slopes of Esquerdes de Rotja

g) Collada des Roques (or Rocs) Blanches (2,252m)

h) Dirt road to Pla Guilhem (2,300m)

i) Turn left across Pla Guilhem on HRP to unstaffed Cabane du Pla Guilhem and Col de la Roquette (2,083m) to meet dirt road again

j) Take waymarked short cuts to meet dirt road at valley floor

Guidebooks: Joosten HRP, Véron HRP

Recognised trail: HRP

Approximate distance: 22 km

Climbing: 650m   *Descending:* 1,110m   *Total time:* nine hours

When we first did this trek in 2006 it was long but comparatively easy. Worsening weather in 2013, however, made it more 'interesting' than intended. We saw vultures at the start, but very little else all day. Nevertheless, we had other matters to concentrate our minds, notably on the plateaux where paths petered out and induced route-finding problems in thick mist. Moreover, from midday we had to contend with rain (sometimes heavy and with hail), and thunder from time to time. Angharad was not even able to pick the bilberries we found in profusion. To cap the hazards encountered, I was given an electric shock when I held the wrong part of the wire that was acting as a gate over the dirt road descending from the Collada des Roques Blanches – just when I thought we were safe! I have described today's major route-finding difficulty in Chapter 4.

Electric wires across the dirt road not withstanding, on reaching it in bad weather you should take it all the way to the refuge and not go wandering off left over Pla Guilhem. Whatever way you choose, however, it's a long descent.

The Refuge de Mariailles[9] has a really nice atmosphere. On a Friday or Saturday evening it may be crowded because it's a base for climbing Canigou. I have shown in Chapter 3 a photograph of the stylish platform bed and described the *Maury aperitif* that we discovered there; also in Chapter 5 the bedlam that greeted our arrival in 2013, together with the start of friendships that blossomed over the following days to Banyuls-sur-Mer.

Day 46 Refuge de Mariailles to Chalet-Refuge des Cortalets (2,150m)

Google overview map: trekthepyrenees.com – Days 45-48 Refugi d'Ull de Ter to Amélie-les-Bains

Trekking Map: Rando Carte de Randonnées, 1:50,000, 10 Canigou; IGN 2349 ET 1:25000 Massif du Canigou

Via: a) GR10 east, on south side of side valley

b) Cross confluence of two streams

The summit of Canigou adorned with the flag of Catalonia

c) Turn right at signposted turn to Canigou

d) Climb Canigou (2,784m) via the *cheminée*

e) Descend by the 'tourist' path to Chalet-Refuge des Cortalets, re-joining the GR10 20-30 minutes away from your destination.

Guidebooks: Joosten HRP, Véron HRP. *Also relevant:* Lucia GR10

Recognised trails: HRP/GR10, then HRP

Approximate distance: 14 km

Climbing: 1,441m   *Descending:* 956m   *Total time:* 7.5 hours

---

[9] http://tinyurl.com/refugemariailles

Walking away from the Refuge de Mariailles, a big sign tells you in French to have a good day, a good walk and enjoy the mountain – *Bonne journée, bon pied, bonne montagne* (photo Chapter 10). It's a nice send-off. Expect to meet many others on the path, especially on a fine weekend, some less fit than others, as Canigou attracts those who do not normally climb mountains. Its dramatic appearance and its status as symbol of Catalonia combine to ensure that it is never lonely.

The signpost indicating the turn-off from the GR10 to Canigou is about 1.75 hours into the trek. Higher up, the path becomes eroded on the approach to the mountain. The best way to avoid the worst of this is to keep following the yellow waymarks and the zig-zags that they indicate.

The near-vertical *cheminée* – rock without a blade of grass to be seen – does not disappoint in terms of excitement. You use hands throughout, but there are plenty of holds and places to put your feet. Yellow waymarks indicate the easiest route. Then, on emerging, to surprise, delight and other emotions, you find yourself about five metres away from the summit cross, usually adorned with the Catalonian flag.

We have climbed the *cheminée* twice. The first time was in 1999 when I was 53. We made short work of it. The second time, 16 years later – September 2014 – it felt significantly more difficult. A thunder clap half way up did not help the nerves. At one point only, however, did we think that we might freeze when the yellow waymarks directed us up a narrow crack in the rock face. Otherwise our adrenalin saw us to the summit. If you want to avoid a lot of mainly cheerful people, try to schedule the climb for a weekday.

The view is of course spectacular. It is, however, a poignant moment. As the gaze extends eastwards to the Pyrenees falling away to the Mediterranean Sea that you are witnessing for the first time, the moment signals that the *hautes-montagnes* end here.

Try also to keep to the zig-zags on the initial steep descent down the tourist route on which counter-erosion work was taking place in 2014.

As the gradient lessened on this path when we walked down, heavy rain hit us, plus much thunder around the summit behind. It stopped as the path rejoined the GR10 to the refuge, and a stunning rainbow appeared (photo Chapter 2).

The clandestine French liberation group, the Maquis, operated from the Chalet-Refuge des Cortalets[10] during the Second World War. It was burned to the ground by the Nazis in 1944 and rebuilt in 1948. An information board

---

[10] http://cortalets.com/

tells the story and there are photographs on the walls inside. It was after visiting the refuge for refreshment after a day ascent of Canigou in 1999 that the crazy love affair with the Pyrenees and its traverse began for us.

The Chalet-Refuge des Cortalets is large. Because it has a good dirt road going to it from the large village of Prades, in the valley below, and can therefore be reached by car and is popular with day hikers, I suspect its main business is providing lunches. Both times we have stayed we have been given a room to ourselves and it has been quiet in the evening with only a few of us having a relaxed dinner together. September 2006 saw us teamed with Bob and Mike – two Brits who were a few days into the GR10 travelling from east to west. We had a laugh together as we stereotyped the guidebooks at that time. Written by 'head-bangers', we agreed. 'The stone chute, while steep, presents no difficulties; rock climbers may prefer to abseil' was how Mike characterised their language. I have never been able to locate this 'quotation' in a trekking guide of that time, but it does sum up the tone with only mild exaggeration.

At the same table in September 2014 the only other guests at dinner were a lovely, young German couple who wanted a night off from camping and an older (though younger than us) French couple who retired to their tent after the meal.

Variant 1 via the Crête du Barbet (purple on text and Google overview maps)

This is the shortest and fastest route between the Refuge de Mariailles and the Chalet-Refuge des Cortalets – 13 km, taking about 6.5 hours in total, depending on length of stops. While ascending significantly higher than the GR10 route, it follows good paths throughout. It is particularly useful if, having left the GR10 with the intention of climbing Canigou, you change your mind on the approach to the mountain. Turn right off the Canigou path at the signpost that indicates the Crête du Barbet, which you reach after a relatively short climb via the Porteille de Valmanya. Cross the Crête at 2,712m and walk on a good path just below it, leading to the Cortalets refuge.

Variant 2 via the GR10 all the way (green on text and Google overview maps)

This is a long (22 km taking about 8.25 hours in total), circuitous route round the lower flanks of the Canigou massif, albeit full of interest. Consider it in bad weather.

From the Canigou signpost carry on along the GR10 to reach the Col de Segalès (2,040m), then head northeast, later north. The terrain becomes rougher underfoot with rock falls to negotiate in places, although the waymarks are there to guide you. You then gain some respite on a dirt road, but this doesn't last long. A little beyond the unstaffed Refuge de Bonne-Aigue (1,741m), the GR10 turns east off the dirt road, leading eventually, after a steep climb through woods, to the Cortalets refuge

Day 47 Chalet-Refuge des Cortalets to Gîte/Refuge de Batère (1,500m)

Google overview map: trekthepyrenees.com – Days 45-48 Refugi d'Ull de Ter to Amélie-les-Bains

Trekking Maps: Rando Carte de Randonnées, 1:50,000, 10 Canigou ; IGN 2048 OT 1:25000 Massif du Canigou

Via: a) GR10 variant to (Ras del) Prat Crabera (1,739m) to join the 'official' GR10

Mountains start to give way to foothills

b) South, then on Balcon du Canigou generally east, then generally south and east to Col de la Cirère (1,731m)

c) Generally southeast to Gîte de Batère (1,500m)

Guidebooks: Joosten HRP, Véron HRP. *Also relevant:* Lucia GR10

Recognised trails: HRP/GR10

Approximate distance: 16 km

Climbing: 450m   *Descending:* 1,050m   *Total time:* 7.5 hours

The GR10 variant to (Ras del) Prat Crabera is clearly shown on the 1:25,000 map and avoids the dirt road of the official route. From here, it's the standard GR10 all of the way (which the standard HRP also follows). For a long, even interminable, time you are on the Balcon du Canigou, an almost level, made-up path that is generally in good shape but eroded in a few places. The climb on a zig-zag path towards the final pass, the Col de la Cirère, also seems long, but the descent from there to the Gîte de Batère takes a refreshingly short 40 minutes.

When we last did this hike in 2013, special effects provided a spectacular start as cloud massed in the valleys below, while a bright sun bathed the mountainsides around the refuge. The cloud rose steadily during the first hour, eventually settling a few hundred metres above us, which made the trek comparatively cool. We met two women on the final stages picking mushrooms. Other fungi were in evidence, while a good crop of wild raspberries to the side of the path provided further diversion. We were also almost mugged for our picnic by a horse that wandered out of a nearby barn.

Also in 2013, Angharad and I wondered about the young couple who had recently taken over the *gîte*[11]. He was full of energy and life, she was heavily pregnant and simply weary. How would they cope and how would their relationship stand up in such a remote place? (We heard a year later that they and their baby were doing well.) I have written about discussions with the motorcyclist from the Ariège, Catalan nationalists and a retired French history teacher in Chapters 2 and 5. What is it about the Gîte de Batère that sparks controversial subjects?

Day 48 Gîte de Batère to Amélie-les-Bains (220m)

Google overview map: trekthepyrenees.com – Days 45-48 Refugi d'Ull de Ter to Amélie-les-Bains

Trekking Map: Rando Carte de Randonnées, 1:50,000, 10 Canigou

Via: a) Col de la Descarga (1,393m)

b) Col de Formantère/de la Formentera (1,133m)

c) Col de la Redoute/ Reducta (875m)

Guidebook: Véron HRP

Recognised trails: HRP

Approximate distance: 18 km

Climbing: 100m

Descending: 1,380m

Total time: 6.5 hours

September flowers and berries all the way to Amélie-les-Bains

Today is pretty much down, down, down on a mixture of dirt roads, tarmac and, for the final hour, footpaths. Behind soars the Canigou massif; below is pastoral and verdant. Looking to the other side of the valley reveals the final sub-range of the traverse. The altitudes on the map indicate that it is not high

---

[11] http://www.gite-refuge-batere.com

compared with what you have been through, but its appearance suggests a different story as it rises abruptly from the low-lying Tech valley.

This HRP route is shown on the map. You diverge from the GR10 at the Col de la Descarga, a few hundred metres from Gîte de Batère. Here, leave the road to go initially north (later east) on a dirt road. Keep your eyes on the map and some time later arrive at the Col de Formantère and then the Col de la Redoute (also called Col de la Reducta). Here, take the main dirt road south rather than the marked HRP route via Montbolo, which goes a little further east. This more direct route is also described in the Véron guidebook. It is still shown as a waymarked way on the map although some of it is on road. Follow it, entering Amélie-les-Bains at a suburban street – Rue Héliopolis.

When we came this way in September 2013, wild flowers lined much of the route, which was also made leisurely by the bountiful blackberries just waiting to be picked and eaten.

The tourist demographic in Amélie-les-Bains sums up the town – once grand, now old and fading and rather sad. While neither Angharad nor I are spring chickens ourselves, we missed the group of chums that had coalesced since the Refuge de Mariailles. They had taken the GR10 route, passing through Arles-sur-Tech, the next town up the valley. We lodged and took dinner alone in the Hôtel-Restaurant des Bains et des Gorges[12], fascinated by the range of medication laid out alongside the plates on the other tables. There are other hotels in Amélie that I suspect provide similar entertainment – portending perhaps the future for us all.

---

[12] http://tinyurl.com/hotelbainsgorges

Days 49 to 51 Amélie-les-Bains to Banyuls-sur-Mer

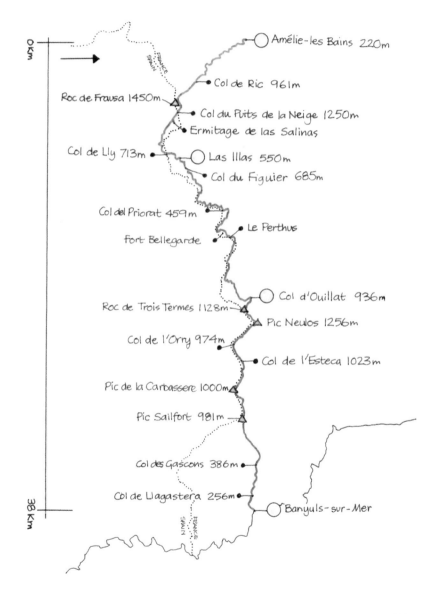

Day 49 Amélie-les-Bains to Las Illas (550m)

Google overview map: trekthepyrenees.com – Days 49-51 Amélie-les-Bains to Banyuls-sur-Mer

Can Felix

Trekking Map: Rando Carte de Randonnées, 1:50000, 11 Roussillon

Via: a) HRP southeast to Can Felix and Col del Ric (961m) to where the GR10 joins below Roc de Frausa (1,450m)

b) GR10 skirting north of Roc de Frausa to Col du Puits de la Neige (1,250m)

c) HRP southeast to Ermitage de Las Salinas (on map, Refuge des Salines)

d) Dirt road southeast, then east and northeast (contouring round the mountain) to Col de Lly (713m) on the frontier

e) North on path descending to Las Illas

Guidebooks: Véron HRP. *Also relevant:* Joosten HRP (from Roc de Frausa)

Recognised trails: HRP with short section on GR10

Approximate distance: 22 km

Climbing: 1,400m   *Descending:* 750m   *Total time:* 9.25 hours

This is a fascinating hike, much of it on old tracks. Don't be surprised on the ascent if you hear a horn and dogs in the distance. It will be a *sanglier* (wild boar) hunt. Otherwise, on the old path through the woods past Can Felix it might seem as if you are the only people in the world. The short section on the GR10 winds through an elegant beech forest as it skirts the Roc de Frausa. You may instead go via the summit of Roc de Frausa by continuing straight ahead (south) from the GR10 junction, then turning left along the frontier ridge

Whichever route is taken, progress seems slow from Amélie to the Col du Puits de la Neige, but unless you are horribly late you should take refreshment down the other side in Spain, at the Ermitage de Las Salinas which has a wonderful almost-medieval atmosphere. In 2013 we threw caution to the wind as we took well over an hour to sample *charcuteries* and associated goodies there. In September it tends to be open only at weekends and special occasions on other days. In 2013, we visited on Catalonia Day[13] – September 11.

You should make much faster time to the frontier at Col de Lly on a dirt road, with parts of the Mediterranean coast now clearly in sight. The col is just off the dirt road to the left and was another 20th century refugee crossing. Memorial plaques on the Col are dedicated to the President and Prime Minister of the Republic of Spain, and the Presidents of the Basque Country and Catalonia. They passed through on 5 February, 1939 in the aftermath of the Spanish Civil War.

Now head north down the path to Las Illas, which is definitely in France despite its name. The village boasts both a *gîte d'étape*[14] and the hotel, Hostal dels Trabucayres[15]. Given that the former does not provide meals (you may cook your own), we have always stayed in the latter. It has bags of charm in an old-fashioned way, including no en suite rooms, and also has a plaque on its wall telling of the passage of the aforementioned presidents in 1939.

In 2013, we were reunited at the hotel with our French friends and a young German couple we had met previously. Bonding through aperitifs and dinner together resulted in more being drunk than intended. The better known sweet red wine – Banyuls – had replaced Maury as the aperitif of choice.

Days 48 and 49 Alternative Itinerary

Google overview map: trekthepyrenees.com – Days 49-51 Amélie-les-Bains to Banyuls-sur-Mer

Trekking Maps: Rando Carte de Randonnées, 1:50,000, 10 Canigou ; Rando Carte de Randonnées, 1:50000, 11 Roussillon

Guidebook: Joosten HRP, Lucia GR10

Recognised trails: GR10 and HRP

This two-day alternative follows the GR10 down to Arles-sur-Tech and then climbs the far side of the valley, meeting the Véron HRP route below Roc de Frausa. Joosten uses this route for the HRP traverse. It is a longer trek and involves more toil. Accommodation is also much more limited than in Amélie-les-Bains. To be blunt, I don't think it's worth the effort, but if you want to try it, it's clearly shown on the 1:50,000 maps. Your overnight stay at the end of

---

[13] http://tinyurl.com/catalonia-day
[14] http://tinyurl.com/gitelasillas
[15] http://tinyurl.com/hostaldelstrabucayre

Day 48 should be the *gîte d'étape du* Moulin de la Palette[16], above and about four hours beyond the village of Arles-sur-Tech, in the valley.

Day 50 Las Illas to Col d'Ouillet (936m)

Google overview map: trekthepyrenees.com – Days 49-51 Amélie-les-Bains to Banyuls-sur-Mer

Trekking Map: Rando Carte de Randonnées, 1:50,000, 11 Roussillon

Via: a) GR10 generally northeast to Le Perthus, mostly on dirt road with some tarmac and one short stretch on footpath

b) D71 east out of Le Perthus, then dirt roads and paths generally northeast

Guidebooks: Joosten HRP, Véron HRP, Lucia GR10 (although none of these describes the new well marked alternative that avoids following the D71 all the way from Le Perthus)

Cork tree above Le Perthus

Recognised trails: HRP/GR10

Approximate distance: 27 km

Climbing: 1,000m   *Descending:* 580m   *Total time:* 9.25 hours

The Joosten guidebook describes today as 'an unpleasant walk', Véron 'without doubt the least interesting of all', and everyone is rude about Le Perthus. What you need, however, is imagination wherever you may be. When we did the tramp in 2013 we found many interesting things that aroused our curiosity. For example:

---

[16] http://ecogitedetape66.com/

- The attempt at corporate responsibility of the *sanglier* hunters, whose plaque (photo Chapter 2) informs that they have provided a picnic area at the side of the dirt road;

- The sign announcing a Naturist Lodge at Mas Nou, and the rules concerning anybody who might consider trespassing;

- A prize pig showing off its body opposite the Naturist Lodge, and even posing for a photograph – presumably it is exempted from the rules;

- The signpost by the France-Spanish border stone 565, disputed by the Catalan defacement, which reads, 'Ni França, Ni Espanya' (Neither France nor Spain – photo Chapter 2);

- The cork trees meticulously stripped of their bark, providing a livelihood for someone somewhere and a natural habitat for the Iberian lynx.

- The Fort de Bellegarde, above Le Perthus, which was built in the 17th century. It featured in wars with Spain during that period, and again during the Second World War where the German Gestapo used it as a base;

- The chequered history of Le Perthus itself as a frontier crossing between Spain and France. A British cinema newsreel – Pathé News – captured the moment in 1939 when thousands of Spanish refugees crossed here in the aftermath of the Spanish Civil War[17].

Le Perthus comprises mostly a string of supermarkets and other shops lining the main drag. Heavy traffic still crawls through, even though the France-Spain 'Catalan Highway' now passes above on stilts. The town appears, however, to be a long way past its sell-by date, that is to say, somewhat down-at-heel.

Leaving the town east on the D71, go through the underpass of the Catalan Highway (A17), where the thunder of traffic above is a useful reminder of the fast lane of a life that has been avoided for a few weeks. You may then walk along the D71 all the way to Col d'Ouillat, but better is to turn right off it a few metres after the underpass onto a waymarked path. Follow the waymarks and signposts and you will reach your destination, barely touching the road on a few occasions.

The Chalet (*gîte d'étape*) de l'Albère[18] at the Col d'Ouillat is a wonderful place in the sunshine, but in the rain (the first time we visited in 2006) its wooden structures exude a miserable, damp smell in sympathy. We have enjoyed the best *charcuterie* ever there at the start of dinner.

You should have an early night as tomorrow to Banyuls-sur-Mer is a hard day.

---

[17] http://tinyurl.com/newsreelrefugee
[18] http://tinyurl.com/chaletalber

Day 51 Col d'Ouillet to Banyuls-sur-Mer

Google overview map:
trekthepyrenees.com
– Days 49-51
Amélie-les-Bains to
Banyuls-sur-Mer

Trekking Map:
Rando Carte de
Randonnées,
1:50,000, 11
Roussillon

Via: GR10 and a)
Pic Neulos (1,256m)

Above Banyuls-sur-Mer, from the Col des Gascons

b) Cols de L'Orry (974m) and de l'Esteca (Col de l'Estague) (1023m)

c) Pic des Quatre Termes (1,156m) and Pic de Carbassere (1000m), but the path avoids the summit of both

d) Pic Sailfort (981m)

e) Col de Baillaury (418m) and the path that goes northeast from the dirt road, rejoining it at Col des Gascons (386m)

f) Road and waymarked shortcuts to Col de Llagastera (256m)

g) GR10 waymarks to Banyuls

Guidebooks: Joosten HRP, Véron HRP, Lucia GR10

Recognised trails: HRP/GR10 all the way (except for our faster variant at the start, to Col de L'Orry)

Approximate distance: 29 km

Climbing: 650m   *Descending:* 1,600m

Total time: 9.5 hours

A tough trek, a bit like a head-butt from a small but nasty thug, ends the traverse. For us in both 2006 and 2013, the start was uninviting, being damp, cool and gusty in thick mist. In these circumstances, rather than the GR10 along the frontier ridge, it's faster and easier to take the dirt road (initially tarmac) that contours below the French side of Pic Neulos, eventually joining the GR10 at the Col de l'Esteca/Estague. You may also join the GR10 sooner by branching off the dirt road to take a path the short distance to the Col de l'Orry, which is what Angharad and I did.

The mist does usually clear gradually through the morning and, by the time you reach the final summit, the Pic Sailfort, a warm sun should be shining. The climb towards this summit provides the first sight of the day of the Mediterranean coast curving north, while from the top you can see Banyuls-sur-Mer nestling far below.

The initial descent from the Pic Sailfort is steep, so be careful – no accidents please on this of all days. On reaching the Col des Gascons, with Banyuls-sur-Mer now in full view (although still at least 90 minutes away), everything suddenly feels real. The previous weeks have not been a dream. Barring an accident, you know that you will make it. As long as joints are still in full working order, you quicken your stride as you pass through the vineyards that may have supplied the aperitif of the previous two days. The intoxication at the moment, however, is the thought of the end. It will almost certainly be sunny and warm, even hot.

The way through the back streets of Banyuls-sur-Mer is inauspicious, but suddenly there is the sea. You do the traditional thing, taking off your boots and dipping your feet.

When we did this in 2006, the water was cool, and suddenly all we could think about was the stones beneath our feet. In 2013, we forsook the ritual. Instead, we bumped into two of our French friends and went to the nearest cafe on the seafront for a beer. Our real highlight came two hours later as we met the full gang for a last supper together. It was warm enough to sit outside and there are no prizes for guessing the aperitif, which was placed on the table in a large carafe. It was a fine convivial occasion, which I describe in Chapter 5. To repeat myself again, friendships forged in the Pyrenees are always intense, but can they ever last?

We have found the Hotel Les Elmes[19] about 1km out of the town centre on the coast road heading north to be a cut above anything else in the vicinity.

Top tips from Chapter 9

1. If, when in Andorra, you are accommodated along the main highway (as is likely), have cash available for taxi rides to and from start and finish points of the daily trek.

2. The ultimate goal is not to reach the top of the mountain, but to still be trekking in your 80s.

3. Sometimes when you have a choice between GR10 and HRP, both ending up in the same place, the former may involve harder work.

---

[19] http://www.hotel-des-elmes.com/en/

10
Do it

'Do it' is a simple instruction to act on an ambition or a dream. It is a suitable title for the final chapter. After all, there would have been little point in writing the book if it did not lead to at least serious consideration of turning a more or less vague initial idea in your mind into a reality, in other words, of going for it yourself.

Is the instruction, however, *so* simple? To me it begs three basic questions. Firstly there is the question of personal rationale – *why* do you want to do 'it'? Then there's the practical side – *how* are you going to do 'it'? Finally, *what* is this 'it' anyway? The answer to the last question might seem obvious – 'it' is the traverse of the Pyrenees from coast to coast; surely? Well, yes, but there are many possible answers that go beyond the obvious.

The *why* and *how* questions form the basis of the 'Do it your way' section that follows immediately. Then comes my personal answer to the *what* question to wind up the book. Your answer will probably be different – but not too different, I hope!

Do it your way – with a plan

Here I take further the idea implicit in the previous four chapters of customising the traverse to your own circumstances. I make practical the notion of treating the traverse of the Pyrenees as 'a concept' that you continually adapt both in your pre-planning and each day on the trek.

I build on the routes that I describe in Chapters 6-9, in which my preferred route represents what I would attempt to do if I decided to embark on a third traverse (it's always a possibility!). I stress the word 'my' because it is not necessarily anybody else's ideal, and, of course I might adapt it as I go along, especially if bad weather kicks in.

Thus, 'my preferred route' provides a kind of model, which you may treat as literally or as metaphorically as you like. Taking it literally means that you decide that it also describes the route you wish to follow, and that's absolutely fine. Treating it metaphorically means that you use it as a starting point for thinking about the route that you would really like to do. This might mean some minor adaptations from my 'ideal'; major adaptations; or even rethinking the whole concept. Also note that Chapters 6-9 provide variations for you to consider that cover one or more days. In other words my preferred route model acts as a kind of tool for helping you plan your own traverse.

I find planning the traverse an absorbing task. Possibly that's because, from an early age, I have enjoyed poring over large-scale maps, especially those of Britain that are produced by the Ordnance Survey. On the other hand, if I'm looking for information about a possible route in the Pyrenees, I find that searching the Internet can be a frustrating experience, although I go through with it.

In planning the trek, you need first to ask yourself some questions, based on *why* and *how* as introduced above. The answers to these questions will form your criteria and, armed with them, the plan will fall into place relatively easily. Yours might differ, but I think the fundamental questions to ask are:

Why do I want to do it?

Because it's there? Because I want a rewarding experience? Because I want to escape for a while from my usual life? Because I want to prove something to myself? Because of some or all of these reasons combined? Do I have a different reason? Your answers will help to determine your attitude towards many aspects of the traverse, for example to accepting lifts or taking taxis or buses on sections that require a tramp along tarmac, or taking easier or more difficult variants. In general they provide a starting point for answering the *how* questions.

How am I going to do it?

The questions that link to 'how' are potentially many. These are the ones that I ask myself.

Am I seeking staffed accommodation every night, or am I planning to camp or stay in unstaffed *cabanes* and refuges, or indeed a mixture of the two?

The answer to this question depends to a large extent on further sub-questions, such as (see Chapter 3):

- How flexible do I want to be?
- How much weight am I prepared to carry?
- How gregarious do I want to be?
- How much money am I prepared to spend on accommodation?

Do I wish to attempt the traverse as one continuous line, starting at Hendaye and finishing at Banyuls-sur-Mer, or is it a broken line, completed over two or more visits?

If the latter, you need to determine suitable break points in terms of when and where. Also, if a broken line, do you want to do it in logical order, or like a jigsaw as we did from 2001-2006? Again, there are possible sub-questions, for example:

- What is my budget? The fewer visits, the lower the travel cost

- How long do I want to be away from home on any single trip? It's obvious, but the longer you are prepared to be away on a trip, the more you can do.

- What other commitments do I have? Angharad and I have had at various times work, home and garden, and grandchildren commitments that have limited our maximum Pyrenean trips to three weeks.

- What do I know about myself in terms of physical and mental stamina? Although you will have 'low' days, overall the traverse should not become a treadmill, or threaten a desperate fear of failure. Nor should it be something to be endured and never enjoyed.

One possibility is to test the water by trekking a short stretch of the traverse over, say, a week. This is what we did in 2001 and, because it was amid the highest of the *Hautes Montagnes*, it gave us the confidence to tackle the rest. Note that our first traverse was over seven visits and not in logical order; our second over three visits, but in logical order. We have never done it in one fell swoop and I occasionally regret that (but not enough to make me dwell on it).

How many days would I ideally like to take overall, bearing in mind that, once started, I will have to be flexible?

We once met an Englishman, above Roncesvalles, in the Basque Country. He was following the GR11 guidebook and was, after only a few days, already one day behind schedule. You shouldn't plan the traverse as a route march on which extra effort will enable a faster journey overall.

How many hours on average do I wish to be on the trail each day, and what is my upper limit?

Personally, I would call a long day on the trail anything over nine hours (including stops). Some long days are inevitable and we have on occasion trekked for more than 12 hours, but I feel that such occasions should not be the norm. For me, an 0800 start, arriving at the night-stop by 1700, is good. It gives a chance to sort your bed, shower and wind down before dinner, including taking in the ambience. If you arrive by 1600 on a fine day you also have chance to do some hand-washing and get laundry dry on hot rocks.

Am I going to build in rest and/or restful days and, if so, where and when?

I have already offered my opinion that I consider complete rest days to be a waste of time unless you are ill or have to break off for some practical task, such as to find a cash machine down the valley or a shop to stock up on provisions. Even then, depending on the logistics of what you want to do, such tasks might not take all day. I prefer restful – that is short and easy – days. Even if you take a complete rest day, my experience is that you will end up going for a walk anyway. After all, that is what you're wired to do, so you might as well put it to good effect and trek even a short distance along the route. On the 'where and when' question, restful days are best following particularly tough stretches, for example Day 35 on my preferred Red Route in Chapter 8. If you are doing the traverse over two or more visits, it's a good idea if the first day of each trip is planned as restful acclimatisation, as well as providing a buffer to deal with unforeseen delays in getting there.

Do I intend to create my own route?

If you are following one of the established traverses – GR10, GR11 or HRP – the requisite directional guidebook that provides step-by-step instructions is very useful, and if that set route is the GR10 or GR11, the white-red paint flashes are indispensable. If the objective, however, is to get from one coast to the other across the mountains, you will not necessarily want to follow the guidebook slavishly or subject yourself every minute of the day to the tyranny of the waymarks. That said, whatever you choose to do, inevitably you will find yourself on these established routes for long periods simply because they go in the right direction. Moving between them requires thought and the map, but there are several trans-frontier trails with fascinating histories.

From questions and criteria to detailed planning

You probably have other questions you want to ask of yourself and trekking companion(s). However, whether you ask the same questions as those above, variations of them, or devise new ones, the important thing is to give some provisional answers so you may plan in detail.

In addition to this book, there are two main sources for detailed planning:

1. The walking maps. See Chapter 4. Although I have said that the 1:50,000 maps are adequate you might wish also to purchase some 1:25,000 maps where these are available, especially those that cover wild, lonely country. For example, the two that I have used most cover part of the near-eastern Pyrenees for the purpose of considering alternative routes to the north and south of the Mont-Roig/Rouch massif:

1:25,000 Institut Geographique National (IGN) map 2048OT *Aulus-les-Bains and St Valier* (the north, French, side);

1:25,000 Editorial Alpina, Mapa-Guia Excursionista, *Pic d'Estats Mont Roig Vall Ferrera Vall de Cardós* (the south, Spanish, side).

Apart from these two exceptions (see also the maps section of the Appendix), use 1:25,000 maps for planning purposes and not necessarily to take with you unless you intend to explore the region a little, rather than simply pass through on the traverse. Compare the line of footpaths on them with those on the 1:50,000 maps.

Of course, the prime purpose of the 1:50,000 maps that you do take is to navigate on the day. We also use them, however, for detailed as well as general planning. Thus, before you set off, or even while still at home, you may check and trace the routes provided in Chapters 6-9 on them. Alternatively, you may use the maps to adapt specific routes from these chapters, often to make them easier. One example of the latter is the final Day 51 described in Chapter 9, where a fast and easy dirt road that is shown on the map may be taken at the start instead of the GR10 path. In general terms, when planning, a map provides the inspiration for a Plan B if the intended trek is not practical, because of bad weather for example.

2. The Internet. You may of course use the Internet to search blogs and so forth to check the experiences of others on the traverse, to see how they have coped with different stretches. We have tended to use it more for information about routes that we have identified, but which are not described in the current directional guidebooks. In other words, we are looking for information about routes that are not the GR10, GR11 or HRP, although they are likely to be trans-frontier trails which connect these. Of course, we also use the Internet for checking accommodation, where being adept at using your favourite search engine will take you to the appropriate websites without fuss.

Personally, I find searching the Internet for new routes a frustrating experience. You are most likely to find 'unofficial' blogs that describe personal experiences, but, as with so much free information on the Internet, they will be of variable quality. You soon obtain a sense, however, of those that are not reliable in their instructions. You might also come across official walking sites that are associated with regional and local government. They may help, especially with details of trans-frontier trails. Note, however, that there is only one *chemin de la liberté* which is commemorated officially each year, although others may attract unofficial gatherings. This 'official' Chemin de la Liberté, which is likely to be prominent in Internet searches, involves a tough three-day trek around Mont Valier in the near-eastern Pyrenees, a mountain that the Pyrenean traverse tends to avoid.

I find myself using different sources in tandem, moving backwards and forwards from one to the other. To illustrate, here is a worked example of my search for a route around the north side of Mont Roig/MontRouch, from Salau in France to Bordes de Graus in Spain, via the Port de Marterat/Tavascan. I undertook the search because our previous forays had involved the 'standard' HRP route around the south side, which is particularly tough and involves wild-camping and staying in an unstaffed refuge. In Chapter 8, I have labelled this latter the 'headbangers route', and coloured it purple! Here is how I went about my search for an alternative.

a) I checked the Véron and Joosten HRP directional guidebooks for alternatives to the standard HRP routes, but there were none. Then I remembered that Véron preferred when possible to trek in France during his early traverses. Thus, I dug out the only English translation of Véron, which was published in 1981 and reprinted in 1991. Sure enough, in it he described among his alternative routes the way from Montgarri in Spain to the Ariège village of Salau, which puts you on the north side of Mont Roig/Rouch. Then for the next day, again among his alternative routes, I discovered the continuation from Salau over the Col de Crusous and Port de Marterat to the Spanish hamlet of Noarre, close to Bordes de Graus. This was a good start, but is probably not open to you, as I suspect that the edition is no longer obtainable (even Amazon said it was unavailable when I checked in May 2015). The description suggested, however, that the route to the *port* was largely pathless until the final section, where it joined what is now a recognised, waymarked trans-frontier trail.

b) I examined the IGN 1:25,000 map OT2048 mentioned above. While the area described by Véron is not completely devoid of paths, they do not add up to a continuous traverse. I did note on the map, however, the Col de Crusous, which has to be crossed according to the Véron description.

c) I did an Internet search to check for more up-to-date information, as follows:

(i) I searched for a trail between my start and end points, that is I keyed in, 'Salau to Bordes de Graus trekking trail'. The top result out of 1,600 was to a site called Muntanyes de Libertat[1] (Mountains of Freedom – see Chapter 1). It described a four-day trek that includes Bordes de Graus, but not Salau. The fourth day was, however, on the trans-frontier trail to

---

[1] http://tinyurl.com/muntanyeslibertat

Bordes de Graus. This was obviously relevant but the link to Day 4 of the 'Muntanyes de libertat' did not work. The next two search results described another four-day trek, the 'Porta del Cel', which again includes Bordes de Graus but goes nowhere near Salau. I already knew it to be a popular trek that had been created by the *guardien* at the Refugi de Certascan. If you spend any time in the summer at Tavascan, Bordes de Graus, Refugi de Certascan, or Refugi Vall Ferrera you can hardly fail to come across people attempting the Porta del Cel. The fourth search result sent me on a wild goose chase to another region and the fifth provided a PDF file of several hiking routes, but they were impossible to read on screen, even with huge amplification. Nor would they print.

(ii) Substituting 'hiking' for 'trekking' gave much the same results. Substituting Noarre (the hamlet close by) for Bordes de Graus provided a Wicilocs site with walks 'near Salau', none of which was the one I wanted. The will to live started to ebb away at this point.

(iii) I substituted 'Port de Marterat' for 'Bordes de Graus'. My reasoning was that Bordes de Graus is too strongly linked with the Porta del Cel and Muntanyes de Libertat treks, which dominated my search results above. Also, my primary concern was the section from Salau to the *port* only, the descent into Spain from there to Noarre, Bordes de Graus and Tavascan being marked as a waymarked path on the map and straightforward, and one which I had done before. Because I was searching for a route in France, I chose 'Port de Marterat' rather than the Spanish version of the name, 'Port de Tavascan'.

(iv) I had two false starts because I spelled firstly 'Martaret' then 'Martarat'. These searches revealed nothing. Finally realising my mistakes, I spelled 'Marterat' correctly.

(v) The top two results out of 114 took me to what I wanted. They were part of a website belonging to 'the bordermarkers of the Pyrenees'[2], where the information I needed was on a page entitled Section 35[3].

Bordermarkers of the Pyrenees is a personal project by a Dutchman called Bef Berns to locate and connect all the Pyrenean border stones as a long distance trail. It's a fascinating website and well worth exploring, if only briefly, for its several features, including links to Google Earth. At the time of my most recent access (June 2015) he had not finished the project and I had to go to his Section 35 – 'All my trips' pages for detailed instructions and useful photographs, where further links to '2013 - August

---

[2] http://www.grpdesbf.nl/index.html
[3] http://tinyurl.com/bordermarker35

– 24 August'[4] took me to where I wanted to be. I discovered crucially that he walked in mist from Salau to the Port de Marterat without becoming lost; that the route is sometimes indistinct; but that it is waymarked with yellow flashes as far as the trans-frontier trail from the hamlet of Bidous. According to Bef, these waymarks are intermittent but also indispensable.

d) With that part of the job done, to my satisfaction and relief, I walked the route with Angharad in July and September 2014. See Chapter 8, Red Route.

While it's well worthwhile looking through Bef Berns' impressive work, do beware of becoming bogged down, sidetracked and distracted. This is very likely on interesting, informative websites. Beware, that is, as long as you don't now intend to throw all previous planning into the waste bin and follow the trail of the Bordermarker!

On the ground (1): the Col de Crusous comes into view from an un-named, vague ridge that is crossed at 1900m en route from the Salau tungsten mine. The route is not straight over the un-named ridge but to the right-hand side (chapter 8).

---

[4] The route is in fact covered by 24 August and 25 August pages. On my latest attempt, however, I accessed 25 August by selecting 'next trip' at the top of the August 24 page because the direct link to 25 August was not working.

On the ground (2): the yellow waymark indicating the route off the Col de Crusous

There are a few lessons I learned from this tale of a 'silver surfer'. There is no exact science to searching the Internet but, from learning the hard way:

A. Be as precise as possible in your search words

B. Ensure that you spell place names correctly, and you might have to try different language spellings for the same spot

C. Give a 'from' and 'to' when searching a route. Otherwise, my editor tells me, Google (and possibly other search engines) will modify the order of the results to where you physically are when conducting the search.

D. Search within one country even if that means that you have to do two separate searches for each half of a route that, for example, passes from France to Spain.

E. Be patient, persistent and methodical

F. If you do find an appropriate site which gives what you want but also much more, do look through it but beware of becoming bogged down, sidetracked and distracted from the task in hand.

G. Finally, if you have a handle on any of these languages, or are willing to use Google Translate with a little care, it's worth searching in French, Spanish, Basque or Catalan as this will throw a different range of results at the top of the search page.

On the ground (3): looking back to the Col de Crusous before descending to the trans-frontier trail coming from Bidous

Between them, this book, maps and judicious use of the Internet should provide the information you need for planning purposes. Should you want more, you might also consult the latest editions of the step-by-step, directional guidebooks to the GR10 (Lucia), GR11 (Johnson) and HRP (Joosten, and Véron if you can read some French.) They are most useful, of course, for checking these standard routes; routes that, as already indicated, you can hardly avoid whatever your intentions. See Chapter 4 of this book for more detail on how we have used them.

Enough of planning, let us now move on to the 'big' *what* questions.

What is 'it'? A place and time to…

To give the glib short answer to this question, I paraphrase the famous lines of the nursery rhyme character Humpty Dumpty in Lewis Carroll's Alice Through The Looking Glass - 'it' means what you choose it to mean. The following is what I choose 'it' to mean:

A place and time to think

'The great gift of walking is that it gives us time to think, letting thoughts and ideas develop at their own speed, at a natural bodily pace.'

These words of Adam Ford in his The Art of Mindful Walking refer to any form of taking a walk, including in city parks. When it comes to walking in high mountains, the exigencies mean that such thinking probably comes mostly at the end of the day, but I'm with Adam in spirit at least.

Of course I think when I'm in other, even sedentary, situations. Yet walking in mountains, especially when I have immersed myself in them for a period of time, as with the traverse of the Pyrenees, has thrown into sharp relief a universal human tension. This is the tension between the unique precious being that I tell myself is me, and my complete insignificance within the scheme of things. The unIque 'I' in the mountains is being on top of the world engaging with nature. The unIque 'I' in the mountains is testing myself to my physical and emotional limits. The unIque 'I' in the mountains has something important to tell others. The unIque 'I' in the mountains is invincible and defies mortality.

On the other hand, the insignificant 'I' in the mountains is nothing, where the mountains don't even bother to show contempt or disdain. They don't care because they can't care. Even human life, my colleagues, my friends and my family, which could care or show interest, don't do so beyond a fleeting engagement. They will congratulate me on my achievement, look at my photographs but never quite engage or fully understand. Without directly experiencing it themselves, they cannot be expected to do so. This particular inadequacy is mine, for I cannot ever communicate adequately what is not shared through experience. I can only communicate to others the sense that *I* make of that experience, and something is always lost in the translation. The only exception is my partner, Angharad, who has shared the experience with me.

On the Pyrenean traverse I have been stimulated to wonder, imagine and make sense of my surroundings more than I ever do in normal life. In the latter, in order to get anything done, so much must be assumed without asking questions, whereas on the traverse the opposite prevails. Yet wonder, imagination and making sense also make me aware of my limits in relation to my physical and mental abilities – and my ability in communication. I am, after all, only human.

The experiences I have had on the traverse have undoubtedly shaped me, the living sentient being. Watching the sun set on an evening from outside the refuge makes my very insignificance feel special as it illuminates the mountains so they appear like the endless waves of a huge ocean. How lucky I am to be here, this speck of humanity. The marmots calling, the herds of shy isards, the frogs by the mountain tarn, the lizards scurrying across the path, the fashion parade of butterflies and the mountain flower meadows – seeing all these makes me wonder who or what I am, and hence to learn about myself.

I have, therefore, been shaped by the traverse of the Pyrenees, but only relatively late in my active life. I am, however, not so insignificant. I in turn shape these mountains when I attempt to make sense of them. Moreover, I shape them literally as well through the impact of my feet on the ground, the air I inhale and whatever I exhale; and the water and other resources I use.

A time and place to share, engage, eat and drink

The ability to wonder, imagine and make sense, of course, is part of what makes me and you human. So too is our ability to communicate and engage socially with each other. Being among the mountains and sharing that being with others simply sharpens those human capabilities, and hence provides gateways to broader and deeper levels of meaning. To paraphrase Nan Shepherd who wrote The Living Mountain in tribute to her immersion in the Cairngorms of Scotland near where she lived (Chapter 1), it is to realise universal truths that spring from local experience in the mountains.

The people I meet, therefore, are integral to the experience. They, who also love these mountains, have their own ways of making sense of them and in turn make me wonder and learn further than I could ever do alone. To adapt a quotation from the French philosopher, novelist and playwright, Albert Camus: 'All that I know most surely about morality and obligations I owe to walking.' Here I have substituted 'walking' for 'football'. As well as all the other things he did, Camus played goalkeeper for the junior team of Racing Universitaire Algerios (RAU – University of Algeria FC) until a bad bout of tuberculosis put paid to any career aspirations in that direction[5].

The adaptation is, I admit, an exaggeration of my own feelings, but it expresses a simple morality of comradeship in shared experience, and of helping one another. This is exactly what I find among the people I meet through trekking in the Pyrenees. To quote from Camus again, this time from his novel The Plague, above all I learn from them that the good outweighs the bad in human beings. They have my profound respect.

---

[5] Some popular T-shirts replace 'morality and obligations' with 'life'. Not being averse to hyperbole, football fans have also widely credited Albert Camus as having played goalkeeper for the Algerian national team, which is wide of the mark. They will be further disappointed by the suggestion from the Camus Appreciation Society that the actual quotation is: 'After many years during which I saw many things, what I know most surely about morality and the duty of man I owe to sport and learned it in the RUA.'

With a French
couple who
offered a lift while
storms were
breaking all
around

People have been kind to us in ways that have moved me deeply. Often it has been the simple offer of a lift in bad weather. At other times it has been on the trail. People have put themselves out for us. Once a Japanaese driver and Jewish family made room by putting two teenage girls in the boot of their car to take us the final kilometres to our destination. On another occasion, feeling exhausted after over 12 hours of tough, lonely trek, a Spanish man wild-camping with his son escorted us a few hundred metres and helped us across the difficult outflow of the lake so that we could reach our destination – the Refugi Enrij Pujol. There was also the time when the *guardienne* and her husband at a French refuge cared for Angharad when she fell ill.

Throughout our trips people have given us fun and companionship. How can I forget the retired British SAS officers, in their 70s, who could clear the dinner table perfectly at a refuge in one minute, having drunk substantial quantities of red wine? They had real style. How could I forget the motorcyclist from the Ariège, who disturbed the peace at the Gîte de Batère and argued with me about 'Anglo-Saxon multiculturalism'? Much of this fun and companionship was fleeting. A few such encounters, however, morphed into friendships, especially with French people on the GR10. With them we learned so much together and about each other through sharing aperitifs made from sweet red wine

Just about everybody whom we met impressed us in their own way, but some people and their acts were amazing – for example, the tour guide we met at the Refugio de la Renclusa, who had carried one of his injured party down the mountain, using his rucksack as a papoose. Also of course, the French couple in their 80s who told us at the refuge breakfast that they were planning that day to take the rough trek to the high mountain pass and back.

Through all of this engagement with one's fellow trekkers, there are, among the fun and light-heartedness, moments of philosophical contemplation. This might be when you sit in silent bond with others outside the Refuge des Oulettes de Gaube after dinner and stare at the glacier adorning the north face of Vignemale, shared in quiet contemplation with many other sojourners. It might also be during conversation, however, such as when we talked about the Pyrenees as mountains of hope and freedom with the two French men for whom Plato was their 'only book'. And of course, we cannot omit the young French man at the Refugi de Certascan who, when we told him that we wished we had attempted the HRP when we were his age, replied: 'I hope I can still do it when I'm your age.' The social contract between young and old still holds in the Pyrenees. (See the start of Chapter 1 of this book).

The moments described above have involved other trekkers. That is inevitable – it is with them that you have a shared experience, even if that experience is sometimes bizarre, such as the early hours snoring scene at the Refugi de Certascan that was accompanied by various attempts to halt it by others in the dormitory.

You meet fewer local people apart from those who provide shelter and nourishment. As you pass through a locality, however, the more astute eyes will catch what is going on beneath the surface. Everywhere has its local politics but mostly you get only hints. As mentioned in Chapter 2, after a hotel dinner in the Ariège, at which the service was found particularly wanting, the North European owner confided wistfully that life with the locals was not easy. In a Spanish valley we discovered a web of dispute between the owner of the mountain, attempts to close a local *refugi* and taxi rights in the village.

In many of our human encounters, food hasn't been far away. Of the hundreds of dinners that we took in the Pyrenees, all bar a few have ranged between good and excellent. Some have been unforgettable, such as the *daube* at the Refuge de Barroude that an English friend described as 'an eight-hour walk for the best meal of my life', the delicious, perfectly cooked food at the Hotel les Jardins de Bakea, and the banquet, including fresh salad and vegetables from the garden, at the Gîte du Presbytère.

Less can be said in praise of breakfasts, especially at refuges, where they are often spartan. An honourable exception, however, was the breakfast at the Gîte du Presbytère.

A time and place to recognise one's limitations

So much for our engagements with others (and the food they produced!). What about us? It never really crossed our minds that we would never complete the traverse, during either 2001-2006 or 2012-2013. However, a few of our longer, rougher, tougher treks pulled us up and made us wonder about our own physical capabilities.

As a result we adapted some of the worst offenders on subsequent visits. For example, we endured the 12-plus hours' trek circumventing the south side of Aneto only once. We now divide it between two days (Chapter 7). The lonely, 11-hours-plus trek on an intermittent path over the Cols de la Cornella, Curios and Calberante to the Refugi Enrij Pujol, and the equally long hours to the Refugi de Certascan the following day now form one of several possible itineraries in this part of the traverse (Chapter 8). More recently, the relatively short 9.5-hour trans-frontier trail over the Port de Marterat/Tavascan had its low moment in 2013 when Angharad declared that she could not hack it any longer and was old and broken. She made it. I think that this particular moment occurred because we had no idea of what was coming next as the path turned in all directions to avoid the impenetrable. Now we think of it as delightful (Chapter 8).

On top of fatigue there are inevitably a few places in these high mountains that you feel scared. Rarely, however, is it linked solely to the inherent nature and situation of the spot you are in – as with the tortuous, steep, unstable descent from the Col de La Cornella, where you know that if you fall and incapacitate yourself it could be a long time before you are found. More often, the time of day and the weather play a significant part. Thus, we were caught once in a vicious thunderstorm on an exposed ridge in the Pyrénées-Occidentales and another time in thick mist and rain on the Hourquette de Héas, where the safe route off that avoided the abyss facing us was not immediately obvious. It is not only current weather that catches you by surprise (and the surprise element plays a large part in the scariness). Weather during days, weeks or months previously may have left its mark. Crossing two unexpected, corniced snowfields before a pass late in the afternoon, where a slide will tip you directly into the lakes below is not the best place to be. If you hear thunder claps while making your traverse of a snowfield, the adrenalin flow is greater.

A time and place to stare

Some places are exciting rather than scary, such as the Passage d'Orteig. Yes, you are walking along a ledge on a rock face and there is an abyss below, but you also have a hand cable. Other places excite because of their surrounding rather than any immediate potential danger. The first distant sight of high mountains from Lindux in the Basque Country, the summit of the Petit Vignemale and the close-up views of its big glaciated brother, the distant sight of the Refugi Enrij Pujol across a wild, lonely glaciated landscape, the hike along the Catalonian frontier ridge accompanied by a pair of eagles: these and many more create a succession of moments that stop you in your tracks.

Excitement spills in my thoughts to beauty. The Pyrenees are beautiful throughout, the scale of which is such as to shrug off Pas de la Casa, La Pierre St-Martin, the Col d'Ibardin and lesser intrusions where the human hand has been very visible. And they are so variable in their beauty. It feels like a profound deprivation not to have the time to stop and stare. You start in the Basque Country with its quiet, gentle charms and villages where you feel you could spend your savings on a property. After about ten days you suddenly gain, as you reach the top of the Pas de l'Osque, the first close-up view of real mountains – the pristine Pic d'Anie and its satellites. It is complemented by the eastern mountain panorama and the first sight of the Pic du Midi d'Ossue willing you forward to see, in three more days, its reflection in the lake in front of the Refuge d'Ayous. From here, it's another four days of stunning scenery before you have views of the Cirque de Gavarnie, which completes the Pyrénées-Occidentales. On the way you cannot miss the unfolding views of the Vignemale all the way up the Valle de Gaube to the Hourquette d'Ossue.

The Pyrénées-Centrales bring you the classic mountain Cirques d'Estaube and de Troumouse, the Posets, Maladetta and Aneto massifs and the Encantats, surrounded by valleys harbouring countless small lakes. Then suddenly you have crossed the Garona and are heading for Montgarri, in its tranquil setting in the higher reaches of the valley of the Noguera Pallaresa. The valley follows

The Pays Basque: descending La Rhune on the HRP on Day 2 of the traverse

the line of the frontier ridge above it, and you cross this next day to see Mont Roig/Rouch soaring above the French Ariège.

In the valleys you now come across many species of butterfly to add to an already colourful scene, while higher up, in the hanging valleys, wild flower meadows may still be in bloom. A few days further on, you cross into Andorra amid jagged mountains, while, looking back, you strain to make out snow-covered Aneto, which you have left behind

Then you cross the higher reaches of the main Ariège valley to enter the Pyrénées-Orientales with the vast landscapes through which you pass and 360-degrees panoramas that you gain from the summits of the Pic Noufonts on the Catalan ridge and the Pic du Canigou. In a few days it will be all over, but not before you have been arrested by the sight of the sweep of the Mediterranean and its bays on the approach to the final Pic Sailfort.

A time and space to come to terms

When you start this trek by the Atlantic Ocean, the mountains, their valleys, lakes, streams and people are both physically and mentally distant. Somewhere among the lonely recesses of the near-eastern Pyrenees I awoke one morning to a realisation that had been creeping up on me – I had not conquered these mountains but become part of them and they had become part of me. They have become the story I tell about myself, a story that is very different from my life in the 'real' world. I have become, in a way, my own anti-reality show.

This realisation reinforces what Nan Shepherd wrote about the Cairngorm mountains in Scotland: the whole range was her 'living mountain', not the individual summits. The same is true for me of the Pyrenees. I have come to terms with these mountains, and through doing so, with myself.

The realisation also reinforces Robert Macfarlane's notion that mountains are places that engender wonder. I add to Shepherd and Macfarlane, however, by including human life in the mountains – from those who live there to those who visit them – as a central ingredient. People are of course present in these books through anecdotes and when recording historical exploration, but they are not presented as a core, integral part. Especially, what I would add is the central idea that people create their truths about the Pyrenees through conversation with one another.

In another book – *Wanderlust: a history of walking*, by Rebecca Solnit – the author presents the case that walking is fundamental to being human, and not only because the simple physical fact of doing so for pleasure, on two legs, separates us from other animals. Walking upright crucially frees the hands to do other things. Generally it frees us to work with them, to labour, but for this potential to be realised it requires a concomitant evolution of the brain to think about the purposes to which we put our hands.

The causal chain of events – walking, freedom for hands to labour, realisation of freedom through brain evolution – is a bit too linear for my liking, but a messy version of it rings true. The human brain did not, however, stop at working with our hands. It went further, enabling us to reflect on our whole lives, not just those parts of life that are connected with labour. It also enabled us to evolve sophisticated forms of communication with other humans.

For the German philosopher Jürgen Habermas, the ability to labour, reflect and communicate makes us human. Rebecca Solnit reminds us that somewhere in this equation lies our simple ability to walk. This is why I love traversing the Pyrenees on foot. It demonstrates the most fundamental human attributes: I walk, therefore I am; I use my hands to put on boots and sometimes mini-crampons, to hold walking poles, open maps and set a compass bearing, therefore I am. I reflect on what I experience, or wonder, as Robert Macfarlane puts it, therefore I am; I share my wonder with others, therefore I am. The process is simplicity itself and because of that it reclaims an innocence that I lost during my working life, when I always had to be 'strategic', to have my own 'agenda', either for personal gain or for the gain of my work group. No wonder that another philosopher, French this time, Michel Foucault, once declared that all strategy was cynical.

Of course, you don't have to traverse the Pyrenees to realise these things, but it certainly brings them into sharp relief. Passing through these mountains of grand scale and grand history, there is so much to wonder, imagine and engage with others about, and so little to be strategic about. Trekking through them 'makes it possible to recover the pure sensation of being, to rediscover the simple joy of existing', as Frédéric Gros puts it in his book, A Philosophy of Walking.

As I write these words I have just returned from an exhibition at the Yorkshire Sculpture Park in northern England. Entitled Uncommon Ground, it comprises works from artists who formed the British land art movement

What are they? Why are they there? Also discovered by the Bordermarker, near-identical engravings appear on several rocks on the lonely, wild trail between Salau and the Cabane de Marterat in the French Ariège (Chapter 8 day 34)

during my formative adult years, 1966-1979. This movement treats walking as a 'creative activity', while one of the contributing artists, Richard Long, describes it as 'simple, practical, emotional, quiet art'. Traversing the Pyrenees fits these descriptions perfectly because, without even trying, it inspires wonder, fires the imagination and sparks conversation. That, surely, is one of the basic functions of all art.

You can do it, so do it

What then does this book add up to? Hopefully, from what I have written above, many things beyond the sense of the physical and mental fortitude required to do the traverse. Through unforgettable moments that are wired into my being, they return to me time and time again whenever and wherever I think about the Pyrenees.

You who are about to embark on this adventure also deserve a complete experience, so create one out of the simple joys and emotions it engenders on the one hand and the complicated thoughts and eternal questions that burst your mind on the other. Create an experience with the Pyrenees as the backdrop rather than this or that individual summit, and understand these mountains as a human story as well as a story of rocks and glaciers. It will be a fantastic experience and your experience. Who knows, you might give them the ultimate accolade and endorsement by doing the traverse all over again. *What is 'It'?* The answer isn't out there, but within ourselves.

Leaving the Refuge de Mariailles, perhaps to climb Canigou (Chapter 9, Day 46)

End words…

Thank you for reading and using my book. If you enjoyed it, I'd be really pleased if you would take a moment to leave me a review at your favourite retailer.

To find out a bit more about me, what I do in another life and books I have published there, go to my website: www.trekthepyrenees.com

This book is also available as an e-book, while chapters 6-9 are available as a separate 'on the trail' guide in ring-bound format. See the above website for further information.

Remember finally that all profits arising from the combined sales of this book, and its e-book and related versions will be donated to mountain charities, especially those associated with the Pyrenees.

Thanks again! Gordon Wilson

Glossary

Please note:

1. This is NOT a dictionary, but an eclectic selection of words and phrases that will be useful for the traverse. Most of them have appeared in the main text or on maps.

2. I have used, with a few exceptions, the spelling for adjectives that describe masculine, singular nouns. Feminine and plural forms of adjectives will have recognisable but slightly different spellings.

3. In a few cases I have not been able to locate the language from which a word derives. Rather than hazard an informed guess, I have simply commented, 'language not identified'.

Mountains
Montagnes (French), montañas (Spanish), muntanyes (Catalan),
Cimes (local French and Catalan), cima (local Spanish)
Sierra (Spanish)
High mountains - hautes montagnes (French)

Mountain peak
Mont (French, Spanish)
Pic (French, Catalan),
Pico (Spanish)
Tuc/Tusse (language not identified)

Flat area
Pla (French, Catalan), plan (Catalan), plat (French), prat (Catalan)

Valley
Gave, vallée (French), valle (Spanish), vall (Catalan)

Lake
Lac (French), lago (Spanish)
Small lake (tarn) – laquet (language not identified), étang (French, Catalan), estany (Catalan), ibón (Spanish)
Reservoir - embalse (Spanish), réservoir (French)

River
Fleuve (French), rio (Spanish), riu (Catalan), noguera (Catalan)
Stream – ruisseau (French), rierol (Spanish, Catalan)
River bank – rive (French), riba (Spanish), orilla (Spanish)
River bridge – pont (French, Catalan)), puente (Spanish), pontet (language not identified), passerelle (French – specifically a footbridge)

Mountain pass
Col (French), collada, collet (language not identified)

Hourquette (French)
Lepoa (Basque)
Pas (French, Catalan), paso (Spanish)
Port, portillon (French, Catalan), puerto (Spanish), porteille (French)

Footpath, 'dirt road', 'Way'
General term for 'way' – chemin (French)
Dirt road/without tarmac -- Piste (French), pista (Spanish, Catalan)
Footpath – sentier (French), senda (Spanish, Catalan)

Path features
Boggy, swampy – marécageux (French), pantanoso (Spanish), pantanós (Catalan)
Easy – facile (French), fàcil (Spanish, Catalan)
Gentle/light – léger, doux (French), suaves (Spanish), suaus (Catalan)
Hard/tough – dur (French, Catalan), duro (Spanish)
Hairpins, zig-zags – lacets (French, literally shoelaces), curvas (Spanish), corbes (Catalan)
'Rock chimney' (scrambling route) – cheminée (French)
Rocky – rocheux (French), rocoso (Spanish), rocós (Catalan)
Scree – éboulis (French), pedregal (Spanish), pedregar (Catalan)
(Quite) steep – (assez) raide (French)

Hiking, trekking
Hike or trek – randonnée (French), senderismo (Spanish, Catalan)
A ramble – une balade

Accommodation
Simple shelter with no facilities except for a platform or bunk bed and sometimes a water source close by – abri, cabane, cabine, orri (French), cabina (Spanish, Catalan)
Mountain refuge (staffed or unstaffed) – refuge (French), refugi (Catalan), refugio (Spanish)
Private rural accommodation in various buildings (meals provided and/or cooking facilities) - gîte d'étape (French)
Room in private accommodation (usually no meals or cooking facilities) - casa rurale (Spanish), casa rural (Catalan), chambre de hôte (French)
Inn - auberge (French), hostal (Catalan), posada (Spanish)
Hotel – hôtel (French), hotel (Spanish, Catalan)

Animals
Chough - crave à bec rouge (French), chova (Spanish), gralla (Catalan)
Eagle – aigle (French), águila (Spanish, Catalan)
Vulture – vautour (French), buitre (Spanish), voltor (Catalan)
Marmot – marmotte (French), marmota (Spanish, Catalan)
No to the bears! - Non aux ours! (French Pyrenees grafitti)

Pyrenean sheep guard dog – patou (French)
Snake – serpent (French), serpiente (Spanish), serp (Catalan)
Wild boar – sanglier (French), jabali (Spanish), senglar (Catalan)
Wild sheep – mouflon (French), muflón (Spanish), mufló (Catalan)
Wolf – loup (French), lobo (Spanish), llop (Catalan)

Greeting, leaving and appreciation

Good day – Bonjour (French), Buenos Dias (Spanish), Bon Dia (Catalan)
Good evening – Bonsoir (French), Buenas Tardes (Spanish), Bona Tarda (Catalan)
Goodnight – Bonne Nuit (French), Buenas Noches (Spanish), Bona Nit (Catalan)
See you later/ until we meet again/ goodbye for now – A toute à l'heure (French), Hasta Luego (Spanish)
Goodbye – Au Revoir (French), Adiós (Spanish), Adéu (Catalan)
Thank you – Merci (French), Gracias (Spanish), Gràcies (Catalan)

Selected Bibliography

Selected titles in English, except for Georges Véron's French HRP guidebook.

Guidebooks to the Pyrenees

Brian Johnson 2014. *The GR11 Trail: The Spanish Pyrenees 'La Senda'*. Cicerone.

Paul Lucia 2004. *The GR10 Trail: Through the French Pyrenees*. Cicerone.

Ton Joosten 2009. *Pyrenean Haute Route: High-Level Trail through The Pyrenees*. Cicerone.

Kev Reynolds 2004. *The Pyrenees: The High Pyrenees from the Cirque de Lescun to the Carlit Massif*. Cicerone.

Georges Véron 2003. *Haute Randonnée Pyrénéenne*. RANDO éditions.

Autobiographical accounts of trekking, climbing and exploring in the Pyrenees

Hilaire Belloc 1909 *The Pyrenees*. Nabu Public Domain Reprints.

Simon Calder and Mick Webb 2004. *Backpacks, Boots and Baguettes: Walking in the Pyrenees*. Virgin Books Ltd.

Steve Cracknell 2009. *If You Only Walk Long Enough: Exploring the Pyrenees*. Lulu.com

Robin Fedden 2000. *The Enchanted Mountains: A Quest in the Pyrenees*. The Ernest Press.

David Le Vay 2012. *The hairy hikers: A Coast-to-Coast Trek Along the French Pyrenees*. Summersdale Publishers ltd.

Mountains of hope and freedom? Refugees and war in the Pyrenees

Rosemary Bailey 2009.*Love and War in the Pyrenees: a Story of Courage, Fear and Hope 1939-1944*. Phoenix.

Edward Stourton 2013. *Cruel Crossing: Escaping Hitler Across the Pyrenees* Transworld Publishers.

Walking and mountains as history and philosophy

Adam Ford 2011. *The Art of Mindful Walking: Meditations on the Path*. Leaping Hare Press.

Frédéric Gros 2014 *A philosophy of walking*. Translated into English by John Howe. Verso.

Robert Macfarlane 2008. *Mountains of the Mind: A History of a Fascination*. Granta Books.

Nan Shepherd (with an Introduction by Robert Macfarlane) 1977, 1996 and 2011. *The Living Mountain: A Celebration of the Cairngorm Mountains in Scotland*. Canongate

Rebecca Solnit 2001 *Wanderlust: A History of Walking*. Verso.

Appendix: Gear, maps and first aid

As used by us on our second traverse 2012-2013

The contents of the rucksack and what I wear

See also the Travelling Light section in Chapter 3. The table indicates what I carried. A comparison with what Angharad carried is given underneath.

Item(s)	Comments
Rucksack	With whistle attached to strap. 45 litres and lightweight at around 1kg (700g lighter than my previous rucksack of similar size).
Head torch	Light and compact. Indispensable when you need to get up in the middle of the night at a refuge.
Wash kit	Shaving stick doubling as ordinary soap, shaving brush, disposable razors (one per week), toothbrush, small tube of toothpaste, small cotton flannel. Light wash bag.
Travel towel	I used to take a very small cotton towel and dry it on the outside of the rucksack each day. However, those made of technical fabric have improved in recent years
Paperwork	Passport, travel and accommodation documents, money and cards.

Overview map	We have a map that shows the whole range (Chapter 4). Its scale is 1:250,000. While no use for trekking, it does show all roads and the area either side of the Pyrenees, so is useful if you need to remove yourself from the mountains for whatever reason, and for showing your overall progress.
Trekking maps	See Chapter 4 and the section below for the different maps available and their scales. You may discard a map once you have walked it!
Compass	Note that some smartphones may now double as a compass.
iPad mini	This is light (about 300g) and tunes into cellular networks when WiFi is unavailable. (Remember that in the mountains the cellular network is often unavailable too, so don't rely on it.)
	More importantly the iPad holds the electronic versions of the necessary guidebooks except for the French (Véron) HRP guide.
	I also use the notes facility for recording my daily diary.
The Véron HRP guide	I photocopy the sheets I need, trim them to remove excess paper, and discard wherever I find a rubbish bin as I go along. (I know of others who tear and discard the pages that are no longer needed from printed guidebooks.) This is a great guide, but only if you can read French. You could equally scan the pages and not take hard copies.
Mobile phone	Given I have my iPad mini, I use a very light, basic mobile for texting and voice only.
Camera	Again light, and one that is used for diving and therefore water-resistant. Check your battery will last the whole trip.
Water bottles	One one-litre and one half-litre. You can't do without water in the Pyrenees. You may top up from streams, but, especially during prolonged hot, dry periods, they may be at a premium.
Sleeping bag liner	Silk, with pillow cover.
Hiking liner socks	Two pairs of each. Wash/rinse as you go.
Hiking outer socks	
Walking shirts	Thin, short-sleeved. Pockets can be useful. Two pairs only. Wash/rinse as you go.
Walking shorts	Reasonably robust as you sometimes have to go down rocks on your bum. Deep pockets for carrying a map are helpful.
Fleece	Light/medium. You might need to wear it when trekking early in the morning. Otherwise its main use is in the evening.
Light trousers	One pair for evenings. Mine detach at the knees for extra shorts.

Two evening shirts	Short sleeves, light cotton.
Three pairs briefs	Cotton for comfort, 60g each, compared to boxer shorts, which can be over 200g each. Alternatively, my editor recommends special walkers' briefs for long walks to prevent chaffing.
One pair evening socks	Cotton
Sun hat	Light cotton. Essential in the Pyrenees.
Storm jacket	As light and waterproof as possible. It's worthwhile throwing money at one. You will hardly ever need to wear it, but when you do, keeping the rain (and wind) out is paramount.
Over-trousers	**Once again – lightweight.**
Boots	I wear leather boots, weighing 1.8kg for the pair.
Spare pair of boot laces	May sometimes double as washing line if not in use.
Sandals	Cheap, flexible and light for evening wear.
Walking poles	Very light, and telescope like tent poles. See Chapter 4.
Mini-crampons	500g for the pair. See Chapter 4.
Suntan cream & lip salve.	Not too big. You can always buy more.
Paper tissues	Small pack of 50.

The total weight of the rucksack I carry, which contains the above minus the clothes and boots that I am actually wearing, but which includes full water bottles and a picnic, is about 9kg.

For Angharad, the main differences are:

- A heavier but smaller rucksack.

- Paperwork: passport and wallet containing cards and money only.

- The first aid kit (see section below for contents and weight).

- No maps, suntan cream or lip salve (we share what I carry).

- Light Kindle instead of iPad.

- Smartphone instead of basic mobile.

- Knitting (two needles and some wool).

The above has assumed that we were not going to camp anywhere. Camping, when we have done so, has required that I carry in addition:

- A one to two-person lightweight tent with carbon and/or titanium pegs and an extra groundsheet for rough ground (1kg). See Chapter 3 for more on the delights of our tent.
- One special lightweight three-season sleeping bag (500g).
- One camping pillow (200g).
- One three-quarter length Therm-a-rest (450g).
- A lightweight camping stove and built-in cooking pot (430g).
- Two 225gm gas cartridges (which you have to buy in France or Spain)
- Matches wrapped in foil to prevent them getting wet.
- Food for two excluding picnic lunch: teabags, fruit, dried food (milk powder, muesli, and ready meals) (500g including matches).

Total = 3.53kg

Except for Angharad's sleeping bag, Therm-a-rest, pillow and share of the food, this extra load would have been carried by me because of the extra room in my rucksack. My total load would then have been a little over 12.5kg which is 44 per cent more than the laden rucksack without camping that I carried in September 2013. That total also includes food for only one night of camping. You can reckon on 500g of food for each extra night for two people.

Trekking maps

Making sense of their diversity

Scale	Produced by	Showing and Covering
1:50,000	Rando Editions Cartes de Randonnées, based on French Institut Géographique National (IGN) data	Shows the GR10, HRP and known variants; trans-frontier trails and other routes. Covers mainly the French and Andorran Pyrenees from the Atlantic to the Mediterranean, with limited excursions into Spain.
1:50,000	Rando Editions Mapa Excursionista with the Institut Cartogràfic i Geologic de Catalunya	Shows the GR10, HRP and known variants; trans-frontier trails and other routes. Covers the Catalonian Hautes-Pyrénées from Gavarnie to Canigou, and in equal measure both sides of the France-Spain frontier and Andorra.
1:40,000	Edita Prames	Publishes the Spanish GR11 Guide + maps.
1:40,000	Editorial Alpina maps of the Spanish Geògraf Salvador Llobert Edicions Cartogràfiques	Shows the GR11 and other routes on both sides of the frontier. We have only used one of these maps (see 2012/2013 table below)

1:25,000	IGN	Shows the same trails as the 1:50,000 Rando editions above, and more (although the HRP is sometimes missing!). Its very limited excursions into Spain are vague.
1:25,000	Editorial Alpina	Shows the HRP, GR11, trans-frontier trails and other routes mainly in Spain. Does not stray far over the frontier into France.

For our traverse in 2012 and 2013, we used the following maps:

Scale	Produced by	Title	Covering
1:50,000	Rando Editions Cartes de Randonnées, based on French IGN data	1 Pays Basque Ouest	These three maps , which overlap with one another, cover Days 1-5 (the western Basque Country) and the first part of Day 6.
1:40,000	Editorial Alpina	Alduides-Baztan	
1:25,000	IGN	1346OT St Jean Pied de Port	
1:50,000	Rando Editions Cartes de Randonnées, based on French IGN data	2 Pays Basques Est	The eastern Basque Country (Days 6-10)
		3 Bearn	Pyrénées-Occidentales: from the start of the Haute Montagne (Day 11) almost to Gavarnie (Day 20), .
1:50,000	Rando Editions Mapa Excursionista with the Institut Cartogràfic de Catalunya	24 Gavarnie-Ordesa	A tiny bit required either side of Gavarnie (Days 20, 21)
		23 Aneto-Posets	Pyrénées-Centrales: from east of Gavarnie to Vielha, east of Aneto (Days 21-29)
		22 Pico d'estats – Aneto	Near-eastern Pyrenees: from Aneto almost to Andorra (Days 28-37)
		21 Andorra-Cadí	Near-eastern Pyrenees/ Pyrénées-Orientales: from Andorra to east of the Ariège valley (Days 37-42)

1:25,000	Editorial Alpina	E-25 Pica d'Estats-Mont Roig	Essential for the Orange Route in Chapter 8, and for planning other routes in this chapter (see below).
1:50,000	Rando Editions Cartes de Randonnées, based on French IGN data	8 Cerdagne-Capcir	Pyrénées-Orientales: from the Ariège Valley to the west of the Canigou massif (Days 42-44).
		10 Canigou	Pyrénées-Orientales: from Refugi d'Ull de Ter Amélie-les-Bains (Days 45-48)
		11 Rousillon	Final 3 days (49-51): Amélie-les-Bains to the Mediterranean

In the years 2001-2006, 2008 and 2009, we used a wider variety, including more 1:25,000 maps. The maps we used in 2012 and 2013 represent a migration towards what is really essential.

For *planning purposes only*, we bought and consulted the following maps for the 2012/2013 traverse but did not carry them with us:

1:50,000 Rando Editions Cartes de Randonnées, Couserans

1 :25,000 IGN 2048 OT Aulus Les Bains/Mont Valier

We consulted them because we were working out different routes around the Mont Roig/Rouch massif in the near-eastern Pyrenees (Chapters 8 and 10). We wanted to check the paths indicated on these maps with those on the map we intended to carry for this section – the 1:50,000 Rando Editions Mapa Excursionista with the Institut Cartogràfic de Catalunya, 22 Pico d'Estats – Aneto.

First Aid Kit (Total Weight 400g)

- A selection of plasters and Compeed blister relief –
- A good bandage, with safety pins
- Ibuprofen tablets
- Anti-histamine tablets for bites and stings
- Immodium for runny tummies
- Antiseptic wipes
- Muscular and joint ache cream. We use a natural product called Traumeel
- Sachets of rehydration salts
- Survival blanket